SALMAN RUSHDIE
SENTENCED TO DEATH

W. J. WEATHERBY

SALMAN RUSHDIE
SENTENCED TO DEATH

Carroll & Graf Publishers, Inc.
New York

First Carroll & Graf edition 1990

Carroll & Graf Publishers, Inc.
260 Fifth Avenue
New York, NY 10001

Library of Congress Cataloging-in-Publication Data

Weatherby, William J.
    Salmon Rushdie : sentenced to death / William Weatherby. —
1st Carroll & Graf ed.
        p.   cm.
    Includes bibliographical references.
    ISBN 0-88184-572-8 : $19.95
    1. Rushdie, Salman.   2. Rushdie, Salman. Satanic verses.
3. Novelists, Indic—20th century—Biography.   4. Novelists,
English—20th century—Biography.   5. Islam and literature—
History—20th century.   6. Censorship—History—20th century.
I. Title.
PR9499.3.R8Z95   1990
823'.914—dc20
[B]   90-1676
                                                               CIP

Manufactured in the United States of America

To Two Free Spirits,
artist James Monroe Parker
and the late Jane Zorza.

Obviously I have a view of the world which is not theirs. I insist on my right to express it as I think fit.

Salman Rushdie

CONTENTS

Prologue: The Prediction   1
Author's Note   5
Part I: The Making of Salman Rushdie   7
  1 A Passage to England   9
  2 Filling a "God-Shaped Hole"   20
  3 Going for Broke   35
  4 The Booker Triumph   41
  5 Mrs. Gandhi and Mrs. Thatcher   49
  6 Defending *Shame*   61
  7 Migrant in Nicaragua   70
  8 Holy Wars and Literary Pirates   76
  9 "For Marianne"   80
Part II: The Making of *The Satanic Verses*   89
  1 Not for the Mullahs   91
  2 Wylie Takes Over   108
Part III: The Making of a World Controversy   123
  1 Book Reviews and Book Burnings   125
  2 Rushdie Fights Back   134
  3 Confrontations and Killings   143
  4 Ayatollah Khomeini's Fatwa   153

 5 Taking Sides   161
 6 American Divisions   178
 7 Breaking the Silence   192
 8 "The Current Level"   204
 9 First Anniversary   217
10 To Sing On   235
Epilogue: Prediction Fulfilled   241
Selected Bibliography   245
Acknowledgments and Source Notes   247
Index   250

PROLOGUE:
THE PREDICTION

Not since Fyodor Dostoevski, tied to a stake in freezing winter weather, faced a firing squad in Czarist Russia has a famous writer been sentenced to death for his writing in such dramatic circumstances as Salman Rushdie.

But Rushdie's plight somewhere in England is even more extreme than the great Russian writer's turned out to be. A messenger on horseback arrived at the last minute to reprieve Dostoevski. The firing squad had merely been a trick to scare him into submission to the Czarist regime, and he was marched off to four years' hard labor in Siberia. No such reprieve has been granted Salman Rushdie since his sentence was read on Radio Tehran, and he could spend the rest of his life on the equivalent of death row, in hiding from fanatical Muslim groups seeking to kill him.

In the West, books have such little influence on political events it seems incredible that a mere novel could cause such an international drama. The condemnation of Rushdie's *The Satanic Verses* as "blasphemous" by the Iranian Muslim leader, the late Ayatollah Khomeini, who ordered the author's immediate execution, has become an event of world significance. It has earned a place in the history of the twentieth century. But interpretations, especially in the West, vary. Some commentators see the controversial event simply as a conflict between Western scepticism—Western "doubt"—and Muslim fundamentalism and faith. Others consider that far too simple a way of looking at it and have called what has become known as the Rushdie Affair a reflection of important trends in our rapidly changing world where so many traditional boundaries are breaking down, bringing different cultures into close—*too* close—contact, without any preparation for living together.

Any quest for the real meaning of the Rushdie Affair should start with E. M. Forster, the great English writer. The author of the classic Anglo-Indian novel, *A Passage to India,* describing the meeting of East and West on Indian territory, predicted something like the Rushdie Affair thirty years ago.

In 1961 I met Forster in his spacious Edwardian-style living room in King's College, Cambridge University. He talked about the growing number of Indian students at British universities and the Indians who were settling in Britain, "both Hindus and Muslims and sometimes unbelievers." Forster had made a study of Islam and summed it up by saying: "Islam, like Christianity, is troubled by the illogical and the idolatrous, but it has made a sterner fight against them. The Caaba, the worship of saints, the Mecca-position, do not succeed in obscuring the central truth: that there is no god but God, and that even Muhammad is but the Prophet of God; which truth, despite occasional compromises, is faithfully expressed in Muslim architecture, and should be remembered by those who would understand it."

Forster had always been fascinated by India and Islam. One of his closest friends was Indian, he spent some of his most creative times in India, and he tried to help Indian writers find an audience in Britain. Rabindranath Tagore, the romantic laureate of the Indian independence movement, had been treated as an exotic star in London, much to Forster's disgust. Londoners preferred "adoration to attention," remarked Forster, and it would be impossible to decide how good a writer Tagore was until the "transient fanaticism" of the fans passed.

He might have said the same about Salman Rushdie whose death sentence made it almost impossible to judge him accurately as a writer. But Rushdie the migrant, spanning both East and West, was beyond Forster's experience. He knew colonial India, forty years before Rushdie was born, when the British still ruled.

"In my day," Forster told me, "Indians in England were exotics. Tagore, Gandhi, there were just a few of them. The movement was all the other way—from West to East. The English went out to India, but you got there after a long sea voyage that prepared you for the strange new world. But now our planet has shrunk so much through air travel and television that strange cultures and faiths are thrown together without any preparation.

"Even in our sea-going days when we theoretically had time to readjust, some of the English went to pieces in India as I record in *A Passage to India.*" He had in mind particularly, he said, an older character named Mrs. Moore, who arrived in India full of goodwill and commonsense, but soon left for home close to despair. "There was always a cultural shock, a breakdown before a mystery forever unplumbed that I symbolize in my novel with the ancient echoing Malabar Caves. Not even a long sea voyage could prepare you for that. But nowadays when there is no interval, when you are immediately plunged into a foreign culture, many of us can't deal with it and there will be surprising conflicts. Bound to be ..."

Forster gave a despairing shrug. "The problem of the twenty-first century, which I shan't live to see, will be simply how to live together in this new, much smaller world. Greater tolerance will have to evolve or the world will become an impossible place to live in. Christians have had problems living together for centuries, but imagine one of the intense, violent Eastern religions forced to exist side-by-side today with Western scepticism—with us conditioned Western doubters."

A bony, birdlike man just over eighty, Forster sat forward in his armchair with a boyish eagerness to share his thoughts. "A Muslim student from India told me the other day that he had difficulty finding any young English students at Cambridge who were true believers. He was rather shocked at the way some students dismissed Christianity with lighthearted mockery. It was a style he wasn't used to. He was used to serious subjects like religion being taken seriously, even solemnly. Imagine what might happen if they dismissed his religion that way."

Forster added wryly, "I received some hostile criticism from Hindus and Muslims about *A Passage to India,* even though I was fairly respectful in the novel. I didn't criticize or challenge or make fun. If I had and there had been the instant international means of communication that exists today, I wonder what the outcome would have been. We have seen writers of a different persuasion put to death in Christian and Communist countries even before our world shrank so much. Now we exist in a new kind of world in which freedom of speech may become impossible.

"There is bound to be a test case involving different philosophies and different countries. As my Indian doctor shouts at the end of *A Passage to India,* 'No foreigners of any sort! Hindu and Muslim and Sikh and all shall be one.' He tells his English friend, 'We may hate one another, but we hate you most.' That of course was before India won her independence. Now perhaps we shall see what difference that has made. The time is coming when we shall *all* have to live together in tolerance or die. Nuclear weapons have made sure of that." Forster giggled nervously. "I'm sorry I shall miss seeing the outcome."

Although it was not an interview, I scribbled a few notes in shorthand on the back of an envelope, but when Forster noticed he reproved me for "a reporter's reflex action." So I gave up and have no record or clear memory of the rest of our talk. At the time, I felt he was expressing the melancholy of an old man who yearned for the world of his youth. But now I appreciate his foresight far better.

Is the Rushdie Affair the "test case" he predicted?

If you follow the course of Salman Rushdie's life, he seems to have been driven relentlessly toward the confrontation that has put him in such peril.

AUTHOR'S NOTE

I met Salman Rushdie in New York City while he was in the middle of writing *The Satanic Verses*. My impression of him was useful for this book because, by the time I began the research, neither Mr. Rushdie nor the other main character in the drama, the Ayatollah Khomeini, was available for interviews. Mr. Rushdie was in hiding and the Ayatollah was dead. My main sources have been dependable witnesses who were well-informed about various stages of Mr. Rushdie's life and about the development of the Muslim opposition. What I found out from these people was generally confirmed by other interviews and background reports. But some of the people I talked with didn't wish to be named, even when they were willing to tell me everything they knew. Sometimes they were apprehensive about "upsetting Salman," and sometimes it was Muslim enemies of Mr. Rushdie they were afraid of upsetting. I hope I have been fair to all sides, but not at the expense of the truth.

W.J.W.

PART I:
THE MAKING OF
SALMAN RUSHDIE

1—A PASSAGE TO ENGLAND

AT THE TIME E. M. FORSTER MADE HIS PREDICTION IN FARAWAY CAMbridge, an Indian youth named Salman Rushdie prepared for his first experience of the outside world.

Aged fourteen, wiry and tall for his age with a pale, intense face, young Salman was leaving the safe refuge of his parents' prosperous home in Bombay to attend Rugby School, an exclusive well-known British public school (a private school in American usage).

Young as he was, Salman wasn't worried about the big change in his life. "I think I had actually wanted to go—I was groomed for it," he recalled later. "Very conventional." He was unusually self-confident for his age and had grown up speaking English, as well as Urdu, one of the main Indian languages, and was familiar with many aspects of British culture. What he had observed of the British in India and had read about them back home suggested he would fit in very well in British society. Their conservative, classbound, rather snobbish ways and their sense of their own importance in the world had much in common with his own view of himself. He had heard horrendous stories about the terrible English weather and their strange inedible food, but he was sure he could learn to live with such things, including even Britain's alien religious faith.

Salman had grown up a Muslim, a believer in the Islamic faith—in Allah as the only God and in Muhammad as his prophet. Christianity to the adolescent Rushdie was a western blasphemer's faith. But he recognized that he would have to tolerate such infidel beliefs while he lived among the British. It never occurred to the innocent youth that one day he would be

9

condemned as an infidel himself, that his experience of the West would shatter what was left of his own faith and teach him what he called "the benefit of the doubt."

So he left his homeland with few doubts, proud of being one of the first generation of independent Indians. He had been born in Bombay on June 19, 1947, almost exactly two months before India—with much rejoicing—gained her independence from Britain. Salman was a premature "Midnight's Child." That was the name he later gave to Indians who were born in the first hour after midnight on August 15, 1947, when India became officially independent. He considered such Indians to be very special, the spiritual trailblazers of Independence, with extraordinary, almost magical powers of perception. He was disappointed to have missed being one of them, and instead to have been among the last Indians born during British rule. It became a Rushdie family joke "that the British left only two months after my arrival."

Salman's parents, Anis Ahmed and Negin (née Butt) Rushdie, were well-off, devout Muslims. After the partition of India and Pakistan, many of their relatives moved to Pakistan where Muslims were in the majority and felt more secure. But Salman's parents decided to remain in Bombay, even though they were a minority among the Hindu majority. Salman's father was an admirer of English education. He had taken a law degree as a young man at Cambridge University and he was still strongly influenced by his years there. At the time of Salman's birth, he was a prosperous businessman with inherited wealth, who could give his family every protection in the teeming, divided city of Bombay.

The difference between rich and poor in Bombay was even more obvious than in most cities. Thousands of homeless slept in the city's streets. About one thousand people, roughly three hundred families, reportedly arrived in Bombay every day from the countryside. The city had neither jobs nor homes for most of them, and public misery was the result. But young Salman saw little of this side of Bombay, except through car or bus windows. He was safe behind a villa's high walls with servants to watch over him—safe in a world of magic, rather than grim reality.

Much of Salman's Bombay was a fantasy city observed from afar, dreamed over and peopled by his very active imagination with fantastic characters, romantic heroes, and grotesque villains. He was particularly interested in the city's large film industry—the dream factory. Its opulent fantasies contrasted strangely with the harshly realistic scenes in the crowded streets. He was a voracious reader, often deep in a book when other boys in the neighborhood were out playing. "I was the kind of boy who got books for presents," he said. "No good at games." His hero was the acclaimed Urdu poet Faiz Ahmed Faiz, and he dreamed of becoming a poet like him, only perhaps writing in English.

A friend of Rushdie's told me that anyone trying to understand him should read the *Arabian Nights*. From the time young Salman learned to read, Aladdin and his magic lamp and the other exotic characters of the *Arabian Nights* were as familiar to him as Robin Hood and his Merrie Men were to young Western readers (and moviegoers). The tales of the *Arabian Nights* usually ended with the appearance of the Annihilator of Men who handed out death sentences like Ayatollah Khomeini was to do with Rushdie. The ancient classic reflected a particular culture, a certain way of looking at life. Rushdie was born in that culture and grew up with much the same viewpoint, identifying with Aladdin and Sinbad the Sailor and a world in which magic carpets could fly. Critics discussing the combination of fantasy and satire in Rushdie's writing have called it magic realism, as if it originated with him, Günter Grass, Gabriel Garcia Marquez and other writers who influenced Rushdie's generation. But it was to be found long before in the great storybook that was Rushdie's constant companion as a boy. The same friend who recommended reading the *Arabian Nights* to gain an understanding of Rushdie said, "I think part of Salman's criticism of the way the world is run came from his deep disappointment at finding Aladdin's lamp wasn't real and that the happy endings of the tales weren't often possible in real life. I think he first thought of becoming a writer when he realized that it was only possible to create such a world in the imagination. Parts of his novels, especially *The Satanic Verses,* are pure *Arabian Nights* in their fantasy and humor, with Salman trying to fulfill the dreams that those tall tales gave him. The humor of the *Arabian Nights* often sounds like Salman. Just take one story—*Kapur the Black Eunuch.*

Both the beginning ('Know, my friends, that when no more than eight years of age I had already cultivated a remarkable habit of telling one big lie a year') and the ending ('That, my friends, is the story of my castration; and peace be with you') seem to me to be pure Salman. The wondrous city of Baghdad has a starring role in the *Arabian Nights,* and to Salman, as a boy, Bombay was his Baghdad and has remained so ever since, certainly in his writing."

Fantasy and realism mixed strangely in the everyday life of Bombay with its incredible mixture of styles and people, and a history that often seemed to have come out of the *Arabian Nights.* There was an equestrian statue in the center of the city depicting the Mahratta warrior-king Sivaji who was supposed to come to life at night and gallop as Salman put it, "awesomely through the city streets." He imagined the statue galloping past his home "down my very own Warden Road," right alongside the segregated swimming pools at Breach Candy (where "pink people could swim in a pool the shape of British India without fear of rubbing up against a black skin"), right up to "huge Mahalaxmi Temple and the old Wilmington Club." Whenever bad times came to Bombay in Salman's boyhood during the early days of Independence, some "insomniac nightwalker" would report seeing the statue move—"Disasters, in the city of my youth, danced to the occult music of a horse's grey, stone hooves." It was like living in a city of the *Arabian Nights.* He was as much influenced by Hindu myths as by Muslim mythology. He was already what he called a "mongrel self, history's bastard" before his first experience of the West. This love of fantasizing was never to leave him. All his writing shows its influence—the influence of a world of the imagination, in which magic carpets are as common as jet aircraft.

It probably also explains much of his great love for Bombay, which he called the "most cosmopolitan, most hybrid, most hotch-potch" of Indian cities. A friend of his father's presented him with a little inch-high block of Indian silver engraved with the map of the unpartitioned continent of India and Pakistan when he was one-day old. It was his "oldest possession," and in England became a symbol of Bombay and India because it went "everywhere with me." This early love of Bombay also explained his preoccupation with the city as reality and metaphor—"the heart of all my work." He had fallen "in love with the metropolis" as a boy.

He was the only son, but he had three younger sisters. "Being the only son and eldest child in a middle-class Indian family does make you tend to think that the world revolves round you," he once commented.

An old Indian neighbor told me he observed Salman growing up. Like so many people involved in the Rushdie Affair, the old man didn't wish to be named. But I checked around and he appeared to be a reliable witness as far as I could tell. He said that "Young Salman, as the only boy, the son and heir, was fussed over and spoiled by both his parents and his sisters and his many other relatives. He was treated as someone very special, one of the elite, a Little Prince." This was a reference not to the famous fairy tale but to a nickname like "a Jewish Princess." The old neighbor said this treatment affected Rushdie's attitude "for the rest of his life, I think. He grew up feeling he had a special role to play in the world, a responsibility to right wrongs and correct the errors of lesser mortals. Isn't that really behind his satirizing in *The Satanic Verses*? He was trying to correct the errors of Muslim leaders. He wanted Islam to live up to its high ideals in every way. The Little Prince was doing his work. But he overdid it and his intentions were misunderstood."

Although his family was devoutly Muslim, Rushdie remembers there was a freedom of discussion about religion, and he contrasts that with the attitude of some Muslim fundamentalists towards *The Satanic Verses*. "I come from a Muslim tradition, and in my family in the Indian subcontinent, there was an absolute willingness to discuss anything, there were not these anathemas, these rules, about what you might not talk about. I know about Islam as well, and these people's Islam is not the only Islam."

The family's discussions were held in both Urdu and English. Salman's father was influenced by the free intellectual atmosphere he had known at Cambridge and which he wanted his son to experience as soon as he was old enough. He also wanted the boy to miss the growing pains and turmoil in India during the early years of independence.

The first step was to prepare the boy for going to an English school and then, his father hoped, following in his footsteps to Cambridge. "In my nearlyninth year I had begun to attend the Cathedral and John Connon Boys' High School on Outram Road in the Old Port district; washed and brushed every morning," he recalled in his novel, *Midnight's Children.* Every morning, too, in white shorts, satchel over his shoulder, his "mighty cucumber of a nose dripping as usual," he waited for the bus to school along with his friends Eyeslice and Hairoil, Sonny Ibrahim, and precocious Cyrus-the-great, as he called them in *Midnight Children.* He imagined himself, not as some mythical Indian hero, but as a "mild-mannered Clark Kent" protecting his secret identity as Superman.

Salman received a good, basic British education from the mission school and had a glimpse there of British ways. Any examples of British snobbery were scoffed at, the British class system a joke now that the British had officially left India. But Salman's jokes were affectionate because he identified with the British in many ways. "I was brought up in a very Anglophile and Anglocentric way," he said. He was, however, offended by the title of one book they studied at school—Joseph Conrad's *The Nigger of the Narcissus*—and he disliked the fact Breach Candy swimming pool tried to maintain a racially segregated policy even after independence for the remaining British residents.

Although he was content at school, he was always pleased when it was time to go home—back to his "kingdom" and "heart of my childhood." You turned off Warden Road between a bus stop and a little row of shops: Chimalker's toyshop; Reader's Paradise; the Chimanbhoy Fatbhoy jewelry store; and, above all, Bombelli's, the confectioners, with their Marquis cake and their One Yard of Chocolates! "Names to conjure with," he wrote in *Midnight's Children,* "but there's no time now. Past the saluting cardboard bellboy of the Bad Box laundry, the road leads us home."

These were to be his last safe, happy days in the family circle that even included a nanny for him. Although he didn't know it then, he would never feel so protected again, so sure of his own position in the world. He would never be the same fussed-over Little Prince again. As he packed his bags for England, he was happily looking forward to a great adventure. His father's attitude suggested that a wonderful experience awaited him.

His mother, however, was more cautious in advising him about his trip because she didn't altogether share her husband's approving view of the English. She even hated to speak English because she said it made her mouth feel tired. She warned young Salman that the English had some strange habits. Sometimes more than one person used the bath water! Salman was amused, sure his mother was exaggerating about the civilized English. He expected them to accept him as one of the elite like themselves. Later he described himself as being conservative and snobbish—"perfect public school material."

He was therefore completely unprepared for his harsh reception in England. It was the start of a new decade—the Sixties—but the country was still recovering from the loss of its empire, and there was often a sour attitude toward people from the former colonies who settled in England—especially toward those easily recognized by their different color. Young Salman was seen as one of them. It was like being thrown in the deep end at your first swimming lesson. One day he was in Bombay saying an affectionate goodbye to his parents and sisters and assembled relatives in the Indian surroundings he had known all his life. A mere day or so later he was thousands of miles away in what turned out to be a very strange, often hostile environment. It unbalanced him. He had prepared with such confidence for his trip. He was ready to put up with the English food and the weather. He even knew some of the names of the English cricket and soccer teams. He felt sure England would be a friendly, familiar place, and that he would soon settle down as comfortably as at home. "I had a cartoon of England in my mind: green cricket patches and all that rubbish." But he arrived in a country he didn't recognize from all his reading, and some bitter experiences awaited him.

It is probably impossible to exaggerate the traumatic effect of his experiences in England on this first visit, and especially what he went through at Rugby School. He was only fourteen with few defenses against a kind of hostility he had never faced before. He soon discovered that for many sons of the English elite, he was not the Little Prince but a "wog," an inferior, colored colonial to be excluded from many of the social activities of the blue-blooded English upper-class heirs. He was greeted with aggressively curious, cold, hostile stares and insulting remarks from many of the English students. Some of the teachers weren't much better, treating him with a condescending superiority as if he came from a primitive culture.

He probably had this reception in mind when years later the hero of his novel, *Midnight's Children,* described himself as "variously called Snotnose, Stainface, Baldy, Sniffer, Buddha and even Piece-of-the-Moon." And there were more choice nicknames, cruel variations of "wog."

Young Salman learned for the first time in his protected life that he was a foreigner, and that was not a popular identity to have in insular England. It meant that you were excluded from much of English life at all levels, in all classes.

This was ironic because, thanks to a Kashmiri ancestor, Salman had pale skin that could have passed for white, although his thick, black curly hair, hooded Mogul eyes, and big nose—"this mighty organ" as he called it—made him stand out as an unusual, exotic figure among the Anglo-Saxon faces at Rugby School.

The ancient public school, part of English history, had given him no warning of what to expect when he first arrived in its impressive setting, one which appeared made for English gentlemen—and the elite of other countries. An acquaintance who knew Rushdie at Rugby in the early days said, "I think Salman came with the romantic view of Rugby School that you find in Thomas Hughes's old classical novel, *Tom Brown's Schooldays.* He thought he was going to be the star of *Salman Rushdie's Schooldays,* I think. He soon learned differently, though his first view of the school may have misled him as it still looks a little like the school described in *Tom Brown's Schooldays.*"

Thomas Hughes's novel was written just over one hundred years before Salman Rushdie arrived at Rugby, and it reflected an idealistic view of Victorian upper-class values with the snobbish elitism softened and the emphasis on making a gentleman of the primitive boy. *Tom Brown's Schooldays* describes its hero's arrival this way: "Tom's heart beat quick as he passed the great school field or close, with its noble elms, in which several games of football were going on, and tried to take in at once the long line of gray buildings, beginning with the chapel, and ending with the Schoolhouse, the residence of the headmaster, where the great flag was lazily waving from the highest round tower. And he began already to be proud of being a Rugby boy, as he passed the school-gates, with the oriel-window above, and saw the boys standing there, looking as if the town belonged to them."

Was this how young Salman felt, too, in the first few minutes of being a "Rugby boy," the romantic view of *Tom Brown's Schooldays* taking the place of the *Arabian Nights*?

Speaking in his heavily accented Bombay English, Rushdie went to Rugby with a very positive attitude—"I didn't even feel foreign"—but he was soon awakened to the reality of life at the school, at least for an Indian boy like himself. "There were other Indians at the school, but either they were the sons of maharajahs or they were stars at cricket, and I was no good at games, which was the only thing you were allowed to be good at."

For the first time he was made to feel he belonged to "a race" and he suddenly became officially "Indian" in a way he never had before. He was apparently considered below even working-class English in status. It came as a great, mind-blowing shock to the Little Prince that he wasn't accepted as an equal. When he walked past English students, he grew used to hearing their sniggers. He sometimes found racist grafitti scrawled where he was bound to see it. He was tempted to pack his bags and return to India, but he decided he wasn't going to give in so easily. He forced himself to live with the hostility, but it meant always being on guard.

He discovered he couldn't even trust the two boys he shared a study with. In his second term, he went into the study to find one of the boys writing WOGS GO HOME on the wall over his chair. It was the last straw for Salman. "I went insane. I grasped that boy by the collar with my left hand, and by the belt with my right hand, and I banged him as hard as I could against the wall he was writing on." The boy was apparently knocked unconscious. Salman's anger slowly subsided. It was typical of the Little Prince not to take such treatment submissively, but to react aggressively and correct the wrongdoer. It was an attitude that grew stronger as he became older and more self-confident.

His rejection and the racial tension at the school inspired him to write about Rugby, pouring out his feelings in a short autobiographical novel entitled *Terminal Report* that featured a conservative, conventional hero—such as he had once been—transformed by his experiences into an aggressive, radical fellow whenever he encountered racial prejudice. It was his first attempt to use writing as an outlet, and it made him think of becoming a writer.

But he got back at the racists his own way—by outshining them in class. "Like in any American Jewish novel, your way of getting revenge is to be three times as clever." It was typical, too, of the Little Prince to prove he was really one of the elite by sheer brilliance. A natural student, he always received high marks and also used his formidable vocabulary to put down the racists with a flood of unanswerable rhetoric that left them openmouthed.

This experience at Rugby made Rushdie a committed opponent of racism wherever it appeared. Britain, the United States, South Africa, India—he was to speak out against racism in all these and many other countries. "Of course, I knew that racism is not confined to the British. I come from a society where racism is commonplace, between one Indian community and another. But you have to combat racism wherever you find it. I've never been one-dimensional about it. I've disliked the rule of fundamental Islam in Pakistan under Zia for the last decade. Fascism is fascism wherever you find it."

Later, in *International Who's Who,* he listed among his Leisure Interests, alongside films, chess and table tennis, "involvement in politics, especially race relations."

Rushdie's time at Rugby, which seemed like an eternity, came to an end at last. His leave-taking of the time-honored public school was the opposite of the one in *Tom Brown's Schooldays.* Tom was divided in his mind between "hero-worship, honest regrets over the long stage of his life which was now slipping out of sight behind him, and hopes and resolves for the next stage upon which he was entering with all the confidence of a young traveller."

Young Salman had no hero-worshipping thoughts, no honest regrets about leaving Rugby. He promised himself that he was going home for good and was never again coming back to England. But he soon learned it was a promise he couldn't keep. England was in his future. He had yet to understand that you can't go home again.

2—FILLING A "GOD-SHAPED HOLE"

WHILE YOUNG SALMAN STRUGGLED WITH THE ENGLISH EDUCATIONAL SYStem, his parents followed their other relatives to settle in predominantly Muslim Pakistan. Salman, lonely at Rugby and missing his good times in Bombay, was very much against their move. Leaving Bombay meant giving up too much.

"I think there were all kinds of terrible reasons like finding husbands for my sisters," he said later, trying to explain the move. "They were beginning to sense discrimination in India— there were a whole series of these half-reasons."

He urged them to stay in Bombay—the only home he knew and a city where most of his friends lived. When they rejected his advice, he didn't hesitate to inform his parents of his strong disapproval of their taking their—his!—home to Pakistan.

The Rushdie family discovered their son and heir had greatly changed and not all the changes pleased them. The fourteen-year-old schoolboy who had left three years before had grown into a very independent young man. His lean, leggy figure had filled out, his self-confidence had grown, and his manner was more forceful in expressing his views. The Bombay accented English he had spoken when he left had been replaced by a superior sounding English that older Indians associated with former British colonial officials. It made Salman sound like an outsider. Indians who studied in England were always accused of imitating the English and rejecting Indian ways, and Salman had picked up more mannerisms than most students because he was adept at impersonations. But above all, his more aggressive attitude showed the effect of his English experiences. His rather conventional, conservative view of the world had become much more militant about the need for change. At nearly eighteen, he had reached the age when sons often rebelled against their fathers and Rugby School had made Salman a real rebel. His father soon had to listen to Salman asserting his critical opinions, especially about religion and politics, announcing his plans for the future, and strenuously arguing if his father disagreed with him. The old, warm, democratic atmosphere of give-and-take in the family circle soon grew cooler, at least between father and son.

Nonetheless, to his father's delight, Salman had won an exhibition scholarship to Cambridge, the university where he had spent several enjoyable, valuable years. But Salman insisted that he didn't want to go to Cambridge. It would just mean more of the Rugby treatment. In fact, he didn't ever want to return to England. He intended to stay home for good. He wasn't sure he would remain in Pakistan with his parents. He might go back to Bombay.

Well, his father wanted to know, if he didn't go to Cambridge, what did he intend to do for a living? Salman's reply was completely unexpected. He might become a writer. He had already done some writing at Rugby. The news greatly upset his businessman father. "What will I tell my friends?" he asked. No, he couldn't take such talk seriously. Salman *must* go to Cambridge.

The outcome of this family disagreement was that his father refused to listen to further arguments, asserting parental authority, and dismissed young Salman's objections as juvenile. Salman didn't seem to realize he had been sent to Rugby just as a preparation for Cambridge. If he hadn't cared for Rugby's snobbery, he would find Cambridge very different, a good preparation for life. He wanted Salman to have the same university experience he had enjoyed. Salman's arguments were firmly rejected. He *must* go to Cambridge. It was one of his father's dreams. He had gone to Cambridge and so must his son.

Rushdie reluctantly began to pack his bags again. Later, he said indignantly about his return to England, "I had to be bullied to come back." He described going back in 1965 as "one of the most disorienting moments of my life." He was convinced it would be Rugby all over again, only worse because all the racist bullies would be older and bigger. He didn't intend to give them an inch, but rather to fight back as he had learned to do at Rugby.

When he arrived in Cambridge for the first time and saw the students in their often hippie clothes filling the streets with their bicycles, he had a big chip on his shoulder and was prepared to strike back at the first hostile encounter. An English student who met him compared Rushdie to young D' Artagnan in *The Three Musketeers*, "... ready, even eager to challenge anyone to a duel who crossed his path. He arrived looking very Indian with long hair. I think he did it deliberately as a challenge to the rest of us. But Cambridge had much more foreign-looking, eccentric-appearing students than Salman Rushdie and he was hardly noticed."

It took Salman a few weeks to settle down and realize that Cambridge was quite different from his gloomy expectations. The Australian writer, Clive James, who was a contemporary of Rushdie's at Cambridge, suggested in his irreverent memoirs, *May Week Was In June,* that undergraduates coming up from public schools—like Rushdie from Rugby—no doubt found the Cambridge colleges, even King's or Trinity, "... the same old thing on an only slightly larger scale: the same turrets, crenellations, lodges, fenestrations, cloisters, clerestories, porticos and porters." But the appearance of Cambridge overall could still have a powerful effect, Clive James pointed out. "The lovely facades, the sweeping lawns, the intricate crannies opening on distant vistas, were meant not just to lull but to disarm: nobody who had once lived in these emollient surroundings would ever again feel sufficiently alienated from society to be anything more troublesome than a reformist. Gradualism was implicit in every carefully repainted coat of arms and battered refectory table. To remain a revolutionary in such a context you would have had to have treason in the blood." The Little Prince from Bombay and Rugby probably arrived with revolutionary feelings, but he was to leave more a committed reformist, not wishing to overturn the world so much as to correct its errors.

Rushdie went to the prestigious King's College where he was most affected by the variety of his fellow students. They came from all classes of British society, as well as from many other countries. He was mixing on equal terms with working-class

Britons for the first time, and he was surprised to find that often he had more in common with their attitudes than with the upper-class students and their elite ways. The university was so big that no one group could dominate its life. There were snobbish associations, clubs, and private groups that a student like Rushdie was excluded from. But there were also lively, radical, artistic, intellectual circles in which being from India was no handicap, and was sometimes an advantage because you were considered exotic and therefore more interesting.

It was the middle sixties and Cambridge, like other British universities, had caught some of the feverish atmosphere of the United States with its hippie-flower children and drug culture, and the new American generation's rebelliousness and rejection of Establishment values. The Civil Rights movement was closely followed at Cambridge, and there was growing opposition to the American involvement in the Vietnam War. Rushdie was very much influenced by this anti-Establishment wave at Cambridge, identifying particularly with the feeling that Vietnam was like the opposition to the Civil Rights movement, just another expression of racism. He "went on anti-Vietnam War demonstrations and did my time as a hippie." But he eventually cooled down and began to pursue his own interests as well as these popular causes. "Mostly I was involved in acting," he said.

He had discovered that his foreign, romantic, dominating presence and his commanding speech made him a natural actor and provided an outlet for his pent-up emotions. He joined Cambridge's Footlights Club, which had nurtured several actors who later became well-known in London. Some of Rushdie's contemporaries in the Footlights Club were also to become famous in London's artistic and media circles, including playwright David Hare and feminist writer Germaine Greer. Rushdie not only greatly enjoyed the work on stage, the self-expression through performance, but also the lively behind-the-scenes social life. Like Clive James, he was first attracted to the Footlights Club during the Societies Fair, which showed university students what organizations were available to join. But you didn't join the Footlights, you auditioned. Rushdie passed this test and became an enthusiastic member.

A fellow actor at the time recalled, "Salman found a free-thinking quality among even us young inexperienced theater people that made him feel accepted without any reservations. Actors are essentially gypsies, they feel respectable society looks down on them, and Salman could identify with that. Moreover, he was a promising player and we all encouraged him, though he was modest in those days about his accomplishments and didn't push himself to the front. He often kept shyly in the background."

Rushdie considered himself "only all right" as an actor—a mere "bulb" in the Footlights. His secret dream was still to be a writer, but Cambridge was full of would-be writers boasting of their masterpieces-in-progress and their friends among London publishers, and so he kept it to himself. "It's a thing you can't tell people. They ask you, 'What are you going to be?', and you say, 'Oh, I'm going to be a writer,' and they laugh or look at you contemptuously. It's not like saying you're going to join a bank. I was also very, very scared of discovering that I couldn't do it. So acting was something I did just in case I couldn't be a writer."

Acting also helped him to settle down and decide he had been wrong about Cambridge. The English university was often "wonderful," but you had to take the bad with the good. "It was a very strange time at Cambridge," he recalled later. "There was a mixture of the old and the new." But even though the radical atmosphere of the sixties shook up everything, the racists and the fools remained. "There were a lot of chinless wonders in blazers who threw people into the river at night. I'm sure they're still there—they endure like the earth."

His "time as a hippie," his bad feeling about Establishments, even those of Cambridge, and his devotion to the Footlights Club probably kept him away from the more glamorous, media-publicized activities of Cambridge. He was still more shy and uncertain than his manner suggested. He certainly didn't become a major figure on campus as might have been expected. He didn't write for the lively undergraduate publications nor did he use his formidable power of speech to become a star of the Cambridge Union's reknowned debates. Some students, ambitious for a political career, rejected dramatic societies like the Footlights, believing the Union to be, as Clive James put it, "the only thing that counted if one had one's eye on high government office." But that wasn't the rebel Rushdie's aim. He saw himself not as a future politician, but as an artist.

A Cambridge academic, who twenty years later tried to trace Rushdie's Cambridge career, said, "I have been asking around about Rushdie at King's. One thing is certain: he was *not* the most popular student! The College Office claims his file 'cannot be located' (which is odd, as there was no reason to think it has been deliberately withheld). Many Fellows who were at King's at the time, such as Professor John Dunn, cannot remember having ever encountered him, and it seems he chose to socialize within an unusually small group of friends. He did join the Footlights, although again he seems to have drifted through without making much of an impact."

James Booth, writing in *Varsity*, reached the same conclusion—that Rushdie's life and academic career at King's College "could not be described as controversial or distinguished. As far as Rushdie's pastimes are concerned, the senior tutor at King's, Dr. Adkins, when asked what aspects of college and university life he involved himself with, replied, 'His files have been lost.' It is known, however, that Salman Rushdie did not write for *Varsity*, nor did he speak in Union debates; instead he was involved in theater, in the era of Clive James and Germaine Greer."

Rushdie was obviously still feeling his way in the complicated Cambridge society that had given him a new view of England—a much more favorable view. The country was as varied as India, which after all had its racial prejudices, too. As soon as he began to compare the two countries, he achieved a much greater understanding of the English.

Back in Pakistan, the Rushdie family was relieved to learn from his letters about his more contented reaction. His parents had feared he might have some bad experience and storm out of the university, refusing ever to go back.

What also helped to settle Rushdie was that he became deeply interested in his Cambridge studies. He later believed it was his good luck to read history rather than English literature. It meant he could select books for pleasure and learn from them as a writer without restricting himself to a set course of reading. That was how he came to read Sterne's *Tristram Shandy* "with a sense of discovery, as if it had been written yesterday." The influence of Sterne's novel was to be seen in much of his writing. It was the English equivalent for him of the *Arabian Nights*.

As part of his studies, Rushdie examined the background of his Muslim upbringing, the history of Islam, and the life of Muhammad from primary historical sources. He wrote a paper on "Muhammad, Islam and the Rise of the Caliph" for part two of his history tripos, or final honors examination. Many of the ancient books he studied were banned in the fundamentalist Islamic world, so he had never seen them before. *Varsity* commented that Rushdie's part two dissertation written in 1968 "possibly provided some of the 'heretical' information" that was to appear later in *The Satanic Verses*.

Muhammad ibn Abdallah, Rushdie learned, was not only "one of the great geniuses of world history" but a successful businessman, a victorious general and a sophisticated statesman, as well as a Prophet who insisted throughout his life on his simple humanity. There were no contemporary portraits of him because he feared people would worship them, whereas he was only the messenger. And it was the message that should be revered. This impression of Muhammad was rather different from that given in India and Pakistan where he had been turned into "a perfect being, his life into a perfect life." It was a revelation to young Salman and influenced all his later thinking about Islam—and his writing about it.

But most important, for the way his life was to develop, this period at Cambridge was the first time he learned about the satanic verses, a fictionalized version of which was to appear in his most famous (and notorious) novel. The phrase, the satanic verses, Rushdie said, came from al-Tabari, one of the canonical Islam sources, who wrote that "When the Messenger of God saw his people draw away from him ... he would gladly have seen those things that bore too harshly on them softened a little." As Rushdie explained, Muhammad then received "verses which accepted the three favorite Meccan goddesses as intercessionary agents. Meccans were delighted. Later, the Archangel Gabriel told Muhammad that these had been 'Satanic verses,' falsely inspired by the Devil in disguise and they were removed from the Koran."

What Rushdie read in these ancient books at Cambridge intrigued him, and the Satanic Verses became "an image which has remained with me for twenty years."

He left Cambridge in 1968 with a Master of Arts in history with honors, a boost to his feeling of intellectual superiority. He had done well even in this highly competitive English university. Ironically, at King's College he had been living only a short distance away from E. M. Forster, who died in 1970 and whose "test case" Rushdie was perhaps to become nearly twenty years later. Leaving King's College for the last time, Rushdie concluded that it had been a "very good time to be at Cambridge, 1965 to 1968. It started with sex and drugs and rock'n'roll and ended with *les événements*. I ceased to be a conservative snob under the influence of the Vietnam War and dope." He had been friendly with several women students at Cambridge, but none led to a permanent attachment—to his family's relief in faraway Pakistan. A former student, an Englishwoman, recalled that Rushdie "could be very defensive and critical and sometimes quite objectionable, but when he gave up expecting to be rejected and relaxed with you, he could be very charming and amusing. He was attracted to English women because they were different, I suppose, to the women he was used to, and because he liked to see the effect on English men when he had an Englishwoman on his arm. He was very competitive even then, very aware of status, and that affected his attitude towards sex, too."

Rushdie said he left Cambridge "with an absolutely cast-iron solution to the world's historical problems. Twenty-one is a very good time to know everything. The fact that you've got this great bulk of knowledge, done a degree and you've just left university and entered the real world encourages you to be very, very sure of yourself. What has happened to me since then has left me progressively less certain about the existence of any single truth."

His history studies reinforced his doubts about being a Muslim, and this made a visit to his family in Pakistan very difficult. How could he describe the intellectual journey from Faith to Doubt he had taken without being dismissed as an imitation Englishman? His parents lived in Karachi in a devout Muslim circle and they assumed that he remained a devout believer, too. He tried to describe his doubts to them without offending them. It was especially difficult to convey to them the effect of his studies at Cambridge. They thought he was being influenced by the godless West. The environment of Pakistan was no help. He didn't feel at ease in Karachi and he missed Bombay, but for his family's sake he tried to settle down and work in Pakistan's new television service. His free-thinking soon clashed with Pakistan's rigid codes. Attempting to televise a production of Edward Albee's play, *Zoo Story,* an American duet he thought would have some appeal, he was informed the word pork would have to be omitted so as not to offend local religious beliefs. The word sex would have to go, too. When he wrote an article about his first impressions of Pakistan for a small magazine, the local press council suppressed it. He was told it wouldn't be in his best interests to publish it.

What also dismayed him was that even some of his Indian and Pakistani friends treated him differently. To some of them, he was a "Europe-returned chappie," corrupted and brainwashed by the godless, materialistic West. They joked about his Cambridge accent. With the patriotic feelings inspired by independence, they treated him as an outsider because of his education in England, the former enemy. Whenever they disagreed about something, it was attributed to his western brainwashing. The antagonism between India and Pakistan also oppressed him. When the Karachi airport was bombed in an Indian air raid, it had a profoundly disturbing effect on him. His two homes were at war with each other. He regarded himself more as an Indian than as a Pakistani, but his family lived in Pakistan so he had reasons to support both sides. "It was really crazy making," he recalled. Thinking rationally about what was going on, he found it impossible to agree with either side. He was continually involved in arguments that got nowhere. He decided it wasn't an atmosphere he wanted to live in or where he could grow as a writer.

He escaped back to England. That in itself showed the deep effect of his Cambridge experiences. England had become attractive to him, a western home where he would be more comfortable with his religious doubts and where he would have a better chance of fulfilling his writing ambitions. To be an Indian writer was too limiting. You were lucky to gain even a small western readership. Since independence, the use of English had declined in India and it was English that Rushdie wanted to write in to reach as wide an audience as possible. London was also a publishing center and there he would have the best chance of establishing himself in the literary world.

But moving to London wasn't an easy decision to make. He knew it was a turning point in his life, that he was leaving perhaps the only real home he would ever know. His relationship with India might remain quite close, but he was sure he would never live there again. He couldn't make his home in Pakistan, he was sure of that now. He was making what he called a "very radical alteration." He was not "who I was supposed to be," he said, explaining "If you look at where I was born and the family in which I grew up and the kind of life that normally happens to people who grow up in such worlds, I stepped out of that world." He had the feeling of reconstructing his life. You wonder, he said, "if there's anything left of the original person or not." It gave him "the sense of character as being mutable." That was to influence his writing and his way of describing character. Everyone was capable of changing, of becoming a new person.

But even if he was no longer a Muslim believer, that didn't mean he could reject the importance of Islam in his life. If you came from India or Pakistan, how could you reject religion? "Religion is the air everyone breathes. If you're trying to write about that world, you can't make a simple rejection of religion. You have to deal with it because it's the center of the culture."

But, Rushdie said, doubt seemed to him "the central condition of a human being in the twentieth century. One of the things that has happened to us in the twentieth century as a human race is to learn how certainty crumbles in your hand. We cannot any longer have a fixed certain view of anything."

That seemed like a justification of his own position—"I am not a religious person any more, formally." In his novel, *Midnight's Children,* he was to write of a patriarch who lost his faith and was left with "a hole inside him, a vacancy in a vital inner chamber." He was really writing of the way he felt himself. He possessed the same kind of "God-shaped hole." Unable to accept what he called "the unarguable absolutes of religion," he tried to fill up the hole with literature, where he went to "explore the highest and lowest places in human society and in the human spirit, where I hope to find not absolute truth but the truth of the tale, of the imagination and of the heart."

His writing became his religion—with the same kind of commitment to expressing the truth as he saw it, and to correcting the sinners. He often acted like a high priest of writing in the years to come. It was an attitude that was to not only win him growing attention, but get him into increasing trouble that would eventually be topped by a death sentence.

But when he first arrived in London, earning a living as a writer was impossible. He returned to acting and soon found work in the bohemian, improvising fringe theater circuit through the actor friends he had made at Cambridge. Swinging London at that time reflected the same kind of mood as the U.S. in the late sixties. The Establishment was still on the defensive even though the drug culture was coming to an end and becoming a big international business instead. There was a sympathetic atmosphere in London for young people trying to make it in the arts. Rushdie joined a radical company at the Oval Theatre in Kensington which specialized in the kind of satirical sketches that the Footlights had done. In many of the fringe productions he worked on—fringe because they weren't central West End productions, but more like Off-Broadway in New York—Rushdie ranged from straight dramas to the *Viet Rock* musical. Although he was modest himself about his acting ability, seeing himself more as a writer, a fellow actor described him as "impressive, with a memorable stage presence and a haunting voice. I remember once he forgot his lines, but I'm sure the audience never realized it because Salman covered up with superb self-confidence and some brilliant fresh improvising. Yet off-stage, he wasn't nearly so confident, much of him still the eager, self-questioning young student and Indian hippie in baggy pants and a stained sweater."

The Indian writer Bharati Mukherjee, who settled in the United States, said Rushdie had "traded top-dog status in the homeland for the loss-of-face meltdown of immigration." In Rushdie's writing, she added, he dramatized the pain and confusion of an immigrant in a language that used all forms of Indian speech at once—"bombastic, babu [an Indian gentleman's speech], bureaucratic, Vedantic [Hindu philosophy], vehement, servile and Sellersish [British comedian's hilarious Indian impersonations], without mocking or condescending, while remaining," claimed Mukherjee, "true to the essentially damaged, ego-deficient, post-colonial psyche."

And mix in some Rugby, Cambridge, and London English and later some American, and you have the complex international East-and-West style of Salman Rushdie. His use of language and even his technique in presenting character and in scene-shifting were also to be strongly influenced by his experience as an actor. Some of the scenes in his novels read like stage directions with dialogue, and sometimes he parodies the entrances and exits of the theater.

No doubt he enjoyed much of his theatrical fringe work and the bohemian life that went with it, but he didn't see his long-term future as an actor. He used the theater as a means of coping with his difficult situation until he was more settled. He was already a British citizen after deciding that he had to make a commitment to this new home. Also, in a country where there was so much prejudice against foreigners—"I think wogs begin at Calais," remarked François Mauriac—especially those of another race, he felt he needed the protection he assumed citizenship would give him.

He had also begun a serious relationship with an English-woman named Clarissa Luard. If he had been deliberately looking for a woman who was easily recognizable as English and represented many popular English characteristics, he could hardly have done better. Tall, slim, articulate and attractive, Clarissa Luard was one of those upper-class English women whose extrovert upbringing made them suspicious of intellectual pursuits. Although her father had intellectual interests, her no-nonsense, extrovert mother, who liked fun things, had influenced her more. Clarissa worked in the rock and pop and fashion worlds of swinging London, but she was sufficiently free of upper-class English prejudices to respond favorably when a clever, attractive young Indian named Salman Rushdie became interested in her. Clarissa's mother and father accepted Salman, but, as an acquaintance recalled at the time, some of her other relatives thought an Indian was a strange choice for her to make when there were so many nice English men available for her.

"To Salman at first," said the acquaintance, "I think Clarissa represented the ideal Englishwoman, and winning her meant a great victory over the English men who treated him as inferior. But then to his surprise apparently, he found himself deeply in love with her and all his belligerent feelings were forgotten. She was no longer an English princess to conquer, but a woman he wanted to share his life with. It was a great tribute to Clarissa. She changed him. I think she helped to unlock the gates that had been blocking him as a writer when he saw everything just in racial terms. Clarissa helped him to see everything—but especially the English—in more human terms. You can't write just from hatred. You need love and that's what Clarissa brought out in him."

It was not long before Salman and Clarissa were carrying on a secret affair, and finally they moved in together and were married in 1976. They both wanted children and soon a son was born. They named him Zafar.

Acting in the fringe circuit was bearable for a bohemian bachelor, but it was too precarious an existence now that he had the responsibilities of a husband and father. Like so many writers before him, Rushdie turned to advertising for a more regular income than acting could provide. Again his Cambridge contacts helped, but there were some disappointments. He failed his copywriting test with the well-established, prosperous advertising company of J. Walter Thompson. "Tell a Martian to make a piece of toast in fifty words," he was instructed. His fifty words weren't catchy enough and he didn't get a job there. It shook his ego at the time, but after he became successful, Rushdie enjoyed telling the story at literary dinner parties where he made the ad world seem bizarrely eccentric, full of the kind of grotesques he put in his novels, and no place for a serious writer. But other job opportunities soon opened up for him. He was a part-time copywriter for Ogilvy and Mather in London, enjoying the freedom this gave him to devote part of the week to his own writing, though he had to learn to discipline himself to be two different writers—a sort of creative Dr. Jekyll and copywriting Mr. Hyde. One of his fellow workers was a friendly, well-read young woman named Fay Weldon. He soon discovered she wanted to be a writer, too, and they exchanged ideas and information about the publishing world. Later, when she and Rushdie were both established novelists, Fay Weldon praised him as an "ex-colleague of mine in an advertising agency" who, she said, was humane, modern, witty and intelligent. Another fellow worker at the time who had no serious writing ambitions recalls that Rushdie never described himself as a copywriter but always as a "writer."

In his spare time away from advertising slogans, Rushdie worked on a novel entitled *The Book of the Fir* about a very successful Muslim holy man. But after finishing it, he decided its experimental style made it "totally incomprehensible" to the general reader, and he abandoned it. He was still trying to find his own style forged by his experiences in both East and West. It would have been easy for him to follow the Anglo-Indian tradition typified by such Western and Eastern writers as E. M. Forster, Rudyard Kipling, Rabindranath Tagore, and, in Rushdie's time, Paul Scott on the western side and R. K. Narayan on the eastern side. You either wrote from an English or an Indian point of view. E. M. Forster was the ideal example of the former and Narayan, with his stories of an Indian town, of the latter. Few Indian writers were known in the West. Narayan had won an audience mainly because Graham Greene, when he was an influential critic in England, read Narayan with enthusiasm and wrote an introduction for a British edition of one of his novels. Rushdie rejected such nationalistic limitations. He intended to write as freely from an English as an Indian viewpoint, merging East and West in his fiction in some new style of his own.

It was then he met someone who was to help him greatly in finding his own style and sense of direction in the literary world. Young writers who know a talented editor in publishing are very fortunate because their exchange usually helps to make the writers more professional and often saves them from writing unpublishable, experimental books and gives them a useful knowledge of the marketplace. A writer as ambitious as Rushdie, who felt insecure as a "migrant" with only an adopted country, was particularly in need of some expert guidance.

You could sense his confusion in his London home, which was full of nostalgic mementoes of India. He still had the little inch-high block of Indian silver engraved with the map of the unpartitioned India and Pakistan that a friend of his father's had presented to him as a baby. It had become a "sacred object," one of the totems that were always placed in front of him as he wrote, conjuring up his boyhood in Bombay. He hadn't let go of India. He was still the man "between." However long he lived in England and became used to its ways, he would never have the feelings he had for India and especially the city he had been born in, because they were deeply rooted in his whole being. Yet he had to face the fact that he had rejected India in settling in England. He had stated a preference by that act. What did it really mean in terms of his life? He had to find the answer before he could know himself as a writer and understand what he wanted to write about. The two worlds he had experienced confused him when he tried to write. India was foremost in his mind, in his imagination, yet he was living in England. He wanted to dramatize his situation, but should it be as a migrant's memoir, a realistic novel or pure fantasy? He was at a literary crossroads and he needed some expert encouragement and advice. He was lucky enough to meet just the right person.

3—GOING FOR BROKE

LIZ CALDER, NOW THE POWERFUL PUBLISHING DIRECTOR OF THE YOUNG Bloomsbury company in Soho Square in London, was a bright, ambitious publicist for the established company of Victor Gollancz in the early seventies. A great reader and a smart judge of manuscripts, she wanted to be an editor and was already on the lookout for her own new, young authors.

She first met Salman Rushdie through a colleague at Gollancz who knew Clarissa Rushdie. "I was commuting and needed a place in London during the week and they had a spare room," she told me. "So I became their lodger. They had a house in Victoria." Soon after moving in, she changed from a publicist to a full-time editor at Gollancz, just in time to sign up Rushdie.

Rushdie showed her some of his recent writing, and she told him about a science fiction competition that Gollancz had organized as a way of finding new writers. Rushdie was immediately interested. "He said he would enter the book he was then writing. It gave him a deadline, which is always a good thing."

Very professional, even then, in meeting deadlines, he finished his book in good time. Entitled *Grimus,* it was to be his first published novel—his start as a professional writer, a crucial stage for any novelist—but in every other way, it was to be a big disappointment. His first real attempt at a novel for publication was a complex combination of science fiction/fantasy and the kind of folk tales he had grown up reading. Some of the grotesque characters could have stepped out of the *Arabian Nights.* The hero was not a handsome prince or a gallant knight, but a striking looking young Indian, but like the princes and knights of the old tales, he was engaged in a mythic search for himself and

35

the meaning of life. Yet in spite of Rushdie's own background, his hero was not an Indian from India but from the United States—known colloquially in the story as Amerindia—and was named Flapping Eagle and was a member of the Axona tribe. Rushdie wasn't ready yet to deal with the Indians he knew or with that side of himself. He felt safer with pure fantasy and a few Muslim echoes and English literary jokes. Flapping Eagle's search—comparable to Rushdie's own as a writer—takes place on a mysterious, almost unreachable country known as Calf Island, which resembles one of the strange planets in more conventional science fiction stories. In this first novel dedicated "For Clarissa," Rushdie went as far as possible to avoid dealing with either India or England directly. He posed some of his own personal problems through Flapping Eagle's explorations, but in an entirely imaginary setting with grotesque characters who were almost entirely creatures of his imagination and far from the everyday realms of East and West. Flapping Eagle's home in Amerindia was left in the mists of the past, a hint only of Rushdie's own personal concerns. He was playing safe, and it showed in both the haphazard plotting and the jerky, clipped use of language, suggesting an experiment in self-conscious literary expression that hadn't quite worked, so different in its constipated jerkiness from the rich flow and masterly play of his later writing.

The opening of *Grimus* is a good example of the general awkwardness of the style: "Mr. Virgil Jones, a man devoid of friends and with a tongue rather too large for his mouth, was fond of descending this cliff-path on Tiusday mornings. (Mr. Jones, something of a pedant and interested in the origins of things, referred to the days of his week as Sunday, Moonday, Tiusday, Wodensday, Thorsday, Freyday, and Saturnday; it was affectations like this, among other things, that had left him friendless)."

Grimus in some ways resembled a play rewritten as a novel because often the narrative and dialogue didn't quite merge. The characters were introduced and left unexplored to walk on and off stage as required. The story showed many of the author's literary "affectations" quite apart from Mr. Jones's. There was a lack of discipline, no consistent sense of a writer in control of what he was describing. *Grimus* had the ingredients of an old folk tale and a fantasy from long ago, but the style struggled to be that of an ironic contemporary social comedy. Mr. Jones could almost have come out of an Evelyn Waugh novel.

The judges for Gollancz's science fiction competition, novelists Kingsley Amis, Arthur C. Clarke and Brian Aldiss, probably didn't know what to make of this attempted literary flight masquerading as science fiction. Liz Calder remembers that Brian Aldiss was the only judge who liked *Grimus;* so it had no chance of winning a prize. "But I liked it very much," she said, "so I persuaded Gollancz to publish it."

The critics, however, liked it even less than the judges. "It received unusually vitriolic reviews for a first novel," recalled Liz Calder. "Isabel Quigley in *The Financial Times* was the only reviewer who liked it." The London *Times* stated, "It is hateful to be unkind to a first novel, but I suspect that under the gaudy feathers there lies a rather sickly, skinny chicken." The prestigious *Times Literary Supplement* described *Grimus* as "an elaborate statement of the obvious decked out in the mannerisms of Oxford philosophy." Liz Calder recalls that both she and Rushdie took the critical rejection very badly. It seemed "as if we were in the wrong job and we sat in a wine bar drowning our sorrows."

Rushdie decided *Grimus* was an "excessively clever book," but contained very little feeling. "I was very distressed by the reviews. *Grimus* had the peculiar effect of completely polarizing the critics; two-thirds of them said it was deeply terrible."

Many a sensitive young novelist still with doubts about his future as a professional writer might have given up after this grim experience. But Rushdie, after nursing his wounds, decided in typical Little Prince style that the critics and the judges were wrong. He had an important role to play in the literary world and he would force them to recognize him. He refused to accept failure. All his competitive temperament came to the fore. He had lost a round, but he would win in the end. This self-confident attitude made several acquaintances describe Rushdie as arrogant, but it came from his determination not to be put down by hostile forces in the literary world any more than he had at Rugby. This attitude was to be his strength during this depressed, discouraging period of his life. His aim was to keep going as a writer in spite of all handicaps, and not allow himself to be stopped. He continued earning a living while trying to begin a new book. But for months *Grimus* haunted him, blocking his progress. In fact, not until four years later, in 1979, did he begin to see a change in critical opinion. When *Grimus* was finally published in the U.S., the reviews there were much more favorable. *The Los Angeles Times* called his novel "engrossing and often wonderful fun," and *Publisher's Weekly* described Rushdie as "a talent to watch."

But long before then Rushdie had shaken off his feeling of discouragement. He used his critics as an incentive—like a red rag to a bull—sure he would soon receive the recognition he believed was due him as a writer. "If you've just written a novel that failed to set the world on fire," commented Rushdie, "You have a number of options. You can stop writing, concentrate on the fads of the market or do something very risky and dangerous— and write what you really want to write."

Being Salman Rushdie, he had no choice. He would go for broke. The first attempt, however, misfired. Liz Calder remembers, "He was then working in an advertising agency, part-time, I think, with two days a week at home working on his fiction. He wrote a book after *Grimus* entitled *Madame Rama,* which was about the movie industry. I read it and I said I didn't think it worked as it stood, though it had absolutely marvelous material in it. He agreed as did other publishers. So he put it to one side." Another failure, but he took it in his stride. Parts of *Madame Rama* had been highly praised by everyone who had read it. He decided he was going to write a novel about India—the whole of India, past and present, ducking nothing—and put all his knowledge and experience and feelings about his native land into an epic tale.

As if in preparation for this mighty task, he and his wife went on a trip to India, Salman's first visit in ten years, though he had been next-door in Pakistan while visiting his parents. The trip provided a tremendous boost for the novel he had in mind, opening doors in his memory that had been shut for years and reviving half-forgotten emotions from his boyhood. Like an indefatigable researcher, he saw as much as he could, introducing his wife to his homeland but rediscovering it for himself as well.

There had been many changes since he had last been there, and he traveled as widely as possible. Weeks of crossing India in crowded buses and staying in cheap hotels brought him in contact with so much he had never known in his protected boyhood. The trip focused on the endless variety and long history of India. But he was annoyed that sometimes because of his patrician manner, his English clothes and English accent, and his pale, almost white skin, fellow Indians thought he wasn't Indian. He was as Indian as they were! He paid a nostalgic visit to his old home in Bombay. "He loved seeing it," recalled Mrs. Rushdie. "I think he was very moved and upset because Bombay had changed quite a lot. He was especially pleased to go back to Kashmir. They had always holidayed there as children." Beautiful Kashmir, where some of his family had come from and where so many childhood memories came back to him at familiar sights! Amid the corruption and conflicts of India, there was still so much to love. He always had a sharp eye for the eccentricity of human beings, and from this visit he took away the memory of many encounters that would enrich his book.

Back in London, he started work at once. He could almost see the big book in which he was going to make his peace with India—and with himself. He knew it would take several years to write and that meant no escape from his advertising work for quite a while. He completed a long first draft at breakneck speed, but wasn't satisfied. He had merely cleared his head. After letting his wife look at it, he threw it away. "It was rubbish," he said. In this first draft, his hero wasn't born until page 115, a *"Tristram Shandy* trick," as he called it. But the "trick" didn't work, keeping the reader too much at a distance and probably bored. So he changed to a first-person narrative with his hero center stage from page one, and this allowed him to comment on past and present events in an ironic, comic way and to range through Indian history in describing his ancestors. But, said Rushdie, he had no intention of writing "a definitive history because there is no such thing. I wanted to leave doubts." Only propaganda had no doubts, not literature, and Rushdie had the highest aim—to turn his memories and observations and deepest concerns into a work of art.

For the style of this massive personal narrative, he successfully blended his Indian and English voices, and he mastered and merged any number of literary influences. "If you are an extra-territorial writer, you select a pedigree for yourself, a literary family." He was particularly influenced by "the great European fantastical, satirical tradition" of writers like Cervantes, Sterne, Voltaire, Gogol, Joyce, Beckett, Günter Grass, Nabokov, and Charles Dickens whom he found "astonishingly modern" in his combination of naturalism and surrealism. He also acknowledged being influenced by Herman Melville and such Latin American writers as Gabriel Garcia Marquez with their "magic realism," which has so much in common with the fantastic vision of *The Arabian Nights.*

So Salman Rushdie settled down in his London home to tame his demons and answer his critics. It wouldn't simply be an autobiographical novel or a dramatization of his view of Indian history under the British and the early, hopeful days of independence, though all that would be in it. He wanted to express his love for his home city of Bombay, its people and its infinitely varied character. That would be the heart of his book.

"I think I saw the Bombay I had grown up in slipping away and that made me go on with the writing," he said. "I felt I had to reclaim the city—and also my own memories of it. I wanted to tell India's story or stories, as well as my own."

Mrs. Gandhi, the Indian Prime Minister, would be among the characters as well as some of his own family. Real people and events would blend with imaginary beings and fantastic deeds. He would give his own hero narrator some of his own life. No one would be able to tell what had actually happened and what he had imagined. Like an old-fashioned magician, he would transform reality. There might even be a magic carpet.

4—THE BOOKER TRIUMPH

WRITING HIS HUGE NOVEL WAS A NERVE-RACKING STRAIN ON SALMAN RUSHDIE and his family because he was shut away in his study at the top of the house for much of his spare time. He tried to write at least seven hundred words a day on his electric typewriter. His wife and son didn't see much of him as he toiled away on the vast book. Sometimes, when he sat back exhausted, he feared he might collapse before he finished.

The hundreds of pages that slowly accumulated contained thoughts and dreams going back to his earliest childhood. There were satirical reflections he had never confided to anyone. It was as if the novel contained his whole life. American writers were always hoping to produce the Great American Novel. Well, this would be the Great Indian Novel covering the whole of that vast country and its history according to Rushdie, as well as portraying his beloved Bombay as he remembered it.

He called his novel *Midnight's Children* after his name for Indians born in the first hour of India's independence. His hero, Saleem Sinai, was one of Midnight's Children, possessing special powers for delving into the past, present, and future. At last the day came when Rushdie typed the final lines of his novel: "... it is the privilege and the curse of midnight's children to be both masters and victims of their times, to forsake privacy and be sucked into the annihilating whirlpool of the multitudes, and to be unable to live or die in peace."

To be unable to live or die in peace—it was a hard conclusion to come to after 552 pages, but Rushdie was confident he had achieved the book he had had in mind for so long. This couldn't be dismissed like *Grimus*. He felt relieved of a great personal burden and believed he had written a novel that was a powerful work of literary art that would receive wide attention in both the West and the East.

Liz Calder, who read his bulky manuscript with great enthusiasm, noted that quite a lot of *Madame Rama* had been absorbed into *Midnight's Children.* The best passages of the abandoned novel had been too good to lose. "I had moved to Jonathan Cape," she recalled, "and Cape more or less took it straight away, though at the time a big fat novel about India wasn't regarded as a very wonderful bet. There is a feeling in the book trade sometimes that certain things don't sell and at that time it was thought books about India didn't sell! But the people at Cape thought it was a marvelous book. We worked together on the editing and he did quite a lot of rewriting at my suggestion. One character was removed altogether. And it was a remarkable success. The hardcover of *Midnight's Children* sold over 40,000 copies. The first printing was 1,750. You can always recognize the first edition because those 1,750 were printed in America and have rough-cut edges. It was then cheaper to print a big book in America. But all the other editions were printed in England."

The reviews were the exact opposite of those for *Grimus.* Rushdie basked in raves. With one book, he had become a major literary figure on the London scene at the age of thirty-four and at last could give up his advertising chores. "I did endless calculations on the backs of envelopes," Rushdie said. "I worked out that, if I was really careful, I could probably live for a year on the basis of *Midnight's Children* and review work. I told myself very few people ever get a year in the bank, and in order for things to work out the way I wanted I had to jump off the cliff." It didn't turn out to be much of a gamble. The success of *Midnight's Children* was greater than even he expected.

The peak of critical approval came when V. S. Pritchett, the veteran novelist, short-story writer, essayist and critic, and a paternal figure in the English book world, wrote a long, enthusiastic review in *The New Yorker* magazine to coincide with the novel's publication in the United States.

"India has produced a glittering novelist—one with startling imaginative and intellectual resources, a master of perpetual storytelling," Pritchett wrote. At the same time he noted "there are strange western echoes, of the irony of Sterne in *Tristram Shandy*—that early nonlinear writer—in Rushdie's readiness to tease by breaking off or digressing at the gravest moments. This is very odd in an Indian novel. The book is really about the mystery of being born and the puzzle of who one is."

Pritchett understood that *Midnight's Children* was not only an Indian novel, but a work that owed much to the West—a unique Anglo-Indian blend of fiction and imaginative autobiography. Pritchett even noticed the early influences of Rushdie's boyhood— "This is pure *Arabian Nights* intrigue," he comments about one bizarre incident. He also found an operatic quality in Rushdie's imagination. But he had reservations about Rushdie's political satirizing in which the Little Prince criticized contemporary Indian leaders for falling below his standards.

Pritchett commented: "The novel is, in part, a powerful political satire in its savaging of both political and military leaders. Saleem's hatred of Mrs. Gandhi—the Widow (that is also to say, the guillotine)—is deep. But I think that as satire the novel is at variance with Mr. Rushdie's self-absorption and his pursuit of poetic symbols: the magic basket in which one can hide secret thoughts, and so save oneself, is an example." But Pritchett felt that Rushdie's symbols "are rather too knowing; he is playing tricks with free association." So much conjuring going on in the hero's imagination could bewilder a reader, "but as a tour de force his fantasy is irresistible."

Pritchett had revealed a conflict in Rushdie. His self-absorption in finding his migrant identity was in conflict with his patrician role as the enemy of injustice and judge of our leaders; the private Rushdie was in conflict with the public Rushdie. Both sides of him were much in evidence in *Midnight's Children* and gave the novel an unusual tension, but the conflict also made parts of the novel read like a political message inserted like an undigested editorial in a work of art.

But these reservations about Rushdie's failure to reconcile his two sides didn't affect the success of his book on either side of the Atlantic. Soon it was also causing great controversy in India— over his personal view of Indian history and his criticisms of the present leadership.

In the United States, he was represented by Elaine Markson, one of the leading literary agents in New York. She met Rushdie first in London about the time *Grimus* was published through Liz Calder, with whom she was friendly. "He helped carry my bags down to a taxi," she said. At the time he didn't have an American publisher for *Grimus,* so she took it on. Even then he talked a lot about the story of his next book, which was to become *Midnight's Children.*

Elaine Markson recalled that Rushdie "talked about his hope of making enough money from his books to give up advertising as soon as possible." She found him very charming in those early days and he was "very gentle when I first met him." She developed a good relationship with him, but "I was aware some people disliked him and thought he had a huge ego." After the success of *Midnight's Children,* he flew to New York on a short visit to help with the promotion of the novel in the United States. Elaine Markson recalled one occasion in New York "shopping with him in the Village for a gift for his wife, Clarissa. He was very funny, very warm. His later themes about race and so on were already there in his mind and in his conversation. Even in *Grimus* all his verbalizing, his brilliant wordplay were there already."

She remembered when she received the bulky manuscript of *Midnight's Children*—"a huge pile of typed pages with hardly any margins or paragraphs. But it was brilliant. I read from it aloud to friends at the beach. It was that rich and funny."

She recalled talking to Rushdie about the possibility of his writing a play about Muhammad, "but he said it wasn't a good idea because you weren't supposed to portray him." This comment showed an unusual caution that he no longer possessed a few years later when he wrote *The Satanic Verses.*

If there were some reservations in Britain about big, fat books about India, American publishers were even more lukewarm because the United States didn't have the close relationship with India that Britain had and therefore, presumably, American book buyers wouldn't be so interested. At first Elaine Markson found *Midnight's Children* difficult to place with a leading New York publisher. Several editors turned it down. "I eventually persuaded Bob Gottlieb at Knopf to take it, but I had to keep pushing him for quite a while. He thought selling it would be difficult, and of course it never did nearly as well as it did in England. But it received incredible reviews simply on its merits because I don't think it had won the Booker then."

The climax of *Midnight's Children*'s reception in Britain was being shortlisted for the prestigious Booker Prize for Fiction, then worth £10,000 (roughly $16,000 at that time). Literary prizes usually received little attention in Britain. Winners of such respected prizes as the Hawthornden and the Somerset Maugham generally rated a brief paragraph in the newspapers. What had helped to popularize the Booker was a well-publicized contest for the prize between two well-known writers the previous year—"heavyweights" as the British media called them—William Golding and Anthony Burgess. After a good deal of politicking by the supporters of both, the award of the prize to William Golding made big headlines. As a result, television had at last recognized the Booker's existence and there were plans to film the final ceremony at which Salman Rushdie was a possible winner.

Apart from *Midnight's Children,* the finalists were:

Muriel Spark's *Loitering with Intent,* about a woman writer in London and "full of witty Spark-isms" according to the London *Times;*

Doris Lessing's *The Sirian Experiments,* the third in her complex series of science fiction;

Ian McEwan's *The Comfort of Strangers,* a slim novel about a young couple on a macabre holiday in Venice;

Ann Schlee's *Rhine Journey,* set in the 1850s and about a family on a Rhine steamer;

Molly Keane's *Good Behavior,* an amusing story of Anglo-Irish gentry in the prewar years;

D.M.Thomas's *The White Hotel,* a literary fantasy about a woman's journey through pre-war Europe.

Doris Lessing said the only book she had read was *Midnight's Children,* "which I like very much." Ian McEwan didn't rate his own chances very highly because the books that won the Booker tended to be "large enterprises, books that go out and capture the world." The judges seemed to like Indian books, he said, "so Salman Rushdie is my tip to win." Molly Keane commented, "I should think the Indian will win. They're awfully fond of Anglo-

Indian books in London, so I'm told. He sounds a jolly good bet."
D.M.Thomas told a reporter, "I haven't read any of the other
novels, though I did start Salman Rushdie. I had seen his good
reviews so I took it on holiday with me, but I never finished it.
It's not really holiday reading. If he wins, I might then finish it.
I'm not a great novel reader."

Among professional gamblers in London, Muriel Spark began
as the favorite, followed by D.M.Thomas, but then Rushdie took
the lead at 2–1 with Spark falling back at 3–1 and Thomas 4–1.
The betting was paltry compared with the money put on horse
racing, but the gamblers were attracted because the Booker was
on television and, as one man put it, "it gives our gambling
business a bit of class."

The judges—Professor Malcolm Bradbury of the University of
East Anglia, science-fiction writer Brian Aldiss, critic ad TV
performer Joan Bakewell, visiting American literary critic Sam-
uel Hynes, and critic and lecturer in English at York University
Hermione Lee—had read seventy-four novels by British, Irish,
and Commonwealth authors published that year, reducing them
to the seven novels on the shortlist. The total number of new
novels published in the same period was roughly four thousand,
but the great majority didn't rate being considered for the Booker.

By the time of the Booker ceremony, Rushdie was still the
favorite with Thomas a close runner-up. Rushdie and Thomas
had much in common, even the great writers who had influenced them. Thomas admired a surrealist "mixture of magic and
naturalism," and that might almost have been the Rushdie of
Midnight's Children talking.

The judges chose the winner at the last minute after three
hours of discussion and argument. Brian Aldiss, who had been
the only judge to like Rushdie's first novel, *Grimus,* in the Gollancz
science-fiction competition, greatly admired *Midnight's Children*
and even identified with much of it. He had once lived on
Warden Road in Bombay near Rushdie's boyhood home and
recalled how it was flooded two-feet deep in the monsoon
season. In Rushdie's huge novel, Aldiss found something of
Henry James's narrative ploys in the development of the story.
Eventually called on to vote, a majority of the judges chose
Rushdie.

Rushdie attended the Booker ceremony at Stationer's Hall in October 1981. He had no doubts about winning. The television cameras caught his solemn, foreign face as he waited for the result to be announced. He looked supremely confident, as if he were sure it was his destiny to win the Booker. With a short beard and his hooded eyes, he appeared an exotic figure compared with the English writers. The TV cameras lingered on him.

Liz Calder sat beside him as Professor Malcolm Bradbury, as chairman of the judges, announced that Rushdie was the winner for his "brilliant experimental novel" and presented him with a leatherbound copy of *Midnight's Children* and a check for £10,000 that represented his freedom to write full-time for at least a year. "It was an enormous thrill for us both," recalled Liz Calder. "It was the most exciting evening." As his editor, she had shared the failure of *Grimus* and now she was there to share the triumph of *Midnight's Children*. Judge Brian Aldiss remembered that Rushdie "gave a very good, modest speech, almost audibly."

The publicity surrounding the Booker award identified Rushdie as a new, glamorous literary star on the British scene. Rushdie responded by playing the role brilliantly in interviews. The whole of London's media seemed to want to meet him. One reporter wrote after interviewing him, "His relaxed and self-assured conversation betokens an incisive intellect and powerful imagination. He is articulate and his command of ideas is impressive; but it is his modesty which is most striking."

In interviews, Rushdie described *Midnight's Children* as a political novel which transcended politics. It was the first winner of the Booker that dealt with India as a subject and not merely as a background. India, Rushdie said, was a colonial corner for English literature and he thought it was time that was stopped. The children of midnight were "basically a metaphor of hope and the purpose of them is to be destroyed by Mrs. Gandhi" (who was then the Indian Prime Minister). Rushdie told a *Guardian* reporter bitterly, "All the corruption and pettiness that were always there were never open. People felt ashamed of it." But in India now "it's very naked power politics: You give your loyalty to whoever pays you the most." The last third of *Midnight's Children*—the most overtly political part—was, he said, designed to make sure that "all this gets on the record."

48

But he didn't want to call it a political novel—"It is capable of multiple interpretations." To prevent it from being "a kind of oracle book," he introduced some trivial historical errors on the part of his narrator, Saleem, including getting the date of Mahatma Gandhi's assassination wrong. The reader may then wonder how much he can trust Saleem's account. "You can even believe that the entire book is a lie and that he may be reinventing history for his own purposes. I don't think he is really." The *Guardian* reporter concluded: "Salman Rushdie has provided us with an authoritative, majestical response to those gloomy pundits who predicted the death of contemporary fiction. The Booker prize has been well won." He added that one could hardly doubt that "a new force has arrived on the British literary scene."

Rushdie had arrived, not only as a major new writer, but as a public personality and celebrity. It was a position that he obviously enjoyed, as if he had been grooming himself for that role all these years. He also saw it as an opportunity to get publicity for his special causes and his dissatisfaction with the way much of the world was run. But probably by becoming famous almost overnight, although he had expected it as his destiny, he did not realize that from then on he would have no real private life and his marriage would be tested as never before. His books, too, would no longer just be of interest to literary critics and serious readers, but would attract the attention of politicians and other opinion makers who appreciated that fame was power.

5—MRS. GANDHI AND MRS. THATCHER

SALMAN RUSHDIE'S LIFE WOULD NEVER BE THE SAME AGAIN. AN OBSCURE writer suddenly thrust under the international spotlight, he was changed forever. People who had had no interest in him, seeing only an Indian immigrant with a Cambridge accent, now began to court him.

Clarissa Rushdie noted with amusement, "We were flooded with invitations from people we barely knew. We met lots of wonderful, exciting people. It was lovely for me. We met Vargas Llosa, Calvino, and Salman met Günter Grass. He went abroad a lot. There were times when I minded very much, but I was doing things at home. My life was child-oriented. I had plenty to do."

Their son, Zafar, was beginning to grow up and take an interest in what his parents were doing. When he asked where his father was, the usual answer was writing or away. *Midnight's Children* was dedicated to him—"For Zafar Rushdie who, contrary to all expectations, was born in the afternoon."

Rushdie became much sought after for literary dinner parties, not only because he was the latest star, but because he was a witty, nonstop conversationalist who could keep a whole table amused by tales of his colorful advertising experiences, including the one about how he thought up "naughty but nice" for cream buns. The actor in him often added hilarious impersonations. Dinner parties in literary London were political, as well as social occasions, where important contacts could be made. And Rushdie was soon well-acquainted with many of the most prominent writers, critics, and publishers. "Salman seemed to collect celebrity connections," said one acquaintance caustically. "He would have made a very good politician except for the kissing-babies side of politics." Literary London was so competitive that Rushdie's success was bound to cause much jealousy and ill will, but this was the price of fame, as Rushdie well knew.

TV and radio also began to take an interest in him, and their interviews brought out the actor in him. The same acquaintance quoted above said, "Salman seemed to be always acting, playing a role as the Distinguished Author to hide his uncertainty under the spotlight in the company of more seasoned celebrities." But his most revealing performance came later when he appeared on the long established radio program, Desert Island Discs, on which celebrities chose records to play and also a book and a luxury item they would like to have with them if they were marooned on an imaginary island. Rushdie chose the complete collection of the *Arabian Nights* tales, usually called *The Thousand and One Nights,* which, he said, "contains all other stories." The luxury item was an eerie choice, considering his later fate. It was an unlisted radio telephone "that would allow me to ring up anybody else without anyone ringing me." He was to find himself in that position in hiding.

More ominous for his future were the influential enemies he was making with his writing and public pronouncements. He acted as if he didn't care, as if he couldn't believe that he might have to pay for his satirical attacks; but prominent politicians like Indira Gandhi, then India's Prime Minister, didn't forgive hostile criticism. The Widow, as Rushdie called her, was slow to react, but soon after *Midnight's Children* was available in India, an Indian cultural attaché conceded, "Yes, we have heard of this book." Mrs. Gandhi held back from using her power to suppress the book completely in India. But she eventually sued Rushdie and his British hardcover and paperback publishers, Jonathan Cape and Pan Books, in the High Court in London over a brief passage in the novel that suggested her younger son, Sanjay, had accused her of neglecting her late husband, who had died of a heart seizure at forty-seven. Mrs. Gandhi won. She accepted a public apology for the cruel attack on her and her son. It must have hurt Rushdie's pride. But The Widow did better than that.

Rushdie and his publishers had to pay the costs of the case and undertake to remove the libelous passage from all future editions of the book, at least those over which they had control. Mrs. Gandhi couldn't sue Rushdie for roasting her as The Widow because such criticism of a public figure was allowed, but she and her political aides marked Rushdie as someone to watch. He might make a bigger slip next time.

Ironically, when Indira Gandhi visited London for a festival of Indian culture, Salman Rushdie received an invitation to a lunch given for her by the British Prime Minister, Margaret Thatcher. Someone at 10 Downing Street must have thought the author of the much-praised novel about India would be of interest to Mrs. Gandhi, and was apparently not aware of the bad feeling between her and Rushdie. According to Rushdie's version of the incident given at dinner parties and on television, he phoned Mrs. Thatcher's office to explain why he better decline the invitation. There was great relief at 10 Downing Street. But perhaps Mrs. Thatcher wasn't informed because the confusion continued. In a speech the following day with Mrs. Gandhi by her side, Mrs. Thatcher referred to *Midnight's Children* as a fine example of the Anglo-Indian cultural bond. She then mentioned Rushdie glowingly, as if Mrs. Gandhi had met him at the Downing Street lunch. Mrs. Gandhi listened, stony-faced.

By telling the story in public with witty embellishments mocking the two prime ministers, Rushdie ensured that he was not only on Mrs. Gandhi's enemies list, but on Mrs. Thatcher's as well. "Mrs. Thatcher will never ask me to lunch again, of course," remarked Rushdie. "She also knows that I've told this story—and Mrs. Thatcher is a vengeful woman."

It would have seemed reckless from anyone else, but such behavior was part of Rushdie's character. He treated prime ministers as equals and spoke his mind with apparently no consideration of what harm it might do to him. In *Grimus,* a character warns that it was erroneous "to look upon oneself as an Olympian chronicler; one was a member of the parade." But Rushdie would never behave like a member of the parade. As he also wrote in *Grimus,* "one tries by one's life and actions to bring a little sense into an inane universe,"—that is an Olympian aim. He also wrote of men "whose curse it is to be different from the rest." Such men were "habitually alone, unloved by most others, incapable of making a friend, since to make a friend would be to accept the other's way of thinking. But perhaps it's not such a curse to be alone; Wisdom is very rarely found in crowds."

Even in *Grimus* there are barbed remarks that would give offense to many people, but in *Midnight's Children* there was no holding back. There was plenty in this novel to upset even his fellow Muslims. For example, "he was by now a true Bombay Muslim at heart, placing cash matters above most other things." There were even jokes about sacred cows. Nothing was sacred to this satirical, crusading reformer; in the tradition of such great satirists as Voltaire and Swift that was considered the right attitude, but it could be dangerous when your targets were powerful, violent people and large organizations.

Rushdie also made enemies through the journalism he pursued. He chose to write for *The Guardian,* the long established, liberal paper, which automatically made him an opponent of the conservative press and conservative political groups presently in power in the Thatcher government. As well as regular book reviews, he wrote occasional articles about his special causes that ranged from Mrs. Thatcher's declaration of war against Argentina over the Falkland Islands to a fire in the London borough of Camden, in which a Bangladeshi woman and her young son and daughter died of suffocation. There had been a number of racial incidents against Asian immigrants, and in areas where they lived, "Wags go home" was frequently to be found painted on walls and doors. The immigrants also found adequate flats hard to find, and even accommodations provided by the local housing authority were not very good. There was evidence that the fire in Camden had been started deliberately. "It is time people stopped having to die to prove to local authorities that they live in hideously unsatisfactory conditions," Rushdie thundered. If the deaths were to be treated as murders, "then many of us would say that the murderers are to be found in Camden Town Hall."

As for the Falkland Islands War, Rushdie said, "I felt I knew England. I felt I'd grown up in it, in a way. But the thing that really shook me was the Falklands' War—the atavistic, jingoistic patriotism that was released. It was terrifying to behold. All the old imperial values were yanked out again, so that the popular press was inviting its readers to sponsor missiles, to send in money to pay for bombs which would then have the newspaper's logo printed inside."

Rushdie added that "it was a hideous event inside English culture, in which perhaps the most hideous thing was that it was impossible to know which way your friends were going to jump." He felt suddenly that he was among strangers, "that in spite of all these years, I didn't know these people no matter how long I've been there, how well I've fit into the society, how well I understand its rules and play its games. And at that point, I began really seriously to think about leaving—and I haven't stopped."

He thought of moving to the United States where the book market was ten times the size of Britain's and he already had friends such as his agent, Elaine Markson. He attended a PEN international congress in Manhattan, at which most of the leading American writers made speeches or appeared on panels to discuss such topics as censorship. There were also a large number of celebrated writers from other countries. It was a well-publicized event and a useful occasion for making contacts. Norman Mailer, the aging enfant terrible, presided. And, as he was a master at the publicity game, the American media devoted far more attention to the congress than was usually given to literary events.

There were a series of rows as if staged especially for the media. On the opening night, objections were made about PEN President Mailer's invitation to President Reagan's secretary of state. A couple of days later Saul Bellow and Günter Grass crossed swords over the question of social commitment. That was a subject Rushdie was deeply interested in, but he didn't rush in to take sides. During the entire congress he remained more or less in the background, taking little part in any of the controversies which was very unlike him; and making only one short speech in a quiet, unhistrionic style, his glasses hiding his striking hooded eyes and making him appear unusually studious for a novelist. It was as if he were paying respects to his peers by playing only a modest role.

I met him for the first time after his speech, introducing

myself as a reporter who was covering the congress for *The Guardian*. But he must have misheard me because he addressed me as if I were a fellow writer at the congress. With his Cambridge accent and slight formality, he seemed very English in that American setting. A friendly man just under forty, reasonably low-key, although with a suggestion of great intensity below the surface, he seemed very knowledgeable about New York. He made many amused references to the latest fads and fashions of the American media. The Indian side of him came out only when he was thoroughly involved in a conversation about something that really interested him, and then the rhythm of his speech had faint echoes of Bombay. We talked about the congress and the writers who were there. He greatly admired Günter Grass. As we chatted, his eyes behind his thick glasses were constantly glancing over the crowd in the auditorium. Norman Mailer passed by with a group of reporters. Playwright Arthur Miller, the tallest writer there and a past PEN president, went by with two intense Europeans neither Rushdie nor I recognized. When Nadine Gordimer and Günter Grass approached, Rushdie excused himself and went after them. I saw him several times later in the day, and he always seemed to be talking to someone—a very lively, sociable man making contacts.

Writers are either loners who avoid the company of other writers—William Faulkner was a prime example—or are very social, political types who feel that making contacts is an essential part of the literary game if you are to become well-known. There was no doubt which kind of writer Salman Rushdie was. The list of organizations to which he belonged was worthy of the most ambitious literary politician, ranging from the Society of Authors to the British Film Institute Production Board.

Later I watched him in a panel discussion with Susan Sontag. The talk was impassioned—over such matters as censorship and imprisoning writers—but Rushdie seemed perfectly relaxed and affable when responding to the audience, which was made-up largely of fellow writers, literary critics, and media reporters. But he wasn't yet a big name in the United States, so the American television cameras didn't linger on him. He didn't appear on the TV news programs I later watched. But he gave the impression of being perfectly at home in New York and could easily settle down to the American way of life and become a big success.

But leaving England was a weighty decision in the early eighties. He had a house, and his wife and young son were rooted there. And he had become quite used to the English way of life. He unburdened some of his pent-up feelings in a long article attacking Mrs. Thatcher. Her huge victory in the last election had made his "sense of alienation" blossom "into something close to full-scale culture shock." He criticized the British people for accepting the Thatcher dominance. "I believe the absence of widespread anger matters enormously, for this reason: that democracy can only thrive in a turbulent climate. Where there is acquiescence, cynicism, passivity, resignation, 'inactivism,' the road is clear for those who would rob us of our rights."

Book reviews are also an easy way to make enemies and Rushdie didn't hesitate to take on some of his peers. One of the most striking reviews was of V. S. (for Vidiadhur Surajprasad) Naipaul's *The Enigma of Arrival.* Naipaul, a distinguished middle-aged writer, born in the then British colony of Trinidad but with Indian ancestors, had studied at Oxford University on a scholarship and settled in London to become a professional writer as Rushdie did ten years later. Naipaul had become an accepted figure in English intellectual life in a way the more rebellious Rushdie never could. He didn't get involved in public controversies like Rushdie did, and so he made many fewer enemies, especially in Establishment circles. He had also won the Booker Prize, had been shortlisted for the Nobel Prize for Literature, and Mrs. Thatcher had made him a knight—Sir Vidiadhur Naipaul (Vidia to his friends). Knighthoods were not highly respected in Britain because the political party in power handed out so many, often to party hacks or business allies. Many of Naipaul's admirers were surprised he accepted a knighthood. *Time* magazine reported that Naipaul was "now widely considered to be England's greatest living writer." He had lived in England for nearly forty years, and had a British wife and an Oxford accent.

A small, nervous man with the low-key manner of an intellectual don, Naipaul was very different in temperament from the tall, intense Rushdie. Both writers were cast as exotic rivals in the London literary scene. They had India in common, but their

Indias were very different. The Indian-American writer Bharati Mukherjee claims that Rushdie and Naipaul, "two magnificent writers," act as mirrors for the collective experience of Third World immigrants who grew up in the emerging light of independence. "Either—following Naipaul—we are less than fully human, pathetic trained monkeys, mimic men; or we are miraculous translations, Lamarckian mutations, single lives that have acquired new characteristics and recapitulated the entire cultural history of our genotype." Naipaul's prose was "as pure a literary English as can be written," whereas Rushdie's was "a fusion of master and slave, imported and native: jangly, harsh, punning, allusive, windy, and grandiloquent." Rushdie considered immigration, despite losses and confusions and its sheer absurdities, to be a net gain, a form of levitation, whereas to Naipaul it was "loss and mimicry."

Naipaul's ancestors had emigrated from India to the Caribbean a hundred years ago. "A hundred years had been enough to wash me clean of many Indian religious attitudes," he wrote in *India: A Wounded Civilization,* "and without these attitudes, the distress of India was—and is—almost insupportable." Rushdie surely would have agreed with that.

But Naipaul wrote with the cool detachment of an outsider, whereas Rushdie always wrote about India as a concerned insider who had been born there. Naipaul thought that "the crisis of India is not only political or economic. The larger crisis is of a wounded old civilization that has at last become aware of its inadequacies and is without the intellectual means to move ahead." When Naipaul met R. K. Narayan in London, the Indian novelist told him cheerfully, "India will go on." It was the same kind of confidence in India's survival that Rushdie had expressed. It wasn't an attitude that appealed to Naipaul. He read a Narayan novel, *The Vendor of Sweets,* set in the mythical town in the south of India that Narayan always wrote about, and Naipaul decided its satire on modern civilization was too gross and Narayan's style was too lacking in irony.

When Rushdie reviewed Naipaul's *The Enigma of Arrival,* he began with lavish praise, calling Naipaul's whopping 1961 novel, *A House for Mr. Biswas,* magnificent. He wrote that Naipaul, a few years ago, had said he still regarded himself as a comic writer and that his highest ambition was to write a comedy to equal *Biswas*. "To read this was to feel heartened," remarked Rushdie. If Naipaul could find a way to combine the warmth and energy of his early books, which culminated in *Biswas,* with the magisterial technical style of his later writing, it might result in "something rather special."

But Rushdie had his doubts. The clouds that seemed to have gathered over Naipaul's world would not be easily dispelled and his affection for human beings appeared to have diminished. *The Enigma of Arrival* suggested the clouds had not lifted, but deepened. Its tone was melancholy. "It is one of the oddest books I have read in a long while," Rushdie wrote. Set in Wiltshire, much of it had to do with rustic England from an immigrant's point of view. Rushdie praised Naipaul's "delicate, precise prose of the highest quality," but added "it is bloodless prose."

He concluded that there was one word he could find nowhere in the *The Enigma of Arrival* and that was love, and a life without love, or one in which love had been buried so deep that it couldn't come out, "is very much what this book is about; and what makes it so very, very sad."

Both Indian exotics and rivals for the literary crown, Rushdie and Naipaul, with their different temperaments, backgrounds, styles, and viewpoints, could never agree. And in this review of Naipaul's book, Rushdie, with faint praise (for Brutus is an honorable man), obviously did his best to put down his distinguished rival. Bloodless and loveless were not words usually to be found in reviews of a Naipaul book on either side of the Atlantic, where he was generally admired.

I saw no comment from Naipaul in the media about the Ayatollah's death sentence so I wrote to him asking if he cared to make one, but I received no reply. It was like Naipaul, perhaps, to reply to Rushdie without naming him and thus avoid a controversy in which the literary Establishment would take sides. Naipaul stated that "There is a way currently in vogue of writing about degraded and corrupt countries. This is the way of fantasy and extravagance. It dodges all the issues; it is safe. I find the way empty, morally and intellectually." As the Bangladesh writer, Farrukh Dhondy, commented, "Whatever else one may think of that judgment (and it certainly had Marquez and perhaps Rushdie in mind), Naipaul is wrong in one respect. Such writing is certainly not 'safe.'" Despite the danger, he added, the one clear message of the Rushdie Affair was "that one has constantly to choose as a writer between supporting an ideology and telling the imaginative truth. Part of that telling is, of course, to find the truth, know it, grasp it, for the moment before it slithers away again." The Rushdie Affair, he said, was "the most massive national and international fight that has been caused since the Magna Carta; and the most desperate and fearful threat ever laid on the life of an innocent man trying to do, quite brilliantly, what he conceives of as his metier, something he cannot avoid doing: being a writer."

When Rushdie wrote an introduction for a collection of articles by *Guardian* writers, he couldn't resist, after praising the newspaper, adding "which is not to say that I do not have my dissatisfactions." There were things to put right there as everywhere else. He also couldn't resist another crack at Mrs. Thatcher. That she was "a racist can no longer be doubted," he wrote. The *New Statesman,* the British left-wing weekly, "said so in a leader [an editorial] so it must be true." Ah, nothing escaped the satirist's whip. Britain "no longer has much in the way of a quality press" and it was now a society "whose most radical voices are heard in the Church of England, the House of Lords, and even, it is rumored, Buckingham Palace."

He also presided over a meeting to discuss Professor Edward Said's book, *After the Last Sky,* concerning Palestine. Professor Said, professor of English and comparative literature at Columbia University in New York and the author of several books on Islam, had become a controversial figure because of his outspoken views about the Middle East. As Rushdie reported at the meeting, Said had recently received threats to his safety from the militant Jewish Defense League in America. Rushdie added, "To be a Palestinian in New York—in many ways *the* Palestinian—is not the easiest of fates." He described Professor Said as "an especially important voice" for those "who see the struggle between Eastern and Western descriptions of the world as both an internal and an external struggle."

Rushdie then told of how one of his sisters, on a visit to California, was frequently asked where she came from. When she said Pakistan, most people seemed to have no idea what it meant. One American said, "Oh, yes, Pakestine!" and immediately started talking about his Jewish friends. Rushdie commented, "It is impossible to overestimate the consequences of American ignorance on world affairs."

Rushdie's father died, leaving little money. Rushdie said once his father had inherited quite a lot "and spent the rest of his life losing it." He had objected to Salman's choosing to become a writer because it wasn't a real job but had finally accepted his son's choice. When he read *Grimus,* he remarked, "What this tells me is that one day you will write a real book." *Midnight's Children* had proved him right. But he would miss seeing his son become the most famous writer in the world.

Another family event shocked Rushdie so much that it influenced the writing of his next novel. One of his sisters came on a visit to London, but it was a bad time to be there. Racial incidents against Asians had increased, and there were riots in the Brixton area where many of the West Indian immigrants lived. The West Indians had grown-up children who had been born in England, but protested they were not accorded the full rights of British citizenship. They were discriminated against in the job market and had a much higher percentage of unemployment than white English young people. Moreover, many London policemen were persistently hostile to them. Rebellious feelings were behind the Brixton riots, which led to mass police action and an increase in racial incidents by white youths. During the Brixton riots, Rushdie's sister, alone in a compartment of an underground train, was beaten up by one of these white gangs and humiliated. The police at Brixton station declined to take any action and a feeling of shame over her humiliation made Rushdie's sister unwilling to pursue it.

Rushdie reacted with fury. The incident embittered him even more about the racism in Britain. He had to find an outlet for his deep feelings and decided he would write a short novel about "a girl who suffers excessively from the emotion of shame, which unleashes in her a violence of which she could not normally be capable."

But the first version was "very, very depressing, unbelievably morbid," and he began to rewrite it "in the language of comedy, and of course it's not really about my sister at all any more." The novel slowly grew into a fantasy about his other home in the East—Pakistan. He called the novel *Shame*.

6—DEFENDING SHAME

SALMAN RUSHDIE DID NOT FEEL THE SAME AFFECTION FOR PAKISTAN THAT HE did for India. So *Shame* was a much more critical work, much of the fantasy seeming to have a bitter, angry tone. Parts of *Shame*, in fact, made *Midnight's Children* read like no more than an affectionate, avuncular view of India and its past errors. Except where he had written about The Widow, Rushdie's attitude toward his huge, sprawling, ancient, native land was more regretful than condemnatory. Bombay, with all its painful divisions, remained a place he was very fond of, a place where so many of his dearest memories were based.

But with Pakistan—his adopted homeland, long since rejected—where he had never wanted his parents to live and which he visited as little as possible, he was unsparing in his view. With Muslims in the majority, he didn't make the allowances that he did in India where Hindus had most of the power. He observed the way religion and politics were often involved, and his satirical view was often as savage as Swift's in the last part of *Gulliver's Travels* where Swift's disgust was so overpowering that he depicted horses as being superior to human beings.

Although Rushdie kept up the pretense of writing about a fantasy land, real Pakistani politicians were easily recognizable and he judged their actions harshly, especially the fallen leaders Bhutto and Zia. General Zia had executed Bhutto and then been killed himself. Rushdie made this grim drama seem like an outrageous farce of political intrigue. Pakistan was "a miracle that went wrong." The supporters of Bhutto and Zia were outraged by the devastating put-downs that condemned the political system of the country. Rushdie made a lot more powerful enemies.

61

"The country in this story is not Pakistan, or not quite," he wrote. "There are two countries, real or fictional, occupying the same space, or almost the same space. My story, my fictional country exists, like myself, at a slight angle to reality."

Rushdie called *Shame* a "modern fairy-tale" and added that "nobody need get upset, or take anything I say seriously. No drastic action need be taken either— What a relief!"

It was as if he knew that one day his enemies would take drastic action.

Shame began like a story from the *Arabian Nights*: "In the remote border town of Q., which when seen from the air resembles nothing so much as an ill-proportioned dumb-bell, there once lived three lovely, and loving sisters." Behind castle walls shutting out the world, they are bringing up an illegitimate child. Only they know which of the three is the mother, the shameful one.

That is only a beginning. Soon the usual lively gallery of Rushdie grotesques is filling the stage, including a woman seeking a terrible, violent revenge for her shame and humiliation. This avenging figure obviously helped Rushdie to exorcise the ghost of what happened to his sister in London.

He often stops the narrative for direct comments about the characters or Pakistan, and many of these are very provocative. He lists some of the bad things he would have to mention "if this were a realistic novel about Pakistan." He refers, for example, to "an industrial program that builds nuclear reactors but cannot develop a refrigerator."

He also satirizes the fundamentalism of politicians who bring back Islamic punishments, such as flogging and dismemberment. Rushdie reports one defender of such practices as insisting they are based on the Word of God and that dismemberment is not performed in any primitive way but rather hygienically.

He constantly stresses the theme of shame and shamelessness— the roots of violence, he believes—in the confused modern world. "Wherever I turn, there is something of which to be ashamed."

He scoffs at some of the primitive ideas in Pakistan. "All this happened in the fourteenth century." In that part of the world, "until quite recently, the thirteen hundreds were still in full swing."

He refers to those who fell in battle and "were flown directly, first-class, to the perfumed gardens of Paradise."

He calls it "a novel of leavetaking, my last words on the East from which, many years ago, I began to come loose," and he added, "When individuals come unstuck from their native land, they are called 'migrants.'" What was the best thing about migrants? "Their hopefulness." And the worst? "It is the emptiness of one's luggage." All migrants were "fantasists."

He also comments of Pakistan, which had a macho Muslim warrior tradition, "It is commonly and, I believe, accurately said of Pakistan that her women are much more impressive than her men."

There are remarks that, with hindsight, would seem like prophecies.

"Your God is great, great in his greatness, and so he may forgive such blasphemy."

"No pardon can be considered until a full confession has been made."

And there are even disrespectful references to the Ayatollah Khomeini.

Referring to the theater, he remarks, "My friends and I had liked *Danton's Death*; in the age of Khomeini, etc., it seemed most apposite."

"Pakistan is not Iran. This may sound like a strange thing to say about the country which was, until Khomeini, one of the only two theocracies on earth (Israel being the other one), but it's my opinion that Pakistan has never been a mullah-dominated society." (Mullahs are Muslims of a class trained in traditional law and doctrine, especially one who is head of a mosque.) Rushdie adds, "What I am saying will probably be anathematized by the present regime in that hapless country."

It was as if he were a little more reckless in each suceeding book, testing how far he could go.

He had signed with Deborah Rogers, one of the leading literary agents in London, to represent him on that side of the Atlantic. But Liz Calder was still his editor for *Shame*, which like *Midnight's Children* was published in Britain by Cape. Liz Calder told me, "Editing went smoothly, there were no problems with it, and it was acclaimed on publication." In the acknowledgments,

Rushdie mentioned the book was written "with the financial assistance of the Arts Council of Great Britain" and owed "a good deal to the entirely non-financial assistance of many others." He ended, "And finally, and as always, to Clarissa, for everything."

The British critics were just as approving as they had been of *Midnight's Children.* Malcolm Bradbury in *The Guardian* called him a major writer, the most brilliant of a group of writers "whose polyglottism of language and style seemed to be transforming everything." Bradbury, who had been the chairman of the judges when Rushdie won the Booker Prize, commented that *Shame* "takes us from the free pleasures of storytelling to the indignation of the bitter modern writer who knows and penetrates the world of mad mullahs, fanatics and hard men who rule everywhere, with a God of some sort on one shoulder and a violent version of statecraft on the other. Like Marquez and Kundera, with whom he is so naturally contemporary, Rushdie shows us with what fantasy our sort of history must now be written—if, that is, we are to penetrate it, and perhaps even save it."

The Times called *Shame* "a pitch-black comedy of public life and historical imperatives," and *The Sunday Telegraph* commented, "It can be read as fable, polemic or excoriation; as history or as fiction." *The Observer* decided Rushdie "has earned the right to be called one of our great storytellers, a magical realist in the tradition of Grass, Calvino, Borges, above all, Garcia Marquez."

When *Shame* was published in the United States—by Knopf like *Midnight's Children*—the critical reception was just as enthusiastic. The *New York Times Book Review* put *Shame* in the exalted company of "those unclassifiable works in which certain writers of the 18th century excelled—Swift in *Gulliver's Travels,* Voltaire in *Candide,* Stern in *Tristram Shandy.*" *Time* commented, "Extravagant mythmaking alternates with passages of first-person political candor. His literary accomplishments are uniquely his own. A Westerner by adoption and choice, looking back on a country where he would assuredly be silenced if he tried to write a book like *Shame,* Rushdie had produced an imaginative tour of obliquities and iniquities."

Elaine Markson remembered that *Shame* sold better in the United States than *Midnight's Children*. The earlier novel "sold about 8,000–9,000 copies in hardcover and paperback rights went to Avon. It had nothing like the success it had in England and France. The printings weren't very large. *Shame* did slightly better with 11,000 and a sale of paperback rights to Vintage."

Shame was shortlisted for the Booker Prize of 1983. No writer had ever won the prize twice, but Rushdie was convinced he would be the first to do so. According to acquaintances at the time, winning the Booker again became an obsession with him, and he talked endlessly about the politics of the prize, who the judges were that year, what kind of fiction they liked, and who would be the favorites. The prize had become important to him in a way no one else quite understood, perhaps not even Clarissa Rushdie. People might scoff at the Booker's significance, it represented only the judgment of a small group, but Rushdie still desperately wanted it; wanted to be the winner with an intense, burning ambition.

Out of sixty-two judges in the prize's history, most had been male and British, and from the literary establishment. There had been a few American judges, but none from such Commonwealth countries as India and the West Indies, although writers from those countries had been on the shortlist several times and had even won the prize. That year three of the five judges were women, only the third time they had been in a majority, and for the first time the chairman was a woman—his old colleague in advertising, Fay Weldon, now an established feminist novelist. She thought the whole thing was a terrible burden on writers, but she found it exhilarating that there was so much good work to choose from. The Booker, she said, had become "a necessary evil." And it certainly brought writers and publishers a great deal of extra publicity that helped to sell books.

Rushdie must have been sure Fay Weldon would be on the side of *Shame,* but some of the other judges were harder to read. Angela Carter, a well-known British fabulist and essayist, shared some of his literary tastes and maybe would vote for *Shame.* She believed we were in "a post-imperial phase of literature." And Rushdie knew she admired *Midnight's Children.* Peter Porter, an Australian-born poet and critic, was a possible intellectual ally as *Shame* would probably appeal to him. Of previous winners, he was said to have liked J. G. Farrell's *The Siege of Krishnapar* and William Golding's *Rites of Passage*. Terence Kilmartin, literary editor of *The Observer* and translator of Proust, was also a possible supporter. He liked the previous year's winner, the non-fiction novel, *Schindler's Ark* by Thomas Keneally, and V. S. Naipaul's *In a Free State*. But Libby Purves—a broadcaster and former *Tatler* editor and at thirty-three the youngest judge—who was regarded as the middlebrow among otherwise highbrow judges, was impossible to predict. She might find *Shame* too highbrow. In interviews, she was indignant about being put down as a middlebrow, but her journalistic background suggested she was no highbrow. "It's not the first time I've read a book since Oxford, you know," she said. In her opinion it was "important that the prize goes to a book that people will read. The whole point of the Booker is to promote fiction to a really wide audience." Where did that leave *Shame*?

The shortlist of novels was described by the London *Sunday Times* as "the most resolutely highbrow in all the fifteen years since the prize was founded." Three out of the six novels shortlisted were by teachers of English—at Oxford, East Anglia, and Capetown universities—a sign, perhaps, of how difficult it was to make a living simply as a professional writer, a fact of literary life that Rushdie knew well from his years in advertising.

Shame's rivals were:

Malcolm Bradbury's *Rates of Exchange,* a comedy about an English university don in Eastern Europe;

John Fuller's *Flying to Nowhere,* a poet's elusive novella set on an island off the Welsh coast during the Middle Ages;

Anita Mason's *The Illusionist,* another historical novel, this one set in the first century A.D. in the Middle East and Rome, with Biblical characters such as Saint Peter among the large cast;

Graham Swift's *Waterland,* an ambitious novel about several generations of Fenland people;

J.M. Coetzee's *Life and Times of Michael K,* a stern view of the near future in South Africa.

This short list was the result of four months of reading by the five judges who each received £1,000 for their trouble (roughly $1,500 at that time).

Rushdie read all the other books and decided *Shame* was superior to all of them, so it all depended on the fairness of the judges in his opinion.

Before he attended the Booker ceremony, he read a passage from *Shame* aloud in Trafalgar Square describing a bomb explosion in New Delhi in 1946. The reading was part of a protest against nuclear weapons, but Rushdie no doubt also regarded it as launching his new novel in public and perhaps influencing the Booker judges with all the publicity. He read vividly, the actor in him enjoying the performance and the reaction of the London crowd.

Clarissa Rushdie accompanied her husband to witness what was to be surely another triumph when he was announced the winner of the £10,000 prize for the second time. There was apparently no doubt in his mind that the Booker was his. He already acted like the winner as he sat waiting, smiling with confidence behind his beard and nodding with assurance to acquaintances who wished him good luck. Filmed by television cameras as a big live news event, the announcement of the winner was made by Fay Weldon. It seemed poetic justice that his old pal should name him. But something had clearly gone wrong in the judges' secret voting sessions. Chairperson Weldon seemed strangely reserved as she came to the winner's name and the reason was easily explained. It wasn't Salman Rushdie. With her old pal glaring at her, she named J.M. Coetzee, the South African writer, instead. The judges, she said, had found Coetzee's novel, *Life and Times of Michael K,* to be a work of remarkable power and great inventiveness. Coetzee, a teacher in South Africa, had been unable to get a leave of absence to be there, so the Booker check for £10,000 was presented to his publisher, Tom Rosenthal, chairman of Secker & Warburg.

Rushdie, clearly astonished at the news, looked as if he couldn't believe it. A fellow writer, who watched the TV report, said, "Salman's disappointment was obvious even on TV. His face with those haunting and haunted eyes froze into a haughty, aloof look, always Salman's way of concealing a blow to his very vulnerable ego. He was probably convinced at first there was some mistake, but when the check was handed over, he must have realized *Shame* had really been passed over, and his Indian paranoid feeling that every failure concealed a conspiracy probably came rushing to the fore and upset his self-control. He probably thought 'Someone has decided I mustn't win the prize again.' There had clearly been very effective opposition to *Shame*, he probably concluded. Seething, he must have felt he had to register a protest against this injustice. His growing anger needed an outlet!"

According to people who were there, the bearded Rushdie stood up, his face livid, and harangued the judges and anyone else who would listen to his embarrassing outburst. His hooded eyes were accusing as his hands gesticulated like an actor's with high emotion. He apparently believed the prize had been stolen from him and given to a compromise candidate. Visions of conspiracies against him were obviously blinding him to the truth—that some of the judges had simply preferred another book—and he was regarded as a bad loser. It encouraged even more the idea of him as an arrogant Man of Destiny convinced he had an important role to play in the world.

Fay Weldon was quoted as saying, "It was a bit of a steamy evening. There were five judges—two for *Shame* and two for Coetzee ... I didn't exactly have a casting vote. Salman didn't speak to me for two years afterwards." Later she told *The Guardian*, "If there is a weakness in him, it is a kind of literary ambition (wanting to win prizes), which was irrelevant because he was so good. But he didn't realize the value of what he was doing. Somehow, the work is greater than him."

It was an embarrassing scene for Rushdie's friends and admirers. Clarissa Rushdie sat at their table, quite expressionless according to a friendly observer. "She sat there looking terribly English while Salman was being a bad loser in a very unEnglish way. The thing about Salman is: if he won the Nobel Prize, he would not be happy until he had won it twice."

When you ask Rushdie's friends about his outburst, they are usually evasive, not wanting to talk about it in case they upset Salman. Most of them blame the media rather than Rushdie, claiming the whole incident was blown up and greatly exaggerated. Asked if she had witnessed what happened, Liz Calder told me that she was at the Booker ceremony, but "I wasn't sitting near him, so I really don't know. He expressed whatever he felt privately."

Well, it wasn't so private according to many observers. "The trouble is, Salman had such a belief in himself," remarked one acquaintance. "After the overwhelming success of *Midnight's Children,* he felt he couldn't do wrong or fail to win anything he went in for. If *Shame* didn't win therefore, it couldn't be that the judges had found a better book. It *must* have been the result of a plot against him. Believe me Salman wouldn't still be alive today if he didn't have that kind of belief in himself, and he has to protect it. His Booker outburst was self-protection."

Delighted gossip columnists seized on the incident as a Booker scandal. Prize-winning ceremonies usually lack drama, except perhaps in France where the Parisian literary scene seems more given to open intrigue, public battles and vendettas, and so Rushdie's outburst was welcomed. It enlivened an otherwise tame literary occasion. Coetzee, far away in South Africa, didn't make much of a story. Journalists were sorry the more newsworthy Rushdie hadn't won instead.

Literary London likes nothing better than colorful, scandalous gossip involving a well-known writer, and so accounts of the incident, suitably embroidered and embellished, were passed around. "Did you hear what Salman Rushdie did when he didn't win the Booker?" It was an example of Rushdie's arrogance and Olympian attitude, although such eagerness about prize winning suggested galloping insecurity and an overwhelming desire to be recognized. Even after being in England on and off for over twenty years, Rushdie still had a "migrant's" insecurity, a sense of not altogether belonging. He may have felt much-publicized awards such as the Booker helped establish him as a public figure beyond all criticism. But when I put this to a friend of Rushdie's, he replied, "I don't think Salman is that insecure. He just likes to win. He thinks it's his destiny. He has a great belief in himself now."

Rushdie tried to ignore all the fuss, brushing off the gossip as untrue or exaggerated. The success of *Shame* critically and in the bookstores helped. Not only was it a bestseller in Britain, but like a consolation prize, *Shame* was awarded the Prix du Meilleur Livre Etranger in France. Rushdie's attitude seemed to be that he had simply expressed his feelings without fear or favor. Wasn't that how he had always lived his life since his early days at Rugby?

7—MIGRANT IN NICARAGUA

INDIA, PAKISTAN, BRITAIN AND, TO A LESSER EXTENT, THE UNITED STATES had been Rushdie's main political interests—and targets. Now, he turned his attention to another continent—Central America—and accepted an invitation to visit Nicaragua.

Ten years before, when he was living in a small London flat above a liquor store, a big house next door was bought by the wife of the Nicaraguan dictator, Anastasio Somoza Debayle. The house became notorious in the street for a burglar alarm that often went off; and for parties that brought guests in Rolls-Royces, Mercedes-Benzs, and Jaguar limousines and blocked the street. The dictator and his wife had long since been deposed and Nicaragua now had a left-wing people's government that was condemned as communist and pro-Soviet by the Reagan administration.

Part of Rushdie's reason for visiting Nicaragua undoubtedly was that the Reagan administration had begun a war against the left-wing government by supporting a rebel army. President Reagan was a friend and ally of Mrs. Thatcher—to Rushdie, another right-wing, reactionary leader whose dangerous ways needed correcting. He originally had a sentimental interest in Nicaragua because the revolution that toppled the ruling dictator and opened the way for the present government had been born exactly one month after his son's birthday. "I've always had a weakness for synchronicity, and I felt that the proximity of the birthdays forged a bond." But the Reagan war made him even more interested because "I was myself the child of a successful revolt against a great power, my consciousness the product of the triumph of the Indian revolution." It was perhaps also true

70

that "those of us who did not have our origins in the countries of the mighty West, or North, had something in common—not, certainly, anything as simplistic as a unified 'third world' outlook, but at least some knowledge of what weakness was like, some awareness of the view from underneath, and of how it felt to be there, on the bottom, looking up at the descending heel."

He became a sponsor of the Nicaragua Solidarity Campaign in London, and so when he visited Nicaragua in July 1986, he didn't go as a wholly neutral observer. He was a guest of the Sandinista Association of Cultural Workers, an umbrella organization that brought writers, artists, musicians, craftspeople, dancers and similarly talented people together. Rushdie was familiar, he said, with the tendency of revolutions to go wrong, to become the thing they had been created to destroy. He knew about starting with idealism and romance, and ending with betrayed expectations, broken hopes. Would he even like the the Sandinistas? But "one didn't have to like people to believe in their right not to be squashed by the United States."

He was there for three weeks, and originally he had no intention of writing about it, "but my encounter with the place affected me so deeply that in the end I had no choice." He found it a beautiful, volcanic country with a population of under three million "and the war continued to reduce it." The few buses "crammed to bursting-point with people" reminded him of India and Pakistan. The roadside shanties put up by the peasants were like those in Calcutta and Bombay.

He spent much of his time with fellow writers, most of whom were poets. He inquired about the relative absence of novelists in this "poet-stuffed country" as he called it, and was told, "There was never time for novels. You could squeeze in poetry between other things. Not a novel."

There was a lot of talk about the United States Central Intelligence Agency as the real threat. Rushdie's reflex action was "simultaneously Eastern and Western"—the Western voice inside him that was fed up with cloaks and daggers and conspiracy theories muttered "Not them again," whereas the Eastern voice inside him understood that although it was easy to make the CIA a scapegoat, "it was also just a bit too jaded, too cynical, to discount its power."

He met President Daniel Ortega, who was also a poet, and asked him about his writing, but Ortega seemed embarrassed by such questions. "In Nicaragua," he told Rushdie, "everybody is considered to be a poet until he proves to the contrary." His main literary effort now was to persuade his ministers and officials to speak clearly to the people.

Rushdie was depressed to find censorship in Nicaragua—the newspaper *La Prensa* had been closed down. "Are such matters as the freedom of the press just cosmetic?" he asked. The official answer was, "Everybody censors the press in wartime." It didn't satisfy Rushdie. He had been in Pakistan during the 1965 war with India and he remembered the "hopelessly and deliberately misleading" information put out by the Pakistan government. He learned to divide Pakistani claims to have shot down Indian planes by ten, and to multiply the admitted losses by the same number, then you had "the illusion of truth." He remembered, too, his outrage at the British government's manipulation of the news media during the Falklands War. He decided in Nicaragua that what had been unacceptable to him in Pakistan and Britain "was also unacceptable here." The issue of freedom of the press was the one on which he "absolutely parted company" with the Sandinistas. It disturbed him greatly that a government consisting of so many poets had turned into a government of censors. But he decided that if Nicaragua was an imperfect state, it was still engaged in a true revolution, in an attempt to change the structures of society in order to improve the lives of its citizens. "And imperfection, even the deep flaw of censorship, did not constitute a justification for being crushed by a superpower's military and economic force." Nicaragua was "a flawed democracy of the left," he concluded.

Rushdie traveled widely in the country and met a fair cross-section of the people with whom he talked through an interpreter, including some grotesques worthy of a Rushdie novel. He ended his visit convinced that the Nicaraguan leaders were men of integrity and great pragmatism, genuine revolutionary nationalists with an astonishing lack of bitterness toward their opponents, past or present.

For the first time in his life, he realized with surprise, he had come across a government he could support not *faute de mieux* but because he wanted its efforts to succeed. "It was a disorienting realization." He added, "I had spent my entire life as a writer in opposition, and had indeed conceived the writer's role as including the function of antagonist to the state." He felt "distinctly peculiar" about being on the same side as the people in charge, but if he had been a Nicaraguan writer, he said, he would have felt obliged to get behind the leadership "and push."

On the plane flying back to Britain, he sat next to a Nicaraguan woman who was married to a Frenchman and lived in Paris. Rushdie described them both as "two migrants making our way in this West stuffed with money, power and things, this North that taught us how to see from its privileged point of view. But maybe we were the lucky ones; we knew that other perspectives existed. We had seen the view from elsewhere."

He felt intensely about his Nicaraguan experience—it was, as he said, the first time he identified with a government and was not in opposition. But he was unsure whether to write about his three-week visit, and if he did, whether it should be one of his long *J' Accuse* articles for *The Guardian* or a short book. A book would reach a wider international audience and probably there could be an American edition, which appealed particularly to him as a way of answering President Reagan and reaching Americans unaware of the situation. To so many Americans, he said, the war in Nicaragua was just something happening on television.

Soon after his return to London, fellow writer Jessica Mitford met him at a dinner party. Rushdie, she said, "a gifted raconteur, kept us enthralled (and sometimes in stitches, for he can be as amusing in person as in his books) with his accounts of Nicaraguan people and places. But he was clearly deeply worried about what to do with the impressions garnered during his brief visit."

Jessica Mitford recalled, "To write or not to write? That was the question he posed to our gathering of some twenty people, most of whom had themselves spent time in that embattled country. Not for him the slippery role of Instant Expert; he can't bear that sort of debased journalism. Yet he felt bound to record what he had seen and heard."

A newspaper or magazine article wouldn't be long enough to cover all the people and places he considered significant. It had to be a book, but a short one. Three weeks didn't justify a long work. It had to be essentially a reporter's observations with a minimum of generalizing and comment.

The finished book was 171 pages, and he called it *The Jaguar Smile—A Nicaraguan Journey* from an anonymous verse about "a young girl of Nicaragua who smiled as she rode on a jaguar," the ride ending, however, "with the young girl inside and the smile on the face of the jaguar." He described the book as "a portrait of a moment, no more" in the life of Nicaragua.

Picador, a branch of the Pan Books empire, had published earlier Rushdie books in paperback in Britain. It was decided the best way to publish *The Jaguar Smile* was as an original paperback with no expensive hardcover edition because then it could be published quickly, which made sense with such a topical non-fiction book.

Sonny Mehta, now editorial director of Knopf in New York, was then in charge of Pan in Britain and edited the book. Mehta told me in New York, "Salman had been out there—I don't know under what auspices. When he came back, he talked with such enthusiasm about it and he decided he would write a small piece. But when he talked and talked about it, it evolved into something much longer. It was decided to do it as an original paperback. That isn't quite so alien in Britain as it is in this country. The book was published in one and a half to two months. It was comparatively straightforward to edit. There was a certain amount of give-and-take, but that's usual. He had a whole list of notes from me and we had a couple of meetings."

This meant it was the first Rushdie book not edited by Liz Calder. *The Jaguar Smile* "was thought to be more suitable as a paperback original," she said, but she was comforted by the belief that she had been promised Rushdie's next novel.

The British critics were generally approving. Jessica Mitford's comment that it was an "absorbing little book" was typical. When *The Jaguar Smile* was published in the United States, Rushdie changed publishers. Elaine Markson told me, "I think *Midnight's Children* with Knopf had been a disappointment and that was why he changed publishers. I took it to Elizabeth Sifton at Viking Penguin. But there were other reasons, too, for the change, including getting more money and that he hadn't liked the way Knopf handled the paperback of *Shame* in Vintage." Viking published the book in both a hardcover edition and a Penguin paperback so it received maximum attention.

The American critical reception was more mixed than the British. Some of the American critics didn't like the attacks on Reagan and the war. A *Newsday* reporter in London described it as a polemic about Nicaraguan political problems and commented, "Even Rushdie, who is not known for his modesty, seems self-conscious about having written a book about a country which he had visited for less than one month." But another writer at *Newsday* was quoted on the Penguin paperback: "A vivid and probing introduction for perplexed outsiders trying to make sense of Nicaraguan dilemmas." *The New York Times* called the book stirring and original and added, "It gives us a picture of the country in bright, patchwork colors unavailable in your usual journalistic dispatches." Penguin also quoted Rushdie's friend, Professor Edward Said, as commenting that *The Jaguar Smile* was "a masterpiece of sympathetic yet critical reporting graced with his marvelous wit, quietly assertive style, odd and yet always revealing experiences."

Rushdie had extended his sphere of activities. He had begun to play a role on the American stage and engage in American political controversies, making his name much more widely known. But this also meant that he made more powerful enemies and and became of interest to both friends and enemies of the United States. It was not lost on his Asian enemies that he had now become part of the American scene with growing influence there.

8—HOLY WARS AND LITERARY PIRATES

THE INDIAN GENERATION BEGINNING WITH INDEPENDENCE IN AUGUST 1947, the generation that never knew British colonial rule, had been nicknamed "Midnight's Children" after Rushdie's novel. When Rajiv Gandhi became Prime Minister in 1984 after the assassination of his mother, Mrs. Gandhi (The Widow), his administration was welcomed in newspapers by headlines such as "Enter Midnight's Children."

Rushdie was proud of having given a name to a whole generation, a feat which few writers achieved. He was also interested to see how close real life and his novel had been. In *Midnight's Children,* he had referred to 1,001 Indian children born in the first midnight hour of freedom. But he had since worked out that the Indian birth rate in August 1947 was approximately two babies per second, so his fictional figure of 1,001 per hour had been a little low.

He was also pleased to learn that readers in Bombay had found his book to be full of revelations about their city. There were even people claiming to be characters in the book. "That book tells many things about Bombay," said a bookseller in the city, "that even we don't know. Only after reading did we know."

When Rushdie became forty in 1987—the same age as independent India—he decided to "take a look at the state of the Indian nation, which was, like me, entering its fifth decade," and make a film about "the real-life counterparts of the imaginary beings I once made up." Meeting midnight's real children would be like closing a circle in his life.

The question he wanted answered with their help was "Does India exist?" In the four thousand years of Indian history, there

76

never had been a united India. But if India didn't exist now in the days of independence, the explanation was to be found in communalism, which Rushdie defined as the politics of religious hatred. He was dismayed to find an India still divided by religious conflicts. Not one of the real-life Midnight's Children he encountered seemed untouched by the conflicts and the violence.

He was particularly upset by the Muslim-Hindu clash over a mosque in a town called Ayodhya in the state of Uttar Pradesh. The mosque was disputed territory because Ayodhya was the home town of the Hindu god Rama and, according to local legend, the spot where he was born was where the Muslim place of worship stood. Hindus and Muslims had been fighting all over north India, and the dispute over the mosque was the main cause of the communal violence.

When Rushdie arrived in Delhi, the old Walled City was under heavy curfew because of an outbreak of violence. The city's leading Muslims had decided Eid, the great Muslim festival marking the end of a month of fasting, should not be celebrated.

Rushdie found that all over India tension between Muslims and Hindus was rising. One Midnight's Child, a clerical worker on the docks of Bombay, told Rushdie that the village he lived in was peaceful and all the villagers, whatever their beliefs, lived in harmony. "Religions are only words," he told Rushdie. "What is behind them is the same, whichever faith it is." But when communal violence came to the Bombay docks, he dared not return to work for weeks.

Rushdie walked through the streets where 350 Sikhs had been burned alive after Mrs. Gandhi's assassination. Charred, gutted houses still contained bones of the dead. One woman had seen her husband's beard ripped from his face before he was killed. "It was the worst place I have ever seen," commented Rushdie, "not least because, in the surrounding streets, children played normally, the neighbors went on with their lives."

Rushdie's India had "always been based on ideas of multiplicity, pluralism, hybridity: ideas to which the ideologies of the communalists are diametrically opposed." He thought the defining image of India was "the crowd, and a crowd is by its very nature superabundant, heterogeneous, many things at once. But the India of the communalists is none of these things."

He asked a Bengali intellectual, one of Midnight's Children, "Does India exist?" Forty years after a nationalist revolution, where could it be said to reside?

"To the devil with all that nationalism," the Bengali replied. "I am an Indian because I am born here and I live here. So is everyone else of whom that is true. What's the need for any more definitions?"

Rushdie said if the idea of nationalism was done without, "What's the glue holding the country together?"

"We don't need glue," was the reply. "India isn't going to fall apart. All that Balkanisation stuff. I reject it completely. We are simply here and we will remain here. It's this nationalism business that is the danger." According to the Bengalis, the idea of nationalism in India had grown more and more chauvinistic, narrower and narrower.

Rushdie concluded that India was increasingly defined as Hindu India, and Sikh and Muslim fundamentalism grew ever fiercer and more entrenched in response. When *Midnight's Children* was first published, he said, the most common criticism in India was that it was too pessimistic about the future. Nobody found the novel's ending pessimistic six years later because what had happened in India was "so much darker than anything I had imagined." The book's conclusion, suggesting that a new, more pragmatic generation would take over from the Midnight's Children, seems "absurdly, romantically optimistic." But India regularly confounded its critics by its resilience, its survival in spite of everything. Rushdie decided that "the old functioning anarchy will, somehow or other, keep on functioning for another forty years and no doubt another forty after that. But don't ask me how." He called the British TV film he made in India at that time "The Riddle of Midnight."

This trip to his native land made a profound impression on him and influenced all his future writing, especially his next novel, *The Satanic Verses.* The religious conflicts, so much involved with politics and the most primitive violence, that he had witnessed in travelling around India helped to shape his view of Muslim and Hindu leaders. Now that he was no longer a Muslim believer, he felt he could observe the religious scene dispassionately. He didn't like what he saw.

As a writer, he had another problem in India and Pakistan— pirates. *Midnight's Children* was widely circulated in Pakistan in a very cheap, illegal, pirated edition that reproduced even the copyright page of the British edition. With a grand impertinent gesture, the Pakistani pirates sent Rushdie a grateful greetings card on the Muslim festival of Eid, a sarcastic tribute to the money his book had made for them. A pirated edition at half the price of the official paperback soon followed in India.

When Rushdie refused to sign a woman's pirated copy of *Midnight's Children* in Delhi, she said angrily, "What do you want anyway? Royalties or readers?" Rushdie replied that he hadn't understood that writers were required to choose between those options. The woman wasn't impressed. Rushdie reflected that it was the only form of theft which engendered little or no sympathy for the victim.

Sometimes pirates put a best-selling writer's name on books by other writers to make them more saleable. Rushdie hoped at least to be spared that. The only pirates he welcomed were those who took copies of his books into countries where they were banned. *Shame* had not been officially banned in Pakistan, but the publishers had been advised if the book were sent to Pakistan, its distributors might have a hard time. A pirated edition was put on sale in bookstores in Karachi and Lahore, but there were massive police raids that frightened the booksellers and dissuaded them from stocking any more copies of the book. One of the biggest displays of pirated editions was on the sidewalk outside the Regal Cinema in New Delhi. Rushdie described them angrily as "purloined ideas, pilfered imaginations, contraband knowledge." When he was told it was "a kind of compliment" to be pirated, Rushdie protested that theft was the sort of flattery he could do without. But it was part of the price of international fame, of the celebrity life.

9—"FOR MARIANNE"

RUMORS THAT HIS MARRIAGE WAS IN TROUBLE HAD PERSISTED FOR MONTHS. At first friends attributed the rumors to malicious gossip. But Rushdie and his wife were seen out together in public less and less. An acquaintance who saw Clarissa at a London dinner party said, "I watched her as Salman took the stage and she bore the patient look of a wife who had heard his brilliant discourse many times before. She played absentmindedly with a bread roll and seemed to have a lot on her mind, none of it happy. Salman paid her little attention as he told his stories and dominated the dinner party. The next time I was a fellow guest, Salman was at the dinner party alone. No Clarissa. When I asked him about her, he acted as if he hadn't heard me."

He was away so much that Clarissa was left more and more to look after their young son alone. She was a lively, sociable woman, but she found herself seldom taking part in her husband's hectic celebrity life. He had also become more demanding, more aware of his own importance. That no doubt made him more difficult to live with when he was home.

The change was to be seen even in Rushdie's appearance. His wiry figure was plumper, as if from all those dinner parties. Although his small tuft of a beard still covered his chin, his dark hair had begun to recede, making his forehead look even more imposing and his hooded eyes and big nose, which he used to joke about, more prominent. He no longer looked like the eternal student, but like a man of distinction. His manner, too, was even more self-confident and assertive. And in any gathering he liked to take center stage if he could. The London *Sunday Times* saw "a glowering, saturnine quality" in his appearance, and observed that "in interviews and profiles he emerged as someone who was driven, obsessive."

He and Clarissa began to live much more separate lives, and in 1987 they were divorced. The marriage had lasted eleven years—years that had seen Rushdie become famous—but it was really over long before the divorce. Somehow Clarissa didn't fit into his new way of life and he was increasingly hard to live with, according to friends who saw the Rushdies at home. Neither of the Rushdies talked much about their breakup in public. When they married, Rushdie had brushed off questions with a brusque "We met and we got married," and he was the same over the divorce. He never liked to talk much about his personal life. He reserved his non-stop conversation for more public matters before an audience, as if he were an actor on stage. But he remained on friendly terms with Clarissa—friendly enough to see their son regularly when he was in London.

Elaine Markson, who had been through a dramatic change of publishers with him in New York, thought the publishing move reflected a deep personal change in him. "In a way, I think, he had a change of life that perhaps started with his divorce," she told me. "Then he went on a personal trip to Australia. I think it was to the Adelaide Festival that was attended by other writers like Angela Carter."

While in Australia, Rushdie became very friendly with a British travel writer, Bruce Chatwin, who had gained a glamorous literary reputation with a series of travel books describing his adventures in out-of-the-way parts of the world. Rushdie accompanied him in a car travelling through vast areas of Australia, a trip described in one of Chatwin's last books, a novel about the Aborigines entitled *The Songlines*. "When you drive through the bush with someone for two months," Rushdie remarked, "you become absolutely intimate friends." He was shocked to learn soon afterwords that Bruce Chatwin wasn't expected to live much longer. He was reported to have caught a rare fatal disease on one of his journeys, but after his death a friend said he had had AIDS.

Malise Ruthven also referred in his book, *A Satanic Affair— Salman Rushdie & The Rage of Islam*, to a report of Rushdie's passionate involvement with an Australian travel writer and novelist, Robyn Davidson. According to a friend, "It's awful when people bring out the most negative aspects in each other. When they parted, he was utterly devastated." A character in *The Satanic Verses* was said to be a satirical picture of her.

Back home, Rushdie seemed very restless to people who met him. A publishing representative said, "He seemed to have gone to another plane and become almost godlike. He couldn't see what he was doing. He wanted to shock, but he lost the sense of reality about what he was doing. The breakup of his marriage affected him."

He scoffed at the recent interest of novelists and filmmakers in India, and particularly at Sir Richard Attenborough's film of *Gandhi.* Dickie Attenborough, he said, "did allow a few Indians to play Indians," a crack at the English actors who had played Indians. Attenborough was reported to be furious—as Mrs. Gandhi had been and so many others.

He aroused more political controversy by vehemently backing Charter 88, an action group demanding a written constitution for Britain. Rushdie said Charter 88 was an attempt to renew the debate about the kind of country people wanted to live in, precisely because the absolute sovereigns, the politicians in Parliament, seemed no longer capable of giving expression to such concerns. It was becoming difficult to believe in the inviolability of people's rights or even in their existence until they could be enshrined in a written constitution.

He was critical not only of Mrs. Thatcher's Conservative Party, but also of the Labour Party, in which he had once had more trust. He was particularly biting about Roy Hattersley, the deputy Labour Party leader and a fellow writer for *The Guardian,* who, he claimed, believed "not only in the absolute sovereignty of Parliament, but of the major parties." Hattersley's hatred of change, he said, "condemns him, I fear, to the fate of the dinosaurs."

The Labour Party leaders, who had regarded liberal Rushdie as one of their literary-journalistic allies, now were as doubtful of him as were Thatcher's Conservatives, or the Indian and Pakistani leaders. Even some of the Nicaraguans grumbled about what he had written about censorship in their country.

Rushdie was one of the first to be invited to join an anti-Thatcher group of established writers, known as the 20th June

Group or the Campden Hill Mob because they met at the home of dramatist Harold Pinter and his wife, popular historian Lady Antonia Fraser, in Campden Hill Square. An expressive, forceful woman, Lady Antonia once would not have been part of such a group or an ally of Salman Rushdie. She had been married to a Conservative member of Parliament and, as a strong feminist, had even voted for Mrs. Thatcher. But marriage to Harold Pinter helped to change her political opinions. Not only had she joined in the founding of the Campden Hill Mob, an attempt to persuade established British writers to think and act more politically, but she publicly criticized Mrs. Thatcher's policies (and compared the British prime minister to Queen Elizabeth I, the sixteenth-century queen who had real power, she said, not like the "powerless, gracious, noncontentious" modern monarchs). She marched in support of Soviet Jewry, organized petitions and tried to help free dissident writers in prison in Europe, Asia, and Africa. So now, without a doubt, she qualified as someone Salman Rushdie approved of and was willing to work with. Both Lady Antonia and Harold Pinter were literary celebrities like Rushdie himself, and much of his socializing now seemed to be exclusively with fellow celebrities or people in the literary-media-political worlds. "Salman doesn't really know many ordinary people outside the London mainstream," observed an acquaintance.

But the restlessness he apparently felt since his divorce continued to affect him. It was understandable because after being a settled married man with a well-run home for so many years, he was now a footloose bachelor, with loneliness to contend with as well as all the domestic arrangements formerly looked after by Clarissa. He was forced more than ever into solitary introspection and consideration of his place in the world. He tried to deal with his situation by keeping busy—by a hectic social life, by travel, by public causes, and by trying to get started on a new novel. London journalists who followed the ups and downs of celebrities noted his moodiness. One journalist described him as "massively egotistical" and as provoking "both adoration and loathing." Many people admired his single mindedness and literary gifts, but "fear his anger and few acquaintances wish to be quoted on him."

It came as no surprise to those who knew him when he soon married again. It was also no surprise that the second Mrs. Rushdie was American because Rushdie seemed to be more and more interested in the progress of his career on the other side of the Atlantic, and talked more often of moving there and of the people he knew there.

The second Mrs. Rushdie couldn't have been more different from the first. Whereas Clarissa was in many ways typically English of a certain class, Rushdie's new wife, Marianne Wiggins, was typical of immigrant Americans with parents of very mixed cultural backgrounds. There was another big difference that was bound to decide the character of this second marriage. Whereas Clarissa had devoted herself to her husband and young son as housewife and mother, Marianne Wiggins was very much a career woman, a fellow novelist just beginning to become well-known in the United States. "Two career writers as ambitious as Salman and Marianne?" said an American editor who knew them both. "Their marriage is set on a collision course. I don't give it a long life unless one of them gives up his or her career, and that's impossible."

The London *Sunday Times* saw Marianne Wiggins as "more than a match" for her husband's writing talent. She was certainly a formidable personality who had had a much tougher start than Rushdie. She was born in the Amish region of Pennsylvania and the ideals of the Amish community probably influenced her interest in improving the world. This shows in her fiction and no doubt helped to establish a relationship with Salman Rushdie. Her father was a failed farmer who lost his land and worked for a relative in a grocery store that failed, too. He preached every Sunday in a church founded by her grandfather, and didn't drink or smoke. But repeated failure eventually drove him to suicide. Wiggins's mother was quite different, a Greek whose family had emigrated to Virginia. When Wiggins was nine, she was baptized into the Greek Orthodox Church. The conflict between her father's Christian fundamentalism and her mother's Greek Orthodox background is reflected in her novels; and probably also helped her to understand Rushdie's religious conflicts, which he was still brooding over while planning his new novel.

As a child, she was often ill—with hepatitis and kidney trouble—and having to be in bed so much, she became a great reader. Her first ambition was to be a playwright like Eugene O'Neill, but at school she was urged instead to become a scientist because of her prowess in mathematics. But a scientist's career didn't attract her and she gave up her schooling to get married. She was seventeen and her husband was twenty-one. He got a job distributing American films in Europe and the young Marianne had her first experience of life outside America. She was only three years older than Salman when he first went to England. She and her young husband lived in Paris, then Brussels and Rome. They had a daughter in 1968. But the marriage didn't last and after they agreed on a divorce, she returned home with her daughter to a country in the middle of the Vietnam War. For the first time, she had to go job hunting. Her first job was in a typing pool at a stockbrokers company in White Plains, New York. Within four years, she was a stockbroker herself, a tribute to her personal drive and ambition. But writing was really what she wanted to do and, like Rushdie, she left the nine-to-five business world as soon as she could for full-time writing.

Babe, her first semi-autobiographical novel, was published by Avon, a mass market paperback company, in 1976, the year Rushdie married Clarissa. It was marketed as a paperback original, which meant it received very little critical attention but had a wider distribution than if it had been published in hardcover. With the proceeds she moved to Martha's Vineyard, the summer holiday resort frequented by writers, where she could live cheaply in the winter and make contacts in the summer.

Her next novel, *West South*, was again semi-autobiographical, making use of her experience in moving to Martha's Vineyard, with a character who rejects the past and begins a new life. It was published by Delacorte in hardcover in 1980, when Rushdie was completing *Midnight's Children*. For her next book, *Separate Checks*, which gave her imagination more scope than her previous books, she again changed publishers. It was published by Random House in 1984, the year after Rushdie published *Shame*. A short story collection, *Herself in Love*, followed soon after from yet another leading publisher, Viking, who were to be the publishers of Rushdie's next novel. Her frequent change of publishers suggested a restless talent like Rushdie's, although she didn't have his status with publishers because she hadn't yet produced a bestseller or a big critical success.

With her daughter in college, she was more free to travel and she decided to try England for a year because her books had also been published there and she liked literary London. Elaine Markson told me she had first introduced Marianne to Salman in New York. "Marianne asked me whom she should invite to a party and I said Salman. They weren't very similar except they shared a sense of the glorious." Born in 1947, the same year as Rushdie, she was an attractive woman who liked shawls and had long, shoulder-length hair, a disarming appearance that concealed a steely self-confidence equal to Rushdie's own. They renewed their acquaintance when she arrived in London, and it wasn't long before she moved in with Rushdie. They were married in January 1988, less than a year after his divorce.

"One night at the Ritz," Marianne Wiggins recalled later, "and we returned to our desks." *Publishers Weekly* in New York called it an exotic marriage. Literary London welcomed a new subject for gossip—how long would dear Salman and Marianne stay together? Would their ambition drive them apart? Journalists were pleased to have an interesting new development in the ongoing Rushdie story. The newly married couple were besieged with invitations to dinner parties. The whole of celebrity London wanted to see how they behaved together—did Marianne sit back, like Clarissa had done, when Salman performed or did she compete with him?

But the popular couple often preferred to stay at home working on their novels in progress. Home was a four-story terrace house in Islington in north London. They usually both wrote at home at similar times. Rushdie's young son lived with them three days a week and Wiggins's daughter came over on vacations from college. Mr. and Mrs. Rushdie sometimes crossed the Atlantic for meetings with publishers and other writers and agents, the people involved in the American side of their two careers.

But mainly they stayed at home writing. She was hard at work on a novel entitled *John Dollar*, reflecting her preoccupation with patriarchal attitudes, religious ritual, colonialism, myth, and the kind of spiritual decline her father had gone through and she had witnessed later in other people. It was to be her most important, most ambitious novel and would show the influence of her parents' large cultural and religious differences and her father's tragic end. The presence of Rushdie writing nearby undoubtedly affected her. She wanted to produce a novel comparable to the big, serious, much talked about works of his.

Her presence also affected his attitude toward his work, according to friends who saw him at that time. His fourth novel was to be his most ambitious, too, and his most daring. In his previous novels, he had seemed to be testing how far he could go, daring a little more each time. Now, he was forcing himself to the very edge of the abyss, determined to hold back nothing whatever the reaction would be, however dangerous. He would risk telling it exactly like it was—or how he had seen it during the last forty years of a migrant's life. It would cover not only India and Pakistan, as in his last two novels, but the West, too. London, "Babylon," would be in this one, Thatcher's London with all the racism and greed, and the London he had learned to love. Also there would be his deepest feelings about his lost Muslim faith and his attitude toward the politics of Islamic leaders. His studies of Islamic history would be in it. He would even risk writing directly about Muhammad. This novel would be his biggest gamble, his greatest risk. He would dedicate it "For Marianne." He already had a title for it: *The Satanic Verses.*

PART II:
THE MAKING OF
THE SATANIC VERSES

1—NOT FOR THE MULLAHS

FAY GODWIN, A PROFESSIONAL PHOTOGRAPHER WHO SPECIALIZED IN POR-
traits of writers, first photographed Salman Rushdie at the time
of *Grimus* when, long-haired and bearded, he looked very young
and Indian and like the struggling bohemian artist he was. As the
former wife of the late Anthony Godwin, who had been chief
executive of Penguin Books, Fay had learned a lot about book
publishing and the ways of writers. And as a photographer, she
had known both the promising beginners—Rushdie was one of
them then—and the often bloated successes living lives of luxury on their bestsellers and film sales.

She had found young Salman Rushdie very nice, she told me,
and they became friendly enough for Rushdie to invite her to his
publication party for *Grimus* and for him to attend all the pre-
views of exhibitions of her photographs in London. But later,
after *Midnight Children*'s success, she saw him as "obviously
overtaken by success, and though friendly enough when I met
him, I felt that he was much more wrapped up in his own life.
But interesting nonetheless."

She took more photographs of him in 1986 when he was in the
middle of *The Satanic Verses*. "He thought there would be some
problems with *Satanic Verses*, but on the same level as *Midnight's Children*. I didn't get the impression he had any suspicion
that all hell would break loose." Her pictures showed Rushdie's
expressive actor's face in varied moods, but "the one I like," said
Fay Godwin, "is the one with what looks like vengeful eyes." She
felt "it was prophetic in a way."

Hindsight sees Rushdie's life during the writing of *The
Satanic Verses* as being full of warning signs that he was playing

with fire. Indeed, the novel itself seemed full of signs, too, with its references to blasphemy by one character—his name was Salman!—who is threatened with a death sentence. Could an author's clairvoyance go much farther than that? It seems almost impossible that Rushdie wasn't aware of what awaited him in the near future. But, as he said, "When I'm writing, it's like being possessed. I write the books that I do because I can't avoid writing them." *Possessed.* He didn't play with fire deliberately. His writing was an expression of the man he had become—the migrant free of ties, at least so he believed.

When *India Today* asked him if there were many coincidences between his work and actual events, Rushdie replied, "There have been unbelievable coincidences. In my novels there are five political figures. All have come to a violent end. Mujibur Rahman in Bangladesh, Indira Gandhi and Sanjay Gandhi in India, Bhutto and Zia in Pakistan. This whole generation either falls out of planes, or gets shot or hanged. None of these people has had a quiet end."

The mention of falling out of planes was a reference not only to Zia's death in an exploding plane, but to the opening of *The Satanic Verses*, in which the two main characters fall out of an exploding plane 30,000 feet above Britain.

Unlike his early days at Cambridge and in London when he kept his writing a secret, Rushdie liked to talk about his work now that he was a success. Other writers were even imitating him. Reviewing a novel by a young Indian writer, a London critic commented that the author had obviously "read them all: Kipling, Forster and Rushdie as well as the B-team (Paul Scott, M. M. Kaye, etc.)." The novel as a whole was "far too derivative (possibly unconsciously) of *Midnight's Children*." Rushdie had become a literary model and not only for young Indian writers. The vastness of his books, covering whole nations and their histories, was beginning to influence young British writers as well to be more ambitious about their subjects and their use of language.

Although Rushdie had left India, the country of his birth still loomed large in his imagination. In nostalgic moments he even talked about returning there to live although since his marriage to an American writer, his friends assumed that if he did leave England, he was more likely to cross the Atlantic. He felt his books filled what he called a great, gaping hole in Indian literature. "India ought to have a great literature like Russia or modern America," he said. "Kipling and Paul Scott are the only writers to have attempted a Cinemascope, panoramic view of it—but neither of them was Indian. What surprises me is that no one had done it before." Now he had. But India was as varied as Europe. Hundreds more vast novels could be written "and none of them would overlap."

His new novel had begun in Britain, in the south of England outside London, but the two main characters were both Indian, and the action was soon back in the East through flashbacks or dreams. But it was Rushdie's first attempt to write of his two homes together in the same book, to blend East and West.

He had begun writing the novel early in 1984 and quickly finished a first draft, but as had happened before with his writing, his first draft was only really gathering his thoughts. "I wasn't very happy with it," he said, "and the Nicaraguan trip came as a godsend. It gave me the chance to get away from my own internal situation. When I returned the problems jamming me had gone away."

The basic idea went back to his Islamic studies at Cambridge twenty years before. One of the major themes was religion and fanaticism. He used Islam as an example because he knew more about that than any other religion. "But the ideas about religious faith and the nature of religious experience and also the political implications of religious extremism are applicable with a few variations to just about any religion."

He expected that "the mullahs wouldn't like it," but he wasn't writing it for them, he said. "I've seen what the mullahs have done in Pakistan over the past eleven years—the level of oppression instituted there by Islamisation. I've seen, too, how almost all the poets in Pakistan were in exile in England during that period. Only now they are beginning to think about going back."

Rushdie said that "a powerful tribe of clerics has taken over Islam. These are the contemporary Thought Police. They have turned Muhammad into a perfect being, his life into a perfect life, his revelations into the unambiguous, clear event it origi-nally was not. Powerful taboos have been erected. One may not discuss Muhammad as if he were human, with human virtues and weaknesses. One may not discuss the growth of Islam as a historical phenomenon, as an ideology born out of its time." These were the taboos against which he was transgressing in his novel.

He couldn't forget the memory of those charred houses and the remains of the Sikhs burnt to death. For twenty years he had lived in the West, which had fought its violent religious wars many years before. He had grown accustomed to the separation of church and state in Britain. It was a shock to go back to India and Pakistan and see no separation. Religion and politics were still as closely involved as they had been in England over three hundred years before. There were still traces of religious persecution in Britain in the conflict in Northern Ireland and in the British law forbidding a Catholic to become prime minister, but the church leaders had no real political power in Britain now and the religious wars were over. How different it was in the East where religious leaders could become political dictators and holy wars were still waged!

Another theme of his novel was religious faith from the viewpoint of someone who would no longer describe himself as religious. "I don't believe that angels appear and talk to people. On the other hand, revelation seems to me to be genuine." He also wanted to write about imported cultures. "The history of the London we live in is a composite history of all the peoples who are now here: Islamic history, Polish history, Caribbean history." He was writing about the city as an artificial, invented space which was constantly metamorphosing. It didn't have roots, only foundations. "There are things that seem not to belong together, except that it is part of the metropolitan experience that such things do not belong together and do live side by side—that you can live upstairs from Khomeini."

He thought again about his multi-layered novel. "It's about the beginning of a religion—the question of temptation, of compromise."

He used some Islamic history, but changed names, he said. He gave the name of an Egyptian temple, Abu Simbel, to the leader of Mecca. He didn't call any of the holy cities by their names. "I wanted to distance events from historical events. Issues are being raised: it is not about whether they were historically true or not. The book is really about the fact that an idea or a new thing in the world must decide whether to compromise or not. Beyond that, the image out of which the book grew was of the prophet going to the mountain and not being able to tell the difference between the angel and the devil. The book is also about the wrestling match which takes place between the two."

Rushdie knew that he wanted figures of good and evil in his novel, but not simple symbols. He wanted them to be ambiguous—good might have some evil and vice versa, the angel might be a little devilish. Plunging out of a doomed plane over Britain, his two main characters were to be the figures representing good and evil, he decided, but grooming them for these roles gave him a lot of trouble at first.

"I had thought that the devil-angel relationship would be straightforward. What I found was that my view of them changed radically. And it was when I came to see how the emotional lives of these two characters connected that I began to know how to write the book. But it took ages."

What caused even more trouble was the character Rushdie called his fictional prophet and whom most readers have taken to be a thinly disguised Muhammad. He called his prophet Mahound, a name used long ago as a derogatory term. But, said Rushdie, "my novel tries in all sorts of ways to reoccupy negative images, to repossess pejorative language." In the novel, he wrote, "To turn insults into strengths, whigs, tories. Blacks all chose to wear with pride the names they were given in scorn; likewise, our mountain-climbing, prophet-motivated solitary is to be the medieval baby-frightener, the Devil's synonym: Mahound." Turning not the other cheek but your enemies' insults around seems typical of Salman Rushdie ever since his days at Rugby School. But doing so in the case of Muhammad was very risky. If Rushdie's intentions were misunderstood or not respected, then he was bound to be in trouble, big trouble.

Anticipating Islamic critics of what he was doing, Rushdie claimed—at least for himself as a writer—that "There are no subjects which are off limits and that includes God, includes prophets. I refuse to think that I should shut my mind off to subjects which are not just of interest to me but which have been my concern all my life." He was not a religious person formally any more, "but I have remained all my life very attached to and interested in the subject of Islam." He guessed some people might be upset by his novel, "but the point is it is a serious attempt to write about religion and revelation from the point of view of a secular person. I think that's a completely legitimate exercise." Besides, Rushdie added, Muhammad was a very interesting figure, the only prophet who existed even remotely inside history. "He is the only one about whom there is some half-established more-or-less factual historical information. That makes him a human being and doubly interesting."

Rushdie said he didn't believe Muhammad had a revelation, but then he didn't doubt his sincerity either. He had had a genuine mystical experience. "But if you don't believe in the whole truth and you don't disbelieve him either—then what's going on? What is the nature of the mystical experience? Given that we accept it happens, and we also don't believe in God or archangels. That's what I tried to write about."

Even in *Midnight's Children*, he had referred to Mount Hira where "the prophet Muhammad (also known as Mohammad, Mahomet, the Last-But-One and Mahound) spoke to the Archangel (Gabriel or Jibreel, as you please)." Rushdie had added, "Muhammad (on whose name be peace, let me add; I don't want to offend anyone) heard a voice saying, 'Recite!' and thought he was going mad." Then Rushdie's narrator, Saleem—one of Midnight's Children with special powers—claimed to hear voices, too—"I was a radio receiver, and could turn the volume down or up." There had been protests from Muslims about this reference to Muhammad when *Midnight's Children* was published, but Rushdie was risking much more in *The Satanic Verses.*

All those far-ranging ideas—from "Proper London" and its multi-national, multi-racial problems to the early days of Islam—were difficult to dramatize in a single novel, however long and complex and varied in style and mood. "Apart from this being my most serious novel," said Rushdie, "it is also the most comic."

Much of the humor came from mixing realism and fantasy, so-called magic realism. A lot of Rushdie's novel was in the fantastic style of the *Arabian Nights*. Right at the start, his figures of good and evil survive a hijacked jumbo jet blowing apart high above the English Channel, plunge earthwards together, and eventually are washed up, very much alive, on an English beach. If they had travelled on a flying carpet, they could hardly have done much better.

But not all Rushdie's problems in writing *The Satanic Verses* came from the book itself. He had his troubled marriage to contend with in the early days. That no doubt affected his concentration on the first chapters. When he said something was jamming his progress, it may have been his deteriorating relations with Clarissa. The break-up was obviously very painful. Nicaragua had been an escape, perhaps, from facing it. He said once his marriage was as good as over in 1984, and that was the year he began his novel in earnest, but produced only an unsatisfactory first draft. It was a long time before he was able to write even the final version of chapter one. And by then, perhaps, he had accepted that his marriage was over.

He divided the novel into nine parts and he called the first part, "The Angel Gibreel," a reference to one of his figures of good and evil and also probably to the Archangel Gabriel. His two main characters continued to become more and more ambiguous. One of them actually grew a devil's horns and hooves and walked about London like that, but it became less and less clear whether he represented evil or whether he was really good.

Finally Rushdie wrote what was to be the opening:

" 'To be born again,' sang Gibreel Farishta tumbling from the heavens, 'first you have to die.' "

Tumbling from the heavens suggests an angel and Gibreel, in fact, acquires a halo. But he is no angel. He is a legendary movie star in India in theological movies about the gods. Gibreel isn't even his real name.

Tumbling with him is Saladin Chamcha, the man of a thousand voices on television and radio, the master of the commercial, and a great Anglophile. He is the one who sprouts the devil's horns.

Merging past, present, and future in East and West, Rushdie finally stages a confrontation between these two characters and at last reveals their true natures. But always at their backs is the figure of Mahound, the Prophet of Jahilia, the city of sand, who receives the revelation in which Satanic verses mingle with the divine until they are recognized for what they are.

The novel is full of asides from the author:
"Question: What is the opposite of faith?
"Not disbelief. Too final, certain, closed. Itself a kind of belief."
"Doubt."

Rushdie the satirist has a great time mocking everywhere from "Proper London" to Bombay and its huge film industry. Gibreel is impersonating gods in his movies. An *India Today* interviewer told Rushdie he recognized quite a few Bombay film stars in the book. Rushdie replied that for Indian readers there would be many "shocks of recognition." he had taken "little pieces out of many characters." Some He made up. One film producer "with a face like a knee-in-spectacles" was partly based on the producer Ismail Merchant, who had made a series of successful literary movies based on famous books.

But the most sensational part of the novel—a mixture of Rushdie's Islamic studies, his general message about religion, and his satirical-magic realism style—was undoubtedly that involving a brothel scene in which the prostitutes impersonated Mahound's wives. "When the news got around Jahilia that the whores of The Curtain had each assumed the identity of one of Mahound's wives, the clandestine excitement of the city's males was intense." Rushdie commented that the brothel's customers kept the secret from the authorities partly because "they would surely lose their lives if Mahound or his lieutenants ever found out that they had been involved in such irreverences." And what of the author? Rushdie undoubtedly must have known that he was on the brink with such scenes. One false step and he could cause great offense and possibly danger to himself. There was a saying, he recalled, that "You can say what you like about God, but be careful with Muhammad." But he went ahead with the brothel scenes nevertheless.

It all comes back to what Rushdie said about being *possessed.* He means by that a total commitment to his writing. He will venture to the brink if his writing and view of the world demand it as they did in *The Satanic Verses.*

"Every novel that I've ever written," he explains, "has come about in the following way. For a long time I think I don't know what I have to write. Then gradually I begin to think of stories, fragments, incidents or characters, quite disjointedly, in such a way that there's no indication that these are part of one story. Then I begin to panic about not having a book to write. And so I try to formalize these vague notions, and I start trying to write things down."

He has a moment of great optimism when he discovers he has at least nine novels to write that are going to occupy him for the next twenty years. Then he tries to decide which to write first. "And then I ache more, waiting, and then everything disintegrates. And I realize I haven't even got one novel, let alone nine."

But suddenly, without quite knowing how, he finds all these fragments of ideas have in fact been part of a larger idea that was really what he was thinking about unconsciously—"and that's the novel I have to write."

So it was with *The Satanic Verses*, although it had a much longer incubation period than the others.

He isn't keen on the term magic realism being applied to his work. "I grew up in a literary tradition—one can mention the *Arabian Nights*, for instance, in which it was clearly understood that stories were untrue—where horses flew and so did carpets. And in spite of that blatant untruth, they reached for a deeper truth. So I grew up in a world in which it was understood that fiction was a lie—and the paradox was that the lie told the truth."

The world, he said, wasn't naturalistic. Naturalism was based on the idea that one thing happened at a time. "But the common experience of all of this is that many things happen at once—that at any given moment of our lives we may be suffering from a hangover, affected by a conversation we had yesterday, worried about a financial difficulty we have to solve in the next couple of months, having this conversation, unwell, crossed in love."

Reality simply wasn't realistic, Rushdie said. And if his novels reflected the grotesque, gargantuan, surrealistic reality in which everyone really lived, "then those are the realistic novels, and the ones that take place in middle-class houses on Long Island are the ones that aren't telling the truth."

100

*   *   *

The unreality of reality is partly conveyed in *The Satanic Verses* through Gibreel the movie star (and angel?). One nickname for Hollywood is the Dream Factory. With Gibreel, it is sometimes hard to tell what are dreams—a scene from some movie he is making, perhaps—and what is actually happening. Rushdie mixes the two together very cleverly: it is part of the way he puts over his message. That is why he is very elusive when he is challenged. Accuse him of depicting something, somebody or somewhere inaccurately, demeaningly, satirically, and it may all turn out to have been intended as a dream, a movie, a distorted surrealistic vision that shouldn't be taken literally. No mirrors are held up to so-called reality in Rushdie's novel. The very beginning—the successful escape from the doomed jumbo jet—is impossible in so-called realistic terms. Nothing short of a miracle would explain it satisfactorily. Even the incredible heroics of the Dream Factory wouldn't go so far as to show a movie star surviving a mid-air explosion and a fall of 30,000 feet unless he were Superman or it was a fantasy, a parody, a prime example of magic realism.

Gibreel became a movie star with the coming of the theologicals. Rushdie comments that "Every god in the pantheon got his or her chance to be a star. When D. W. Rama [obviously a survivor from Rushdie's abandoned novel, *Madame Rama*] scheduled a production based on the story of Ganesh, none of the leading box office names of the time were willing to spend an entire movie concealed inside an elephant's head. Gibreel jumped at the chance. That was his first hit, *Ganpati Baba*, and suddenly he was a superstar, but only with the trunk and ears on."

After six movies playing the elephant-headed god, Gibreel then had to put on a long, hairy tail "in order to play Hanuman the monkey king in a sequence of adventure movies that owed more to a certain cheap television series emanating from Hong Kong than it did to the *Ramayana*." After Hanuman, Gibreel enjoyed a phenomenal success deepening his belief in a guardian angel at his side. But a grave illness reflecting a spiritual crisis made him give up his career. "His images simply faded off the printed page." The great publicity machine that had made him a superstar—almost a god himself to movie fans—gave him up.

"It was the death of God. Or something very like it; for had not that outsize face, suspended over its devotees in the artificial cinematic night, shone like that of some supernatural Entity that had its being at least halfway between the mortal and the divine? More than halfway, many would have argued, for Gibreel had spent the greater part of his unique career incarnating, with absolute conviction, the countless deities of the subcontinent in the popular genre movies known as 'theologicals.' It was part of the magic of his persona that he succeeded in crossing religious boundaries without giving offense."

Rushdie gives examples of Gibreel's roles in his major theologicals. "Blue-skinned as Krishna he danced, flute in hand, amongst the beauteous gopis and their udder-heavy cows; with upturned palms, serene, he meditated (as Gautama) upon humanity's suffering beneath a studio-rickety bodhi-tree. On those infrequent occasions when he descended from the heavens he never went too far, playing, for example, both the Grand Mughal and his famously wily minister in the classic *Akbar and Birbal*."

Rushdie sums up that for over a decade and a half Gibreel had represented to hundreds of millions of believers "the most acceptable, and instantly recognizable, face of the Supreme. For many of his fans, the boundary separating the performer and his roles had long ago ceased to exist."

Inevitably then, when the novel switches abruptly from the first part, "The Angel Gibreel," to the second part, "Mahound," many readers have been uncertain whether this new section is to be taken literally as an account of the Prophet or is perhaps a theological movie not to be taken seriously. Is Mahound on the same level as Gibreel's Krishna or Gautama or the incredible escape from the jumbo jet or the flying carpets of the *Arabian Nights*? Is it one of Gibreel's movie scenarios or even a dream out of his past and his reading about Islam?

"Gibreel when he submits to the inevitable, when he slides heavy-lidded towards visions of his angeling, passes his loving mother," begins the "Mahound" section. It is obviously the world of memory, of dreams—and of doubt. In Rushdie's universe, even the angels have doubts, challenging God's will. "He calmed them down, naturally, employing management skills à la god. Flattered them: you will be the instruments of my will on earth, of the salvationdamnation of man, all the usual etcetera. And hey presto, end of protest, on with the haloes, back to work."

Angels, he added, were easily pacified. "Human beings are tougher nuts, can doubt anything, even the evidence of their own eyes. Of behind-their-own eyes. Of what, as they sink heavy-lidded, transpires behind closed peepers ... Angels, they don't have much in the way of a will. To will is to disagree; not to submit; to dissent.

"I know; devil talk."

All that is a build-up to the entrance of Mahound, first seen as "the businessman: looks as he should, high forehead, eaglenose, broad in the shoulders, narrow in the hip." His name, readers are told, is a dream-name. Here he is neither "Mahomet nor MoeHammered." Here he is known by the Devil's synonym of Mahound in the same way that insults are turned into strengths.

A dream-name. That seems a clear warning that it is the world of the Dream Factory or Gibreel's own personal dreams, if he can ever divorce his unconscious from his movies. At the end of the section, Mahound the businessman is left "climbing his hot mountain in the Hijaz." The mirage of a city shines below him in the sun. Movies, dreams, mirages ... is Mahound to be taken seriously or is he a mere figure in Gibreel's imagination, part of his drama of good versus evil?

Rushdie provides no easy answer. When Mahound seems most like a dream figure, Rushdie then introduces parallels with the life of Muhammad that make him seem to be portraying the Prophet. Then when readers might assume he is retelling Islam history, more fantasy is introduced bringing back the impression of a mere dream, of the excesses of Gibreel's dream factory in Bombay.

It is Rushdie's message conveyed in the most dramatic terms: "Doubt, it seems to me, is the central condition of a human being in the 20th Century."

Another great theme of *The Satanic Verses*, a telling variation of Rushdie's message, is migration, "its stresses and transforma-tions, from the point of view of migrants from the Indian subcon-tinent to Britain." With Rushdie, this is as much an obsession as his interest in Islam. He tried in this novel "to give voice and fictional flesh to the immigrant culture of which I am myself a member." He said of his two characters plunging into the English Channel, "I wanted to start with the most spectacular act of immigration I could imagine. The point about the book is the ambiguity of Good and Evil. The devil figure in the novel is by no means the evil figure and the angel figure is, in a way, responsible for more evil. As we have found it harder to define what is, we have found it harder to say what is good. If you can't agree what is the case, it is very hard to decide what is right and wrong."

According to "one way of seeing things"—a typical Rushdie remark because doubt demands more than one viewpoint—a migrant, a person who "sets out to make himself up," is taking on the "Creator's role" and is therefore unnatural, "a blasphemer" (another warning of things to come).

But from another angle, added Rushdie, you could see heroism in the migrant's struggle, in his willingness to risk: "not all mutants survive." (Had he also in mind the risks of the author of *The Satanic Verses*?)

Or, said Rushdie, consider a migrant socio-politically. "Most migrants learn, and can become disguises," which are "our own false descriptions to counter the falsehoods invented about us, concealing for reasons of security our secret selves."

The migrant in hiding: another warning about the future.

All authors leave traces of themselves in their books and Salman Rushdie is an unusually personal writer. But, as with everything else in *The Satanic Verses*, nothing is sure: doubt is paramount there, too. It is often impossible to know with some of his seemingly personal anecdotes how much is from Rushdie's life and how much is pure imagination.

At least in describing Gibreel's face, Rushdie seems to be joking about his own appearance as he did in *Midnight's Children*. Reduced to life size, set amongst ordinary mortals, the face was "oddly un-starry." Those "low-slung eyelids" could give Gibreel/Rushdie an exhausted look. There was, too, "something coarse about the nose, the mouth was too well fleshed to be strong, the ears were long-lobed like young, knurled jackfruit. The most profane of faces, the most sensual of faces."

It is when readers begin to follow what might be thought to be the author's footsteps that confusion arises. Take the key figure of Saladin Chamcha who plunged to earth with haloed Gibreel and grew a devil's horns. He had long ago constructed a migrant's face for himself to suit the English he lived and worked among. His father in India wrote disapprovingly to him that he had Saladin's soul kept safe—"The devil has only your body. When you are free of him, return and claim your immortal Spirit. It flourishes in the garden." His parents, noted Saladin, were Muslims "in the lackadaisical, light manner of Bombayites," and he asked himself, "Is it I who have been the subject of devilment, am I the one possessed?" *Possessed* like the author?

Saladin was in London in 1961 as was Rushdie, who was on his way to Rugby School. On the plane from India, Saladin read science-fiction tales of interplanetary migration, Asimov's *Foundation* and Ray Bradbury's *Martian Chronicles*. That seems like the future author of *Grimus*. "He imagined the DC-3 was the mother ship, bearing the Chosen, the Elect of God and man, across unthinkable distances." Were those the Little Prince's thoughts, too?

In London, Saladin shivered in his hotel room, as Salman probably had done. Saladin was a "secular man" determined "to live without a god of any type" and become "a goodandproper Englishman." Rushdie shared the secular identity, but was his ambition ever to become "a goodandproper Englishman"? At boarding school Saladin's classmates "giggled at his voice and excluded him from their secrets"—he certainly shared that with Rushdie—and to defend himself, he began to act, to find masks his classmates would recognize, "paleface masks, clown masks," that fooled them into thinking he was *okay*, he was *people-like-us.*

Rushdie's description of Saladin's first experiences with English food seems heartfelt. Saladin came down one day to breakfast to find a kipper on his plate. He had no idea how to eat it and none of his classmates helped him. He wasn't allowed to leave the table until he had eaten the kipper and it took him well over an hour. It then occurred to him that England was like a kipper—a peculiar-tasting smoked fish full of spikes and bones—and nobody would ever tell him how to eat it. "I'll show them all," he swore. The kipper was his first victory, the first step in his conquest of England. That seemed like Rushdie—"I'll show them all!"

Back home in India, Saladin has "such big-big criticisms" about everything from Indian movies to Indian food, his mother observes, "My God, he really got an education," England-returned "and talking so fine and all." Is this Rushdie making fun of himself on his first trip back home—like Saladin "conqueror of kippers," Saladin "of the England-returned upper lip"? Saladin's attitude was clear. Damn you, India, he cursed. To hell with you. I escaped your clutches long ago, you won't get your hooks into me again, you cannot drag me back. Were those Rushdie's feelings, too, at that time in his life?

Saladin had begun to hear in India's Babel an ominous warning: don't come back again. "When you have stepped through the looking-glass, you step back at your peril. The mirror may cut you to shreds." The fears of a migrant—and yet another warning to himself.

There is a letter from Saladin's father that surely has echoes of Rushdie's early experiences as a father. "One dandles the bonny babe upon one's knee," Saladin's father wrote, "Whereupon, without warning or provocation, the blessed creature— may I be frank?—it *wets* one." Any exasperation quickly died away, "for do we not, as adults, understand that the little one is not to blame? He knows not what he does."

Saladin was deeply offended when his father compared him to the "urinating baby." By the time of his graduation, he had acquired a British passport, and he wrote his father he intended to settle in London and look for work as an actor. His father replied: "Might as well be a confounded gigolo. It's my belief some devil has got into you and turned your wits." He concluded: "Answer me this: What am I to tell my friends?" An echo of what Rushdie's father reportedly commented when told Rushdie intended to be a writer.

Saladin met Pamela Lovelace just before the end of the sixties "when women still wore bandannas in their hair." That was about the time that Rushdie first met Clarissa. Pamela stood in the center of a room full of Trotskyist actresses "and fixed him with eyes so bright, so bright." He monopolized her all evening and she never stopped smiling, but she left with another man. Clarissa was reportedly involved with someone else when Rushdie first met her. Saladin dreamed of her eyes and smile, the slenderness of her, and her skin. He pursued her for two years. "England yields her treasures with reluctance. He was astonished by his own perseverance, and understood that she had become the custodian of his destiny, that if she did not relent then his entire attempt at metamorphosis would fail." When at last she agreed to marriage, he rushed it before she could change her mind, but he "never learned to read her thoughts." When she was unhappy, she would lock herself in the bedroom. He called her a clam and thought of the locked bedroom door as representing "all the locked doors of their lives together, basement first, then maisonette, then mansion. He needed her so badly, to reassure himself of his own existence, that he never understood the desperation in her dazzling, permanent smile, the terror in the brightness with which she faced the world."

Whether this description of Saladin's relationship with Pamela contains echoes of Rushdie's first marriage, readers never know for sure. Certainly the past that Rushdie gives Pamela (parents' suicide, etc.) is different to Clarissa's and sometimes more like Marianne's, and Saladin and Pamela "never managed to have children" whereas of course the Rushdies had had a son.

All that seems certain is that because the Saladin-Pamela relationship comes so early in the novel, it was probably written about the time his marriage was most troubled. He describes Saladin and Pamela as being "on the rocks," maybe because they couldn't have a family, "maybe we just grew away from each other, maybe this, maybe that."

Throughout the separate adventures and final confrontation of Gibreel and Saladin, there are continual reminders of the author. Gibreel loses his faith like Rushdie. "There came a terrible emptiness, an isolation." When Gibreel prays for recovery from a serious illness, "he felt nothing, nothing, nothing, and then one day he found that he no longer needed there to be anything to feel." He wasn't punished for his sinfulness and he started to recover. "Don't you get it?" he shouted to a woman. "No thunderbolt. That's the point." The woman laughed at him. "You're alive," she said. "You got your life back. *That's* the point." Always doubt, never certainty in Salman Rushdie's world.

"What follows is tragedy," Rushdie writes toward the end. "Or at least the echo of tragedy." The full-blooded original was unavailable to modern men and women, so it was said. So he settled for "a burlesque for our degraded, imitative times, in which clowns re-enact what was first done by heroes and by kings."

That is the view of the world of Rushdie the satirist, and it certainly describes the style of *The Satanic Verses.*

But what is most memorable are the frequent references to blasphemy ("punishable by death"). How can one forget the confrontation between Mahound and "some sort of bum from Persia by the outlandish name of Salman?" This Salman has been drunkenly critical of Mahound over his women and the Satanic verses. Mahound catches up with him and "the Prophet begins to pronounce the sentence of death."

Salman pleads for mercy.

"Mahound shakes his head. 'Your blasphemy, Salman, can't be forgiven. Did you think I wouldn't work it out? To set your words against the Words of God.'"

Salman "blubbers whimpers pleads beats his breast abases himself repents."

He offers to show Mahound where his real enemies are and he is finally reprieved.

Few readers will escape an eerie feeling at Salman Rushdie's prophetic sense of what was to happen to him. Life imitated art to an astonishing extent but not, so far, all the way. The real Salman has not yet been as lucky as his fictional namesake.

2—WYLIE TAKES OVER

WHEN SALMAN RUSHDIE FINISHED *THE SATANIC VERSES,* HE SAID PROUDLY of his fourth novel, "This is the first time that I have managed to write a book from the whole of myself. It is written from my entire sense of being in the world."

He showed the book when still in manuscript to a few trusted friends and discussed the controversial Islam aspects. His friend, Professor Edward Said, read *The Satanic Verses* in typescript when Rushdie was still working on it. "He didn't anticipate what Khomeini would do," Professor Said told me. "My impression was he was expecting the novel to have an impact. He said it would shake up the Muslims. But he never expected it to bring about a threat to his life."

For a book that meant so much to him, Rushdie wanted the best international marketing possible in the East as well as the West. He wanted Muslims to read his novel. But he was particularly concerned to get maximum exposure in Britain and the United States, where the most profitable sales were likely to be. *The Satanic Verses* had taken nearly five years to write and he was in need of money. He was confident his novel could be a big international bestseller, provided it was written and talked about enough.

Liz Calder had seen chapters along the way and expected to be its editor. She confided to her friend Salman that she intended to leave Jonathan Cape and co-found an entirely new publishing company to be known as Bloomsbury with headquarters in Soho Square in the heart of London's West End. Rushdie responded enthusiastically, keen to switch from Cape to Bloomsbury to remain one of her authors, loyal like most writers to his longstanding editor rather than the company. Liz Calder therefore felt safe in planning to lead off her first Bloomsbury list with *The Satanic Verses.* The prospect was very pleasing. Publishing a major novel by a celebrated author would ensure that the Bloomsbury launching became national news. It was like a reward for her loyal support of Rushdie over the last ten years.

But a spoiler was waiting in the wings. This was an American agent named Andrew Wylie. His arrival in Rushdie's life changed all Rushdie's professional relationships, although it took some time for Rushdie's women backers—his two agents as well as Liz Calder—to appreciate that Wylie had moved in on their turf.

Aggressive agenting like Wylie's was only possible because publishing had radically changed its character and the way it did business over the last twenty years. Once an industry of small independent companies, publishing was now largely dominated by big corporations who had taken over many of the old companies. Millions from oil, newspaper chains and other industries gave publishers much more money to work with as long as there was a healthy return. Advances grew bigger and bigger as the major publishers competed for the established bestselling authors.

Publishers had once prided themselves on nursing promising young writers, who in return remained loyal when their books began to sell. Advances were calculated as a reasonable percentage of what a book might make. But loyalty and reasonable advances seemed to have gone out of much of commercial publishing as the big corporations came in. Publishing became more and more like Hollywood in its way of doing business, with the big companies acting like the major film studios and the best-selling writers behaving like movie stars. As in Hollywood, agents ran much of the show in this new kind of publishing. Some agents with their sales talk about Big Books and Big Bucks even sounded like Hollywood.

The few remaining independent publishers found competition increasingly difficult, as did some of the more low key agents who sometimes lost clients to rivals promising Big Bucks. Where did this leave writers who did not have bestsellers—that is, the vast majority? They found it harder to get published and, when published, much more difficult to have their books become bestsellers. A book, of course, has to have the ingredients of bestsellerdom, but the publisher also has to spend money on advertising and other special marketing before a book can become a bestseller. "Bestsellers in America are *made*," John le Carré once remarked.

If a book doesn't sell well, publisher and author tend to blame each other—the publisher says the book didn't have it, and the author contends the publisher didn't make a big enough effort. That is when an agent looking for authors steps in. Even the most successful authors have some grievances, and a clever agent plays on such feelings to make a switch seem sensible.

The old loyalties generally depended on a close relationship with an editor, such as Rushdie had with Liz Calder. But editors now changed jobs so frequently it was often compared to musical chairs. Authors sometimes followed them from company to company, but more often an agent moved in to establish a similarly close relationship.

There was always one agent in New York signing up famous names and obtaining record advances, who was the current hotshot front-runner according to the media. The newspapers reported their big deals and the magazines profiled them. At one time it was Candida Donadio, who made a record paperback sale of Mario Puzo's *The Godfather*. Then it was lawyer Morton Janklow, breaking records with Judith Krantz's *Princess Daisy*. Now it was Andrew Wylie with a whole stable of writers he had wooed from other agents.

Time profiled Wylie under the heading "The Naughty Schoolboy," a description of him taken from veteran agent Sterling Lord, who sees the Wylie type of agent as pushing "the ethics back a little farther." *Time* also quoted another veteran agent, Scott Meredith, who represents Norman Mailer among other well-known writers, as saying Wylie was "probably the most dishonest agent in the business." Morton Janklow said, "Wylie is to the literary business what Roy Cohn was to the legal business." Wylie called Janklow the literary equivalent of a heroin dealer for representing pop bestsellers by authors like Judith Krantz. "They have no lasting value and two years after they've been published are worth nothing," Wylie added. He prided himself not only on increasing an author's income, but on representing distinguished literary writers.

7 Days, another New York-based magazine that profiled Wylie, described him as a barracuda agent and reported him as saying that the problem of publishing was not big advances or who had the upper hand—writer, agent or publisher. The real issue was Front List (the current list) versus Back List (old books still selling). The current bestsellers might do well on the Front List, but made no money on the Back List. Wylie said he thought publishers were learning short-term business was bad business.

The *Tatler* in London also profiled Wylie and called him "Wily." Readers were told that "Publishers fear him. Authors adore him. Rival agents live in dread of the man." The *Tatler* described him as "supposedly the most powerful literary agent" in New York and therefore in the world. The *Tatler*'s writer, Lucretia Stewart, gossiped about Wylie getting drunk with a young British client at a publisher's party and opening a window and inviting his client "to piss with me on New York." And both men urinated through the window.

There are countless such stories about Wylie's allegedly eccentric, bizarre behavior in the pursuit of clients, many of the stories told with lip-smacking enjoyment by rival agents. Bill Buford, editor of *Granta*, the Cambridge magazine and a Wylie client, said Wylie's appeal was that he got clients "money that they have never got before." That was why Philip Roth left the prestigious independent company of Farrar, Straus and Giroux and joined the corporation-owned Simon and Schuster—for a much bigger advance. But many publishers doubt Simon and Schuster can make back the large advance and then Roth may be in a difficult situation. Did Wylie consider all the literary implications, or was his mind only on the money? The answer depended on whether you were for or against Wylie.

The *Tatler* summed up that Wylie "is so much a creature of our time, an embodiment, as one less than enchanted writer put it, of all that is despicable and grasping about the Thatcher/Reagan era. Or, as another agent (a prejudiced source of course) once said, 'Wylie is utterly without principles.' "

But Wylie's clients denied these charges. He was certainly a very controversial figure. A pale, slim man with thinning reddish hair and glasses, he could talk like a tough negotiator or a literary charmer. The son of a senior editor at the independent

Houghton Mifflin company, a Harvard graduate with a major in French literature, he showed little of this background in his style as an agent except in his references to the literary names on his clients' list. Literary clients also often praised him for carefully reading their work and commenting intelligently on it. He liked to put down other agents as un-literary, as if they were all doing what he was accused of—putting the Big Bucks first. But he also scoffed at what he called the outdated "little East Hampton approach to publishing." East Hampton is a popular New York literary resort on Long Island where, according to Wylie, publishers and agents "share summer houses so that they can get together and shaft the writers." But that way of doing business, he said, had now "gone by the board—I'd like to think partially as a result of our efforts."

Wylie became an agent after publishing a book of his own and being dissatisfied with the agent who represented him. His first successes were with literary survivors of the Beat generation—six-figure advances for poet Allen Ginsberg and novelist William (*Naked Lunch*) Burroughs. And he wooed other well-known writers. Rival agents claimed he sometimes got the promise of a hefty advance for a writer and only then approached the writer, telling him or her what he could get if the writer became his client. Wylie denied doing that. When accused of wooing writers away from other agents, he snapped, "This is not Texan ranching; these are not cattle with a brand." Typical of his clients' attitude was writer Susan Sontag, who described him as "the best agent in America, as his partner, Gillon Aitken, is the best in Britain. Wylie is aggressive and very literate. He reads what you write and discusses it. He has been criticized for being aggressive, but surely that's part of an agent's job."

Salman Rushdie was a natural attraction for Wylie. He was a serious literary writer, an international celebrity ideal for the growing global market, an obvious case for bigger advances if he was available. Most publishers would want him, and where you could arrange competitive bidding, Big Bucks were inevitably the result. Wylie also admired Rushdie's writing. *The Wall Street Journal*, in a profile of Wylie, claimed that to woo Rushdie away from his current agents who were also friends, Wylie recited from memory the opening pages of Rushdie's earlier novels and told Rushdie that "every time he passed a bookstore, he bought copies of Mr. Rushdie's earlier works."

The *Tather*'s profile quoted Wylie's British partner, Gillon Aitken, as commenting, "Perhaps Andrew's not always as controlled as he should be, but he did become genuinely obsessed by Salman's work. He couldn't go by a bookshop without going in to buy copies of Salman's books. The book that affected him was *Shame* and he started looking around to see what was happening to this writer in America and he formed the conclusion, which I think was probably accurate, that Salman was not being adequately represented and ultimately not being published well in the United States. And he did make a move to Salman to the extent that he telephoned him."

A meeting was easy to arrange. Rushdie's wife, Marianne, had already signed with Wylie. She claimed her former agent had sided with the publisher over the jacket design for her book, *Herself in Love*, which she hated. Wylie apparently asked her if she would switch to him if he succeeded in getting the jacket changed. He did so, and she switched and credited Wylie with boosting her career and getting her a better contract for her novel in progress, *John Dollar*. Salman no doubt heard about it and must have been favorably impressed.

According to the London *Sunday Times*, Wylie conducted a long campaign to sign up Rushdie. He reportedly told Rushdie he deserved much bigger advances than he had received so far, and if *The Satanic Verses* didn't get at least a $250,000 advance in the United States, he was being badly represented. People who knew both men well said Wylie and Rushdie had a lot in common— they were both provocateurs and dissenters. Wylie's view of publishing was bound to appeal to maverick Rushdie. They soon became friends.

Secrets are hard to keep in London's publishing circles. Liz Calder must have quickly learned that Andrew Wylie was wooing Salman. It was bad news for her and Bloomsbury. Wylie would want *The Satanic Verses* to be auctioned. She had only a personal assurance from Rushdie that Bloomsbury could publish the new novel. She apparently tried to get the assurance formally spelled out on paper, sending Deborah Rogers the outline of an agreement for Bloomsbury to publish *The Satanic Verses*.

But Deborah Rogers, who had her own worries about Wylie, couldn't help. Rushdie told her that he wanted to withdraw from the agreement. Liz Calder heard nothing from him directly, but the exchange with Deborah Rogers confirmed her fears. Her concern increased when she heard that Rushdie had fired Elaine Markson and made Andrew Wylie his American agent.

Elaine Markson's angry reaction can well be imagined, but she had cooled down by the time she discussed it with me in her cozy Greenwich Village office. "He was very carefully and vigorously courted by Andrew Wylie," she said quietly. "One becomes philosophical about writers who change agents. I saw Salman just before he changed to Wylie. He was here in New York. When he switched agents, he wrote me a very nice, warm letter."

Although Markson spoke as if determined to say nothing critical of Rushdie, her deep feelings about being dropped for Wylie seemed to come out when she reminisced about Rushdie's early days as a writer and how she had tried to help him to become better known in New York.

"I remember I had a party in this office and introduced him to Kurt Vonnegut," she said in a low voice. "He didn't know many people then, but he was very engaging and very talkative. I didn't see him as a man of two worlds, but of one world. He doesn't forget his roots. He mingled with the people of Oxford and Cambridge and all that, and became part of the English literary scene, the climate of England. But he kept his Indian roots and didn't forget where he came from. I remember a meal of Indian food he cooked—and cooked very well.

"What happened with *The Satanic Verses* showed he wasn't living in two worlds. If he had been living in the Eastern world, he would have understood better what might happen. I remember a lunch in New York when he told me the plot of *The Satanic Verses* and I didn't have any sense of the Muslim side. He talked mainly about the two leading characters. I didn't get a feel of the controversial quality of the book. Perhaps he kept that to himself or at that time it wasn't developed or wasn't the important side to him. *The Satanic Verses* as a title meant something to him, but he didn't talk about it.

"He fitted in very well in the literary community here and in England. He was very good company, very funny, a real asset at dinner parties." She paused with a faraway, thoughtful expression. "I'm not sure he's as much fun today, but in the old days he was great fun."

Deborah Rogers lasted a little longer than Elaine Markson, but inevitably her turn came because Wylie wanted his British partner to represent Rushdie. Like Elaine Markson, Deborah Rogers was quietly philosophical to me about being dropped, but at the time she must have been very angry at Rushdie's allowing her to become a Wylie victim. She spoke of its being humiliating. She told me: "I represented only *Shame* and *Jaguar Smile.* It was unfortunate about the break. Of course writers are entitled to change if they want to and we still remain good friends. We had a good relationship so it was irritating and caused some bad feeling because it all became rather public, though it was not my doing. The whole thing got out of hand because the press seized upon it. It was humiliating for me and enraging for Salman. The fact of Salman's going was quite rational. He had appointed Wylie in America and Wylie very understandably wanted the global picture and to have his own representative in London." But according to the *Tatler*, she had earlier said of Wylie, "I really don't want to talk about him. To talk about that man gives him more credibility than he deserves."

I asked Deborah Rogers if she thought Rushdie had changed much over the years she had known him. Elaine Markson had spoken of the effect of his divorce. "I don't think people change," Rogers replied. "I think they just reveal more of themselves. Salman is a complex, interesting, multi-faceted person. You only have to read one line of his to know that. He's not a pedantic kind of person in any way, but has extraordinary kinds of areas of impression. I don't think he's changed. I think he's revealing a different side of himself."

Where did all this leave Liz Calder? That apparently was what she was wondering. She had heard nothing from Salman, so she wrote directly to him, reportedly an anguished and angry letter. He still didn't reply. But she learned that, as she expected, Wylie wanted to auction *The Satanic Verses* to get the highest advance and that meant Bloomsbury couldn't have it unless she outbid all the other publishers.

When I spoke to Liz Calder, she was as calm and philosophical as Rushdie's two ex-agents. She made only a passing reference to being hurt and she didn't mention Wylie by name. With *The Satanic Verses*, she said, she had "every reason to think I would publish it at Bloomsbury. It is very difficult and complicated to understand why that didn't happen and why he changed publishers. He felt the time had come to test the waters. Bloomsbury was a brand new company and we had a series of misunderstandings, Salman and I. He was encouraged by his new agent to go into the marketplace. I was extremely disappointed and hurt. We had a falling out, but since then have made up. I don't think I want to talk about it. It happened just between us. None of the experiences I had with his first three books were anything but extremely rewarding. There was never any talk of our parting, which is why it came as a blow to me."

Wylie could be abrasive with critics of his methods, but Rushdie's tactics with his former representatives and friends was to stay out of their way, to avoid any confrontations. Ultimately, given his attitude toward his writing, he would probably justify his actions as necessary for the marketing of his most important novel. Sometimes he even talked like Wylie, reflecting his ideas about publishing. He said publishers demanded a strange kind of loyalty from writers, trying "all kinds of emotional blackmail." Many agents, he added, had too close a relationship with publishers. That was not a view shared by most agents, who thought Rushdie was using rationalizations picked up from Wylie to explain what he had done. "Andrew took a decision not to be part of the club, which is why I wanted him as my agent," said Rushdie. "I think that the level of cronyism that exists in publishing on both sides of the Atlantic is so high as to be in my view unacceptable."

The British media made a great drama of Wylie's takeover and gave the American agent the full treatment. As the *Tatler* put it, "It was Wylie's acquisition of Salman Rushdie as a client that both made the British aware of him and left the literary establishment reeling." The *Tatler* claimed it was as much Wylie's means as the end—losing Salman—that left Deborah Rogers "feeling bruised and betrayed."

Defections were nothing new in the book world, but this was unusually acrimonious, according to the London *Sunday Times*.

"Feelings were wounded, the breach remained unhealed and Rushdie seemed to feel there was a vendetta against him. But whatever the feelings of others, one thing was plain: his overriding ambition on behalf of his own work. His new book, he knew, would be *the* book, though he could not have foreseen in what manner *The Satanic Verses* would etch his name on history."

The Guardian reported that "there was some resentment that he allowed the rights of *Satanic Verses* to be auctioned by Andrew Wylie, said with horror in Bloomsbury [the symbol of literary London as well as Liz Calder's publishing company] to be ruthless—a quality that publishing fogies believe appropriate to secret agents, not literary agents." This was written long after the acrimonious event and seems overly defensive toward former *Guardian* writer Rushdie. More than publishing fogies were critical of Wylie.

The way was now clear for offering *The Satanic Verses* to carefully selected publishers with prestige and money on both sides of the Atlantic. Wylie, from his office high above West Fifty-seventh Street in Manhattan, was in charge. He and his British partner talked to the selected publishers about Rushdie and the new novel, exploring the extent of their interest, especially in financial terms.

The final stage was to hold an auction with the publishers bidding against each other. Some publishers had suggested that the sales of Rushdie's earlier books didn't justify the kind of large advance Wylie wanted for *The Satanic Verses*, especially as the new novel was not written in a popular style, but was a very literary, intellectual work. Wylie and his partner, with Rushdie's consent, decided to offer at the auction world hardcover and paperback English-language rights, which covered the main international markets and, it was hoped, would justify Big Bucks even to the more cautious publishers. But Wylie made one condition—they didn't have to accept the highest bid. That gave Wylie and Rushdie some freedom to choose the right literary publishers.

Wylie had talked confidently to Rushdie about at least a $250,000 advance, but most New York publishers and agents who had read Rushdie's complex novel thought Wylie would be lucky to get that and certainly no more. This view was confirmed when such a shrewd judge of the marketplace as Roger W. Straus, the president of Farrar, Straus and Giroux, the small, prestigious and independent company, soon dropped out of the auction.

"I was the first to be offered *The Satanic Verses* here," Roger Straus told me in New York. "I read it and then someone else did, one of the editors. We agreed it was an interesting but failed work of art. But Rushdie's a writer we'd like to publish. *Midnight's Children* was marvelous. So we were willing to go to $50,000 or $60,000. But Wylie wanted six figures and eventually that left Sonny Mehta and Peter Mayer, I think."

To Roger Straus's surprise, the bidding soared and reached nearly seven figures. Not only Mehta of Knopf and Mayer of Viking-Penguin were bidding, but several other American and British publishers or groups of publishers. Wylie refused to discuss the bidding or the publishers involved in the auction. Secrecy was part of the game because publishers who didn't get the book didn't wish to flaunt their failure. Even the favorites, Mehta and Mayer—favorites because of their long personal connections with Rushdie—didn't make public their top bids.

Sonny Mehta, who had worked with Rushdie on *The Jaguar Smile* for Pan Books in London, was Indian, born of prosperous parents, and Cambridge educated like Rushdie. He obviously identified closely with his fellow Indian's writing, calling Rushdie "one of the few significant writers of his generation." Knopf had published *Midnight's Children* and *Shame* and then had lost Rushdie to Viking-Penguin for *Jaguar Smile.* Sonny Mehta hoped to bring him back to the company.

An informal man, with a short beard like Rushdie, Mehta was impatient with office routine, even though he was a top executive. He brought a with-it reputation from swinging London, which he renewed in Manhattan with swinging literary cocktail parties. His company style was criticized by some longtime Knopf people and some top agents who complained he didn't always return their phone calls, but it was a style that would appeal to Rushdie. Mehta also enjoyed editing books as well as the wheeling and dealing of Big Bucks sales. That, too, would appeal to Rushdie. He had only recently arrived at Knopf as the boss and was keen to sign up some impressive books and authors to strengthen his position. Rushdie's novel was important to him for that reason, too.

The bids kept going up and Mehta kept raising his own. He reportedly stayed in the auction up to a whopping $800,000, but when I talked with him, he told me, "I don't remember the figure correctly. That's common with me when I don't get a book. I wipe it out in my memory. But we made a very aggressive bid with a very substantial offer."

I asked Sonny Mehta if a big six-figure offer hadn't seemed too risky a gamble for that kind of novel because no one then could know it would receive such worldwide publicity. Mehta replied, "It was almost a year before the death sentence. The book was complex, but I don't believe Salman has ever written a simple book. You either believe Salman is one of the most important writers working the language or you don't. I happen to believe he is. There were parts of that book that was the best writing I had read of his. I anticipated the book would arouse a certain amount of controversy, but I don't think *anyone* expected that kind of direct action. A certain amount of trouble, yes, but not that." Asked if Rushdie had changed much in the time he had known him, Mehta replied, "I think he's institutionalized a little, but he remains an enormously challenging writer, a person deeply involved in the society he operates in. He has an idea of the author as a part of society and of the country, and that influences very much his notion of context."

With this belief in Rushdie and his book, Sonny Mehta bowed out of the auction with great reluctance. He bid as high as he thought realistic or even perhaps beyond. Any publisher involved in an auction of that kind must have a gambler's instincts, but also must know when it's time to quit. Mehta obviously didn't think *The Satanic Verses* could make back more than his final offer.

That left Peter Mayer, the head of Viking-Penguin, as the front-running favorite. He was just as great an admirer of Rushdie's work as Sonny Mehta. His involvement with Rushdie went back as far as *Grimus*. In 1979, when none of the leading New York publishers wanted Rushdie's first novel, Mayer had published it himself with his small family publishing company, Overlook Press. He couldn't show his faith in Rushdie as a writer more than that, and Rushdie remembered it. Later at Penguin, Mayer had bid for the British paperback rights to *Midnight's Children*, but Picador with Pan Books behind it bid much higher. "It's the big one," a Picador executive had told Liz Calder, and so Picador was willing to pay big money. Peter Mayer felt the same way about losing *Midnight's Children* as Sonny Mehta felt about not getting *The Satanic Verses*. He had greatly admired Rushdie's novel about India. "It came as a revelation of the kind of writing that was emerging in the English language, but not out of England," said Mayer. "It was big in every sense. And it was another view of India which you could not have got from any Anglo-Indian writers."

Mayer was determined not to lose the new novel. Although Viking-Penguin would neither confirm nor deny the report, it was generally accepted in New York publishing circles that Mayer's final bid was $850,000. That kind of offer for that type of novel showed how badly he wanted it.

The last stages of the auction were kept strictly confidential. The difficulty seems to have been that there were higher bids than Viking-Penguin's from trans-Atlantic hardcover and paperback publishers, who put together complicated joint package deals in which they all shared the cost. The London *Sunday Times* reported that "Collins and Weidenfeld & Nicolson had put together larger joint packages with American houses." Would Wylie recommend that Rushdie take the biggest bucks? Or would Rushdie's friendship with Peter Mayer and Viking-Penguin's international network with offices in most parts of the world, including India, be more important than the extra bucks?

Wylie recalled his condition that they needn't accept the highest bid, and they decided to go with Peter Mayer and Viking-Penguin. Publication would be in Britain first in mid-September, in time to qualify for the 1988 Booker Prize. The American edition would come out the following February boosted, Mayer hoped, by glowing British reviews and the winning of a second Booker by Rushdie.

When Roger Straus learned that Peter Mayer had paid so much, he asked him over a private lunch why he thought Rushdie's novel was worth that. Surely it was a very big gamble for Viking-Penguin. "Peter said there are some writers you feel belong with Penguin and he felt very strongly that Salman Rushdie was one of them," Roger Straus told me. "Peter said he was determined to get *The Satanic Verses* and thought the book would make back the big advance given enough time in all editions. He had bought world English-language rights, hard and soft. Of course Penguin is the only truly international publisher and that was bound to help in marketing the book. Peter needn't have worried about the size of the advance as it turned out, but who could foresee that then?"

The *Tatler*, in its Wylie profile, also quoted a Wylie client as claiming that Viking-Penguin "desperately needed a lead title for autumn 1988, which is why Andrew was able to get so much."

Roger Straus, a sociable, sophisticated cosmopolitan, had met Rushdie, but he felt no particular friendliness toward him. "He's not really the kind of man I'd like to spend an evening with. He's like an actor. He likes attention."

Peter Mayer obviously felt very differently about Rushdie, but then his background was very different from that of Roger Straus, who had not only been born in the United States but to a wealthy patrician family. Mayer was a migrant like Rushdie. His Jewish parents emigrated from Nazi Europe soon after the rise of Hitler, and Peter Mayer was born in London in 1936. The family moved to New York when Mayer was three and his father prospered there as a glove maker.

Mayer went on scholarships to Columbia University in New York, Oxford University in Britain, and the Free University of Berlin. A passion for Joseph Conrad's sea stories made him join the merchant navy, but he soon gave that up. He worked as a copyboy for *The New York Times* and wrote advertising copy for *Esquire* magazine—he and Rushdie could exchange advertising stories. Book publishing came next, and at twenty-eight he was running Avon Books, which he turned into one of the most successful New York paperback publishers. He bought the rights to the grown-up children's tale, *Jonathan Livingstone Seagull*, that had done unexpectedly well in hardcover, and paid a stunning $1 million. Many veterans of New York publishing said it was an impossible gamble. But he made a success of it. The memory of it probably boosted his confidence over *The Satanic Verses*.

After an unhappy time at Pocket Books, part of the Simon & Schuster empire, he became chief executive of Penguin in London in 1978. At first it wasn't easy. Many of the British employed by Penguin resented him as an American intruder and, with his New York directness and casual style, he broke Penguin rules of decorum and protocol. But the company's genteel decline was stopped. Mayer popularized the Penguin list and modernized the appearance of the books. He even bid for some of the pop bestsellers and experimented with format as he had done at Avon. Despite his casual manner and offbeat style, his eyes were always on the bottom line. Anything that wasn't profitable in swinging, conservative Britain couldn't be subsidized for long. Longtime Penguin supporters criticized him for abandoning much of the Penguin political list, which traditionally had dealt with current British problems but were often published at a loss. A lifelong pacifist with liberal leanings, Mayer had turned into a successful trans-Atlantic publisher.

A sign of his success was that in 1987, nine years after taking over Penguin, he was confident enough to move his main office to New York. Even some of his sternest critics at Penguin admitted that he had more than survived. They were even reluctant to condemn his spending a fortune on *The Satanic Verses.* Publishing logic suggested it was a disastrous decision and would lead to a great loss, but such was their respect for Mayer's cautious, canny record that they wondered if he knew something they didn't and had made a smart move they didn't yet understand.

"No deal in publishing history has excited so much comment, analysis, resentment and envy," commented the London *Sunday Times* under the headline PORTRAIT OF THE NOVELIST AS A HOT PROPERTY. "By the standards of Jackie Collins or Shirley Conran, it certainly wasn't a big advance; but by the standards of the literary fiction market, it was enormous." To get it back, bookstores on both sides of the Atlantic would have to sell far more copies of *The Satanic Verses* than they had of *Midnight's Children* or *Shame.* That didn't seem likely as the quarter of a million words of Rushdie's novel went off to the printers. It was what booksellers called a hard read.

PART III:
THE MAKING OF
A WORLD CONTROVERSY

1—BOOK REVIEWS AND BOOK BURNINGS

LONG BEFORE SEPTEMBER 26, 1988, WHEN *THE SATANIC VERSES* OFFICIALLY went on sale in British bookstores, Salman Rushdie's novel had circulated widely in bound page proofs among reviewers and other interested parties. It was much discussed at literary dinner parties in early September. Journalists from the East stationed in London began to scramble for early copies to check rumors of what was in the novel.

The Satanic Verses was launched with a Viking-Penguin publisher's party, and even then there was much to celebrate. The first British reviews concentrated mainly on the dazzling literary quality of Rushdie's book and could hardly have been better if Peter Mayer had written them. Everyone at Penguin began to feel the Booker Prize was a sure thing. As one of Rushdie's acquaintances remarked, "It's *Midnight's Children* all over again."

Typical of the critical acclaim was Angela Carter's long review in *The Guardian*. A writer herself, she had been one of the judges when *Shame* failed to win the Booker. She wrote that *The Satanic Verses* was "an epic into which holes have been punched to let in visions; an epic hung about with ragbag scraps of many different cultures." She called Rushdie's novel a "populous, loquacious, sometimes hilarious, extraordinary contemporary novel," and she referred to its "roller-coaster ride over a vast landscape of the imagination."

Like most British reviewers, she paid little attention to the Islamic aspects of the novel. She mentioned Gibreel's "strange, terrible dreams in which he features as his own namesake, the archangel" and that form a "phantasmagoric narrative within the novel" and have a cinematic quality befitting a Bombay super-

125

star's unconscious. "The vexed question of the Lord's song and how to sing it" in a strange land concerned most of Rushdie's characters, she pointed out, because they were mostly displaced persons—expatriates, immigrants, refugees. But the portrayal of Mahound was not discussed. It was not a matter of great importance to a British reviewer. *The Satanic Verses* was reviewed strictly as an outstanding work of literature.

The London *Times* thought Rushdie's novel was about the question of evil, so did the *Sunday Telegraph*. But the Islamic sections clearly baffled some British reviewers. The *Sunday Tribune* found the novel compelling to read and yet at times verging on incomprehensibility. *The Times Literary Supplement* found that in the absence of a more formal structure, the novel was held together by a bemusing cat's-cradle of cross-referenced names and images. *The Independent* reported that it was on the London scenes that the bulk of critical labor was expended, perhaps because the critics were more familiar with the material, perhaps because an obvious autobiographical streak aroused the sometimes hostile curiosity which the famously successful author has been known to attract.

The *Illustrated London News* compared the book to a loud and garish Bombay movie with "a frantically coy approach to sex." Even if some critics felt Rushdie's style and power were beginning to flag, he still commanded a remarkable degree of respect. The influences he showed were listed as Joyce, Calvino, Kafka, Frank Herbert, Pynchon, Mervyn Peake, Gabriel Garcia Marquez, Jean-Luc Godard, J. G. Ballard, and William Burroughs. *The New Statesman* called it a "collection of rented spare parts," and *The Independent* recalled that *Midnight's Children* was "substantially an unconscious duplicate" of Günter Grass's *The Tin Drum*. But *The Independent* added that "Nevertheless Rushdie can be seen to be wreaking something new with his material, and often doing it impressively well." Reviewers concluded Rushdie's novel and the protests against it came out of different worlds—literary London and Islam. Rushdie certainly wouldn't have agreed with them.

It was left to two of India's news magazines, *India Today* and *Sunday*, to treat the novel as a political work and controversial religious commentary. They knew what would most interest their readers. *India Today* thought the news was so urgent that it didn't wait until publication day, but reviewed the book over a week before. Madhu Jain, the reviewer, described *The Satanic Verses* as "an uncompromising, unequivocal attack on religious fanaticism and fundamentalism, which in this book is largely Islamic." Rushdie, he wrote, "takes a very irreverent look at Islamic folklore and fact." The *India Today* review concluded, *"The Satanic Verses* is bound to trigger an avalanche of protests from the ramparts."

The Indian news magazine followed up with an interview with Rushdie asking him, "Do you fear a backlash from the mullahs?" Rushdie replied, "Even *Shame* was attacked by fundamentalist Muslims. I cannot censor. I write whatever there is to write."

Sunday also interviewed Rushdie before the novel's official publication. Shrabani Basu, the interviewer, claimed that already *The Satanic Verses* had caused a lot of controversy because of the references to Muhammad—"There was even the possibility that it may not be published in India." Rushdie replied, "That's news to me—I haven't heard it from Penguin. But it would be absurd to think that a book can cause riots.... That's a strange sort of view of the world." The interviewer said the situation in India was particularly delicate, and Rushdie told him, "Well, the point about the book is that there is a view in it that I take—and that is that everything is worth discussing. There are no subjects which are off limits and that includes God, includes prophets."

These reports in the two Indian news magazines were read in India by Syed Shahabuddin, an ambitious Muslim member of Parliament. He immediately condemned Rushdie's novel as an "indecent vilification of the Holy Prophet." In one scene, he complained, the prophet's wives were portrayed as prostitutes. "The Home Minister was shocked when I showed him the passage." He demanded that the Indian government ban the book. "The book should also be restricted in England," he said. "No civilized society should permit it."

The Indian Prime Minister, Rajiv Gandhi, whose Congress Party was unpopular, faced a general election soon and he needed all the support he could get. He dared not risk offending India's one-hundred million Muslims. On October 5, just over a week after the book's publication in Britain, the Indian government informed Penguin in London that it had banned Rushdie's novel in India. Similar bans soon followed in Pakistan, Saudi Arabia, Egypt, Indonesia, South Africa, and other countries with large Muslim populations.

Zamir Asari, the Penguin representative in India, said he hadn't expected the ban—the book obviously had literary merits—but Penguin would abide by the ruling. But he warned that when a book was banned, which was rare, it sometimes led to a strange situation. D. H. Lawrence's novel, *Lady Chatterley's Lover*, was still banned, but it could be bought in a pirated edition and was even recommended in some university courses.

Leading Indian newspapers and magazines deplored the ban as a philistine decision as *The Hindu* put it. Many Indian publishers and booksellers condemned it and were supported by International PEN and Index on Censorship. Rushdie's friend, dramatist Harold Pinter, organized a protest in London supported by such fellow writers as Kingsley Amis, Tom Stoppard, and Stephen Spender.

Rushdie was sufficiently upset by this ban in his native India to write the Indian prime minister a long open letter defending his book and addressed to "Dear Rajiv Gandhi." He accused the Indian government of having given in to two or three Muslim politicians, including Syed Shahabuddin, "whom I do not hesitate to call extremists, even fundamentalists." He pointed out that an official statement explained that *The Satanic Verses* had been banned as a preemptive measure. "Certain passages in my book had been identified as being capable of distortion and misuse, presumably by unscrupulous religious fanatics and such. The banning order had been issued to prevent this misuse. So now it appears that my book is not deemed blasphemous or objectionable in itself, but is being proscribed for, so to speak, its own good!"

Rushdie commented, "This is no way, Mr. Gandhi, for a free society to behave." The right to freedom of expression, he added, was at the very foundation of any democratic society.

He insisted his novel was not "actually about Islam, but about migration, metamorphoses, divided selves, love, death, London and Bombay." It dealt with a prophet who was not called Muhammad living in a highly fantasied city made of sand in which he was surrounded by fictional followers, "one of whom happens to bear my own first name." Moreover, wrote Rushdie, this entire sequence happened in a dream, the fictional dream of a fictional character, an Indian movie star, who was losing his mind. "How much farther from history could one get?"

In this dream sequence, Rushdie added, he tried to deal with revelation and the birth of a great world religion, and his view was "that of a secular man for whom Islamic culture has been of central importance all his life."

He deeply resented his book being used as "a political football." He told the prime minister: "In my view, this is now a matter between you and me." What sort of an India did the prime minister wish to govern—an open or a repressive society? "Your action in the matter of *The Satanic Verses* will be for many people around the world, an important indicator." He saw the choice as confirming the ban or admitting it had been an error and moving swiftly to correct it—"That will be an honorable deed and I shall be the first to applaud."

Muslim leaders in Britain had followed events in India closely and started to take action themselves. Hesham El Essawi, chairman of the Islamic Society for the Promotion of Religious Tolerance, informed Penguin that he regarded *The Satanic Verses* as an insult to Islam. Faiyazuddin Ahmad, public relations director of the Islamic Foundation in Leicester, bought the novel when he knew India was banning it. The allegedly blasphemous passages were photocopied and sent to the leading Islamic organizations in Britain. Copies were also delivered to the forty-five embassies in Britain of the member countries of the Organization of Islamic Conference, including Iran. Ahmad then met with the leaders of the Islamic Conference at their Saudi Arabian headquarters in Jeddah. All member countries were then urged to ban the book.

Dr. Syed Pasha, secretary of the Union of Muslim Organizations in Britain, called a meeting of the Union's council members who decided to start a campaign to get the novel banned in Britain. Dr. Pasha asked the British prime minister to prosecute Rushdie and Penguin under the Public Order Act (1986) and the Race Relations Act (1976). "Never have we encountered such a ferocious and savage attack on our Holy Prophet, using abominably foul language," Dr. Pasha told the Prime Minister. Mrs. Thatcher replied there were no grounds in which the government would consider banning the book. "It is an essential part of our democratic system," she wrote, "that people who act within the law should be able to express their opinions freely." Sir Patrick Mayhew, the attorney-general, decided the book constituted no criminal offense. Dr. Pasha then demanded the Home Office should ban the book. The Home Office refused and said no change in the law of blasphemy, which applied only to Christianity, was being considered. The British blasphemy law was a result of the conflicts between different branches of Christianity and was really intended to protect the Church of England of which the British sovereign was the head. Dr. Pasha hoped to get the law changed to include Islam so Rushdie could be charged with breaking it. He also appealed to booksellers to withdraw the book from sale.

Muslims claimed the situation was comparable to recent Christian protests about an American film, *The Last Temptation of Christ*, which had a controversial portrayal of Jesus. There was no reference, however, to another film entitled *Muhammad— Messenger of God*, which had led to violent protests by Muslim groups in the United States, even though Muhammad was never portrayed directly. But perhaps that should have alerted Rushdie and Viking-Penguin to the kind of reception they could expect.

Dr. Zaki Badawi, principal of the Muslim College and chairman of the Imams and Mosques Council, asked the 382 mosques in Britain to support a ban. Dr. Badawi said at one time they were thinking of commissioning a play about Islam, perhaps about the dilemma of Muslims in Britain, and he had thought of asking Rushdie to write it, "but I am afraid we can't do that now."

Muslim organizations asked Penguin to pulp all copies of the novel and not reprint, to offer an "unqualified public apology" to the world Muslim community, and to pay damages equal to the profits from all copies already sold in Britain and abroad. If Penguin refused, Muslim authorities were to be asked to freeze the company's assets in their jurisdiction. Penguin was accused of masterly indifference and of telling protesters that the company didn't recognize Rushdie's novel "in your description," that the book had been widely praised by literary critics and "We have no intention of withdrawing the book."

Muslim leaders asked all fellow Muslims to send telegrams and letters and to phone and call personally on Penguin. The ideal would be for Rushdie to go to a Muslim country where he could be prosecuted under Islam law, but if he remained in Britain, he should be left to his "charmed circle of 'literary critics'" because the Muslim leaders sensed "a milling anger about the outrage committed by him." Such remarks served only to work up the protesters still more.

Increasingly frustrated in their efforts to get the book banned, British Muslims staged angry demonstrations in several towns in the industrial North, where large Muslim communities lived. More than 7,000 people gathered in Bolton to watch a copy of *The Satanic Verses* being publicly burned. In Bradford, where more than 50,000 Muslims lived, another copy went up in flames outside the local police headquarters. The atmosphere in Bradford was so tense and the Muslims leaders' speeches were so fiery that the police advised W. H. Smith, the British chain booksellers, to withdraw copies of the book temporarily from display in their Bradford shop to prevent possible danger to their staff and damage to the shop from demonstrators. Some local politicians, who represented areas with large numbers of Muslim voters, fanned the flames by denouncing Rushdie's book and speaking sympathetically of the book burnings.

The media had tended to ignore the early Muslim protests, but the book burnings were front page news. They awakened memories of Nazi and fascist demonstrations in the thirties. *The Independent* wrote that the Muslims' campaign "not just against the book but against Rushdie personally does them no credit." They should not seek to impose their feelings about the book on the "rather larger non-Islamic part of the population." Was the Islamic faith not strong enough to withstand some controversial fictional analysis in a book of literary merit that was "written as a moral parable?"

The Guardian criticized members of Parliament who had denounced what the paper called Rushdie's "superb anti-racist novel" and attacked the "outrageous suggestion" of the member of Parliament representing the book burners of Bradford that the laws of blasphemy be extended "to allow non-Christians to drag people like Rushdie before the courts for offending against their faith, no matter what it may be."

This newspaper coverage was described by Muslim leaders as patronizing and intimidating. It failed to cool the anger of the demonstrators. There were more book burnings climaxed by a massive rally in London in Hyde Park, the traditional center of free speech in England. More than two hundred policemen were there. Protesters marched to Penguin Books and the Prime Minister's residence at 10 Downing Street. Appeals were to be made to the House of Lords and the European Court.

The Tablet, the Catholic intellectual journal, gave a Christian answer to the Muslim extremists. Malise Ruthven wrote that the allegedly blasphemous passages about Mahound and the brothel scenes concerning his wives were not intended to be insulting as the Muslims insisted, but were "an imaginative way of charting the migrant's path from faith to scepticism, his shifting perspective of women, his attempted exorcism—consciously or otherwise—of childhood archetypes." *The Tablet* writer added, "The rage with which this magnificent, challenging novel has been greeted by a number of Muslim organizations proves that Rushdie has touched upon some extremely raw nerves in a community experiencing the very dilemmas and transformations he portrays."

Both Rushdie and Penguin continued to receive threatening letters and phone calls. Rushdie tried to ignore them and live as freely as he had before the protests began. He accepted an invitation to make the keynote speech on apartheid and censorship at a book fair in South Africa. He was packing his bags ready to go to London Airport to take a London-Johannesburg night flight when he learned his visit had been cancelled. Some militant Islam fundamentalist groups had threatened a holy war against the *Weekly Mail*, the organizer of the book fair, if blasphemer Rushdie arrived. Several bomb threats against the paper and Rushdie were received. The invitation was then withdrawn because Rushdie's physical safety couldn't be guaranteed. Nadine Gordimer, a friend of Rushdie as well as a leading South African writer, said the Muslim extremists had been offered the chance to present their point of view, "but they were not prepared to be reasonable." Rushdie said he was sad not to be going to South Africa because his visit was intended as an act of solidarity against apartheid, which he had long condemned. The speech he was to have made was entitled "Wherever They Burn Books, They Also Burn People."

Rushdie took every opportunity—in newspaper and magazine articles, speeches, interviews, and television appearances—to defend his book and himself. Unable to accept the "unarguable absolutes of religion," he had replaced them with literature. "The art of the novel is a thing I cherish as dearly as the book burners of Bradford value their brand of militant Islam," Rushdie said. So the battle over *The Satanic Verses* was "a clash of faiths in a way." Or, more precisely, a clash of languages. "As my fictional character 'Salman' says of my fictional prophet 'Mahound,' 'It's his Word against mine.' "

The saddest irony, according to Rushdie, was that after working for five years "to give voice and fictional flesh to the immigrant culture of which I am myself a member," he should see his book burned, largely unread, by the people it was about, people who might find some pleasure and much recognition in its pages.

"How fragile civilization is," Rushdie reflected. "How easily, how merrily a book burns!" Inside his novel, its characters sought to become fully human by facing up to the great facts of love, death, and "with or without God," the life of the soul. Outside his novel, the forces of inhumanity were on the march. "Battle lines are being drawn up in India today," one of his characters remarks. "Secular versus religious, the light versus the dark. Better you choose which side you are on."

Now that the battle had spread to Britain, Rushdie warned, "I can only hope it will not be lost by default. It is time for us to choose."

He was beginning to realize what he was up against at home as well as abroad.

2—RUSHDIE FIGHTS BACK

LIVING WITH CONSTANT THREATS—BY MAIL OR PHONE OR PUBLIC DEMON-strations—had upset the peaceful, industrious routine of the Rushdie household. Marianne was completing her own new novel, *John Dollar*, and wanted no disturbances. She therefore rented a small apartment five blocks from home, a quiet place where she could write in peace and which could serve as a refuge for both of them if they needed it.

Rumors soon started that their marriage was on the rocks and the second Mrs. Rushdie had moved out. "What did I tell you?" remarked a journalist who knew them both. "Two big demanding egos, two ambitious novelists, Salman getting all this worldwide attention while Marianne remains in the background—their marriage *couldn't* last."

But the Rushdies insisted that there was no truth in the rumors, that they were only trying to adapt their private lives as well as they could to their new, rather frightening situation. They pointed out they were planning an American trip together early in 1989 for the publication in February of both *The Satanic Verses* by Viking-Penguin and *John Dollar* by Harper and Row. Meanwhile, they were trying to live a normal life as far as possible, but there were certain precautions they had to take.

Bomb threats meant that Rushdie had to cancel some public appearances, including a return visit to Cambridge he had been looking forward to. He had intended to sign copies of *The Satanic Verses* in Cambridge and give a lecture to three hundred language students at the European Centre on Panton Street, but a bomb scare began just hours before he was to speak. One of the organizers said, "Although the risk was minuscule, we were

134

ushdie and his second wife, American novelist Marianne Wiggins, in their Islington
ome in North London shortly before they went into hiding. (*Terry Smith/Camera
ress*)

ushdie in 1975, the year he published his first novel, *Grimus,* and still had an Indian
air style. (*Fay Godwin*)

Mrs. Indira Gandhi, former Prime Minister of India, who sued Rushdie in London over *Midnight's Children* and won. *(Globe Photos)*

Bestselling novelist John le Carré was one of the few writers who criticized Rushdie over *The Satanic Verses. (Globe Photos)*

ramatist Harold Pinter, a friend
nd political ally of Rushdie's,
cted as his stand-in at a public
ecture in London. (*Globe*
hotos)

Mrs. Margaret Thatcher, Prime
Minister of Britain since 1979,
whom Rushdie called "Mrs.
Torture," but who nevertheless
provided him with Scotland
Yard protection. (*Globe Photos*)

Ayatollah Khomeini of Iran sentenced Rushdie and his publishers to death fo "blasphemy." (*Globe Photos*)

"Women Against Fundamentalism" remind anti-Rushdie demonstrators in London tha thousands have been killed in the name of Islam in Iran. *(Peter Francis/Camera Press*

Muslim protestors in London call for a boycott of "Penguin the Satanic Press" and hang an effigy of Rushdie from a home-made gallows. (*Peter Francis/ Camera Press*)

Muslims in Bradford in the North of England carry pictures of the Ayatollah and burn copies of *The Satanic Verses* watched by British policemen. (*Camera Press*)

Rushdie in Indian clothes, a reminder of his role as a migrant author bridging East and West, seen here soon after he finished *The Satanic Verses*. (*Camera Press*)

The author of *The Satanic Verses* at home in his book-strewn study in London; one of the last pictures before he disappeared with Scotland Yard detectives for protection to become the most famous writer in the world. (*Terry Smith/ Camera Press*)

Norman Mailer speaking at the PEN American center. U.S. writers hold a public reading from *The Satanic Verses* in New York to show their support for Rushdie. Everyone was searched for weapons before being allowed to attend. (*Adam Scull*)

Andrew Wylie, regarded as one of the toughest, most controversial literary agents in New York, negotiated a record contract for *The Satanic Verses*. Rushdie was strongly criticized for dropping his previous agent in favor of Wylie, seen here in his Manhattan office.

Peter Mayer of Viking-Penguin, publisher of *The Satanic Verses,* who was an early Rushdie admirer. (*Jonathan Player, NYT Pictures*).

not prepared to risk the lives of three hundred students for the sake of a lecture." But bookstores in Cambridge continued to sell the book. Rushdie agreed with the decision to play safe. He took the Islamic threats very seriously. As the London *Sunday Times* noted, "He was struck by the extent and efficiency of their organization, and taken aback by the hatred and loathing in their vilification."

Rushdie himself admitted, "In many ways I've been gratified to be in England during all this. In Pakistan I'd be dead." He hoped other British religious leaders, bishops and rabbis, might be able to help, but the cultural gap between them and the Muslim extremists was too wide. A Muslim pointed out that, unlike the Nazis who looted libraries and bookstores, the Bradford demonstrators had bought the copies of *The Satanic Verses* they burned. "Thanks a lot," said Rushdie.

He was aware the Muslim extremists had huge resources, some of the campaign against him operating out of the Regent's Park mosque, and Saudi-financed; some of it from the Muslim Education Trust of Yussuf Islam, the Muslim name of the American pop singer, Cat Stevens, who had been converted to Islam and had spoken out against Rushdie. "It is brilliantly managed, incomparably better organized than anything I've ever seen on the Left," said Rushdie.

At least the Muslims' campaign had brought *The Satanic Verses* so much publicity that it had become a bestseller. Over 40,000 hardcover copies had been sold and Penguin were busy reprinting. Peter Mayer was winning his gamble.

Rushdie's novel had also been shortlisted for the Booker. The prize money had gone up to £15,000 (roughly $25,000) presumably to make up for inflation. But Rushdie's interest in winning the Booker was to stress the literary merit of his book as an answer to the Muslim extremists who classed it as "filth." Peter Mayer also wanted the book to win to boost sales even more and help the American edition.

The Satanic Verses and five other novels had been selected from more than ninety submitted by publishers. Four of the authors had been on earlier shortlists and two of them, Rushdie and Penelope Fitzgerald, were former winners. No one had yet won a Booker twice. Michael Foot, the veteran Labour Party leader and journalist, was the chairman of the judges. The other judges were Sebastian Faulks, literary editor of *The Independent*; Philip French, producer of Critics' Forum, a highbrow television program, and film critic of *The Observer*; Blake Morrison, poet and literary editor of *The Observer*; and Rose Tremain, novelist and potential Booker winner in the future. A more literary team than usual, the judges were tipped to select a serious novel. The favorites were *The Satanic Verses* and Peter Carey's *Oscar and Lucinda*, set in nineteenth century Australia, a fantastic, funny, crowded love story by an Australian writer who lived in Sydney and who had had a previous book shortlisted in 1985.

The other novels on the short list were:

Utz by Rushdie's dying friend, Bruce Chatwin, a "quest" story twisted into a set of art historical puzzles that made use of Chatwin's earlier experience of the art world in London;

The Beginning of Spring by Penelope Fitzgerald, the engaging tale of a disrupted romance of a British couple living in Moscow in 1913:

Nice Work by David Lodge, a follow-up to his *Small World*, which was shortlisted in 1984, a campus novel that also takes in the outside world;

The Lost Father by Marina Warner, the story of a London museum curator who goes to California in search of the truth about her grandfather's death.

Rushdie attended the Booker dinner at the Guildhall, but he didn't have the same obsession about winning as he had when *Shame* was shortlisted. More important concerns preoccupied him now, symbolized by the bodyguard he took with him for this public appearance. The threats to his life put everything in a more realistic perspective.

The final judging was held in the twenty-seventh floor boardroom of Booker's headquarters in Victoria and was over in a record twenty-five minutes. The chairman, Michael Foot, began by backing *The Satanic Verses*, but the other four judges were unanimous in choosing Peter Carey's *Oscar and Lucinda* as the winner. Michael Foot argued that the daring picture of contemporary life made Rushdie's novel outstanding, but the other judges, although they admired Rushdie's book, refused to budge. It was four against one. Michael

Foot finally gave in. "I surrender," he said. "I think I've got to."

Rushdie listened grave-faced as Peter Carey's novel was announced as the winner. There was no outburst from him this time. The presence of his bodyguard was a constant reminder of his new position. He behaved with silent dignity as if he were above this literary contest, concerned only as to how far the Muslim extremists would go against him. The television cameras filming the ceremony made more of him than of Peter Carey the winner. Rushdie had become the leading figure in a drama as suspenseful as any TV soap opera. People had begun to ask how the death threats, bomb threats, hate mail, and book burnings were going to end.

Voices threatening to kill Rushdie on his answering machine at home had forced him to change his phone number and keep his address a secret as much as possible. He was taking no chances, but he didn't want his enemies to think he was giving in to them. At first he was convinced that people would read his book and the extremists would lose support, and his life would slowly return to normal. But his optimism didn't last. He was particularly affected by a demonstration in Bradford at which a copy of *The Satanic Verses* was nailed to a post in a central square of the city before being set on fire. His book had been crucified. For Rushdie it was the last straw.

"One simply cannot remember the last time a book was burned in the streets of England," Rushdie said. "You would have to go back really a long time. They didn't just burn it; they nailed it to a post first. They crucified it. To me it evoked Nazism. The Inquisition. It made something snap inside me. It made me start fighting back."

He decided to meet one of his Muslim opponents face-to-face for the first time. The British Broadcasting Corporation staged a television debate in Birmingham. Hesham El-Essawy of Britain's Islamic Society for Religious Tolerance represented the Muslims. Rushdie spoke angrily about the misrepresentation of his book in Muslim protests and about the threats against him. He snapped at Essawy, accusing him of helping to organize "a campaign of vilification and fabrication." Essawy replied sharply that books like Rushdie's "should carry a health warning." Rushdie didn't like that. The debate, as Rushdie said afterwards, soon "deterio-rated into a slanging match."

A small crowd of noisy protestors with such signs as "Satan Rushdie" gathered outside the television studio waiting for Rushdie to come out. BBC officials phoned for police protection at the front door. Rushdie was escorted from the building to the train station for his journey back to London. Also on the train was his recent opponent, Hesham El-Essawy, who approached him with hand held out "in peace" and asked Rushdie "to bring this matter to an end by agreeing to a simple erratum slip in the book for historical and factual mistakes." Rushdie refused and, according to Essawy, said, "You want me to apologize. I will never apologize. I said what I said and will never stand down."

Rushdie left behind him in Birmingham even greater antago-nism toward him. "Nobody could guarantee what would happen if he came and walked down the street," said Sherafsal Khan, president of the Muslim League of the United Kingdom in Bir-mingham. "There are notices in every mosque ridiculing this man. In his devilish book he has insulted the Savior of Mankind. We are united against this Mr. Rushdie."

Rushdie said he understood the grievance of "my people" and knew that they would be provoked in England. After all, "funda-mentalist Christianity is not that different." But he hadn't foreseen "the scale of protest, how much they would want to attack it."

But the more the book was attacked, the more it sold in British bookstores. Some booksellers didn't display it, but kept their copies underneath the counter, and yet they sold out, too. A week after the Bradford demonstrators staged a book burning, *The Satanic Verses* shot from seventh place to the top of bestseller lists. "It serves them right," said Rushdie.

The demonstrations were also having another effect. The fate of Rushdie's book might not mean anything to most English people, but their prejudice against foreign immigrants of differ-ent races and cultures, strong in the case of the Muslims, was growing at the sight on television of fiery un-English demonstra-tions. The hardworking Muslims had striven to make a place for themselves in British society and now they were losing much of the respect and goodwill they had earned. They were interfering with the British tradition of free speech.

Rushdie commented, "The zealot protests serve to confirm, in the Western mind, all the worst stereotypes of the Muslim world."

But there was another side of Islam that was heard from as the weeks went by. Rushdie's morale was boosted by a growing number of letters that he received from Muslims who liked his book and disapproved of the demonstrations against him. "They write to me to say we're not all like those people who burn books," Rushdie said. These correspondents added that they were ashamed of what the Muslim extremists were doing, of the way in which they were bringing shame on the Muslim community in Britain by behaving in this extremely uncivilized manner. "So the idea that what I'm saying is somehow outside Islam is one that I resist," Rushdie said. When people dared to speak out against the extremists, arguments in the Muslim communities showed opinions were not nearly as rigid as the demonstrations suggested.

Jordanian novelist Fadia Faqir, who had a novel boycotted by Muslim fundamentalists in Egypt, wrote in *The Guardian* that some of *The Satanic Verses* was as offensive to Orthodox Muslims as the film, *The Last Temptation of Christ*, was to devout Catholics. But the film was not stopped from being shown and Rushdie's novel should also be published and read. "If some Muslims in Britain and elsewhere find the book abusive, it is time for them to be intellectually militant in their positions, to launch a scholastic offensive to refute Rushdie's argument, and present their point of view in an equally powerful way." She referred to one of Rushdie's characters who said a poet's work was "to name the unnameable, to point at frauds, to take sides, start arguments, shape the world and stop it from going to sleep." That was certainly what Rushdie was trying to do.

The New York Times called him "Fiction's Embattled Infidel." Gerald Marzorati, who interviewed him for *The New York Times* in London, was surprised that Rushdie was willing to show him around Brick Lane in London's East End, where 40,000 Asians lived, mostly Muslims from Bengal and some of Rushdie's bitterest opponents. Much of *The Satanic Verses* takes place in a London district called Brickhall, a neighborhood that Rushdie said "is and is not" Brick Lane. When Marzorati suggested it might not be safe for him to walk around Brick Lane, Rushdie told him, "You cannot let something like this take over your life, or you have lost." Marzorati thought he sounded "frustrated, beleaguered" and asked him was he sure he wanted to go. "They're not going to know my face from the book jacket," replied Rushdie. "They're not allowed to buy the book."

Rushdie had shaved off his beard and wore thick glasses. He was hard to recognize. But Marzorati was favorably impressed. "You see in his small gestures and phrasings a hint of formality once adhered to," reported Marzorati, "but this has given way to gentlemanly casualness." English cartoonists who depicted him with his beard as Satan got him wrong. His heavy-lidded eyes were too soft, and there was no hardness either in the way he held himself or in the way he spoke.

They drove to Brick Lane in Rushdie's Saab. Rushdie pointed out a mosque that had once been a synagogue. The shops had signs in Arabic script. "The thing you have to understand about a neighborhood like this," said Rushdie, "is that when people board an Air India jet and come halfway across the planet, they don't just bring their suitcases. They bring everything. And even as they reinvent themselves in the new city—which is what they do—there remain these old selves, old traditions erased in part but not fully. So what you get are these fragmented, multifaceted, multicultural selves. And this can lead to such strange things." Was Rushdie thinking of his own life? "I know how you can be here and, in a way, still there." In his previous novels, he had to "make my reckonings" with the other parts of the world he had come from "before I had the platform from which to approach this country" in *The Satanic Verses.* But going back to the East "inside me when I've written" nourished him more than anything else, back to the real East, the Islamic culture he had grown up in. The extremists' Islamic culture was "something new and dangerous." They were defining Islam in a way that merely fed Western stereotypes—"the backward, cruel, rigid Muslim, burning books and threatening to kill the blasphemer."

Marzorati also described a dinner party at Rushdie's four-story home. Marianne had cooked a New England-style Thanksgiving feast. Literary critics and writers were in the kitchen gossiping with the cook. The guests included two American writers, Michael Herr, author of *Dispatches* about the Vietnam War, and Tess

Gallagher, a poet who was in London for a memorial service in honor of her late husband, writer Raymond Carver. Rushdie was in good spirits, among writers he liked in the safety of his home. He proposed an amusing toast over the American dinner of turkey and sweet potatoes.

Marzorati recalled the story of the Indian schoolboy and the kipper in *The Satanic Verses*. Rushdie confirmed it was autobiographical. "Yes, I'm afraid it's only slightly embellished. And I've never eaten another one." He said he was afraid the Islamic fundamentalists would succeed in reducing his novel in people's minds to a pamphlet. But later he thought that in burning the novel, as if it were merely a pamphlet, the extremists had gone too far. "It is such a charged image. It got people concerned about me, sympathetic towards me, who had been content to sit on the sidelines." He had written the novel from the part of him that loved London and the part that longed for Bombay. He had to come to terms with a plural identity. "We are increasingly becoming a world of migrants, made up of bits and fragments from here, there. We are here. And we have never really left anywhere we have been."

W. L. Webb was *The Guardian*'s literary editor when Rushdie was reviewing books regularly for the paper. He now joined the controversy on Rushdie's side, summing up the situation this way: "For the first time, a very intelligent novelist with a sophisticated and influential audience all over the world has brought to bear on Islam, its culture and its history, all the subtly and powerfully expressive techniques of Modernism, whose hallmarks are iconoclasm on the one hand and profoundly searching exegesis on the other. (There are, of course, also many passages in the parodic vein of Post-Modernism)."

Webb recalled that an Islamic group had declared a jihad, a holy war, on Modernism, and he was reminded of Soviet attacks on Modernism as bourgeois formalism. Webb commented, "As Stalinism recedes and the culture of one kind of world faith begins to recover its nerve, another militant ideology revives heresy hunts, telling its faithful to stop their ears."

The Jordanian novelist Fadia Faqir reported that a secret Saudi Islamic group stated as its dogma, "We believe that our religion is right and anything else is wrong." Anything else in practice meant communism, secularism, nationalism, existentialism, modernism, and even structuralism. This group referred to "the West's cultural invasion" represented by such allegedly decadent movements as Modernism, and many Arab novelists, poets and intellectuals had been banned as heretical in Muslim countries and escaped into exile.

British television's *Bandung File* suggested that the heart of what the Muslim extremists were angry about (and, of course, not only extremists) was not the specific insults to Islam in Rushdie's book, but had to do with his "whole notion of doubt" that was offensive to all the great religions. In reply, Rushdie repeated one of his favorite themes about doubt in the twentieth century and applied it to Modernism—"Everything we know is pervaded by doubt and not by certainty. And that is the basis of the great artistic movement known as Modernism. Now the fact that the orthodox figures in the Muslim world have declared a jihad against Modernism is not my fault. It doesn't invalidate an entire way of looking at the world which is, to my mind, the most important new contribution of the twentieth century to the way in which the human race discusses itself. If they're trying to say that this whole process has gone out of the window—that you can't do that, all you have is the old certainties—then, yes, I do argue."

3—CONFRONTATIONS AND KILLINGS

SALMAN RUSHDIE AND VIKING-PENGUIN STILL RECEIVED THREATS AND HATE mail in large quantities, but neither showed any sign of backing down. Rushdie was still appearing in public even if he sometimes felt the need for a bodyguard, and Viking-Penguin was shipping the book to bookstores and reprinting it. It was some of the booksellers who lost their nerve, returning their remaining copies to the Viking-Penguin warehouses or keeping the book half-hidden by their displays of other novels.

W. H. Smith, a huge chain with over 400 bookshops, had already withdrawn *The Satanic Verses* from its Bradford bookshop and claimed sales were beginning to flag generally, as if that justified withdrawing the book from its other bookshops. But when a well-publicized row broke out in Parliament over the blasphemy laws and Muslim demands, the company seemed to have reconsidered its policy. It obviously didn't like the way it had been criticized for its timidity. *The Guardian* sarcastically quoted Smith's marketing director as coyly remarking, "I think the recall program will now take longer than planned." The real heroes were some of the small, independent bookshops, which displayed the book in the middle of their windows and ignored any protests.

The Guardian commented that the real struggle would be in Islam, the brunt of it borne by that culture's writers and intellectuals. In Britain, it was merely a matter of "how a no longer very brave or liberal political culture responds to local manifestations of the struggle."

The Muslims still remained militant in Britain, especially in Bradford, but they were becoming increasingly frustrated with

143

nothing to show for their efforts. But so far the threats and protests had gone no farther than book burning and bomb scares. There had been discussions in the media about freedom of speech and whether any limitations could be accepted in a free society. It seemed as if the situation in Britain at least was beginning to calm down.

In New York, Peter Mayer prepared for the American launching. Independent booksellers, who accounted for roughly two-thirds of the hardcover fiction bestseller sales during 1988, claimed to have ordered a total of almost 200,000 copies. Rushdie's other books in paperback were also being reprinted as the demand for them rose, too. An experienced wholesaler predicted at least half a million copies of *The Satanic Verses* should be sold in hardcover, making the book a huge bestseller. But Viking-Penguin was more cautious, pointing out that orders were not sales and books not sold could be returned to the publisher for full credit.

Already added to the costs of publishing *The Satanic Verses* were the large expenses for security to protect Viking-Penguin employees and buildings in Britain and many other countries in the West and the East. There was the prospect of large security expenses in the United States, too. Viking-Penguin's Manhattan headquarters had already received protest letters and phone calls from thousands of American Muslims, and the FBI was investigating several bomb threats. Although publication day wasn't until the middle of February, copies of the book began to appear in American bookstores early in January and sales were brisk, thanks to all the publicity. The book was already third on the bestseller list of the *San Francisco Chronicle* and fifth on those of *The Boston Globe* and *The Chicago Tribune*. But this meant the American Muslims were already being worked up by the book's appearance in prominent displays. Peter Mayer was expecting trouble when Rushdie arrived for a series of public readings from the book in major cities and on major campuses. He and the rest of Viking-Penguin would be content if the protests went no further than book burning, as in Britain.

The publicity photograph of Rushdie released by Viking-Penguin for the American publication showed him with a beard and a mustache (though he was by then much more clean shaven). His hairy face, hooded eyes, and an enigmatic expression made him appear almost satanic, which may have been the intention—one of those Rushdie jokes like his remarks about his huge organ of a nose.

The American reviews were more revealing than the British in dealing with the Islamic sections and the alleged blasphemy because reviewers had the advantage of hindsight and knowing the violent reaction among Muslim fundamentalists. But like the British, most American reviewers tried to treat the book primarily as a novel—as literature—and Rushdie as an artist, rather than as a provocateur. Most American readers of book reviews didn't have much interest in Islam's dogmas.

Time called it "a long, challenging novel" that disproved "Kipling's bromide about East, West and the twain never meeting. They have met, all right, in [Rushdie's] experience and imagination, with results that are alternately comic, poignant and explosive." The Muslim critics had misinterpreted it. "There is no ridicule or harm in this novel, only an overwhelming sense of amazement and joy at the multifariousness of all Allah's children."

Newsweek thought the novel brilliant and controversial. "Rushdie enjoys an impressive but perhaps not enviable reputation for producing huge, critically acclaimed, unreadable books. True, *The Satanic Verses* is full of extravagant language, rampant fantasies and kaleidoscopic plotting; nonetheless, it's remarkably easy to follow and a constant delight to read. Rushdie is a master storyteller and a thoroughly refined stylist." *Newsweek* added, "As Rushdie's accusers maintain, there is indeed a powerful political subtext in this book; but it's not the one they're complaining about. No dreams or confabulations dress up the narrative when Rushdie details his vision of British racism." The implication seemed to be that the British have far more to protest about than the Muslims.

Newsweek quoted Rushdie as saying, "I knew that the very theocratic, medievalist Islam that is being pushed out through the mosques was not likely to take very kindly to the book I was writing, but I didn't foresee a reaction on this scale. If you don't believe—and I don't—that some kind of disembodied supreme being sent an angel to dictate a book to a seventh-century businessman, named Muhammad, you're in trouble."

One of the most revealing reviews was in *The Village Voice*, written by Bharati Mukherjee, an Indian migrant from Calcutta, and also a novelist who deals with the Indian migrant experience in the United States. She won the National Book Critic Circle award in the United States for her collection, *The Middleman and Other Stories.* "Her exploration of the nature and effects of immigration is impressive, informed as it is by profound if understated feelings as well as by intelligence and wit," wrote Rushdie about her earlier collection of migrant stories entitled *Darkness.* She chose to review *The Satanic Verses* as the last volume of a trilogy, the other volumes being *Midnight's Children* and *Shame*, a view of his work that Rushdie now agrees with although it hadn't occurred to him while he was working on *The Satanic Verses.*

Claiming that the great writers of our time were "apocalyptic farceurs, comic voices unraveling an elaborate tapestry of the sheerest horr," she named Günter Grass, Gabriel Garcia Marquez, Appelfeld, Beckett, Nabokov, Primo Levi, Flannery O'Connor, and Thomas Pynchon—"Fantasists and blasphemers all, carrying their dispute with God to a final, collective grave." She added that "there is only one other English-language author who belongs in their company, and his name is Salman Rushdie."

Rushdie's last three novels were a trilogy, "a vast, comic, morbid masterpiece of conceptual and architectural brilliance." Its subject ranged from Hindu and Islamic myth and the tarnishing of the bright ideals of Indian independence and Pakistani godliness to the metamorphoses of the immigrant and the death of British decency. Its style was a "fevered fusion" of appropriate and appropriated "nativisms, Britishisms, puns and coinages."

In spite of *The Satanic Verses'* much-reported brush with Islamic orthodoxy, it was "a *very* Muslim book," a blatant fantasy, a reenactment of an Islamic myth of creation, fall and redemption. Censorship on religious grounds was cruel to Rushdie, not because it denied him an audience, but because "it trivializes his message." She added, "As a satirist he must be doing something right: he faces literary deportation from all three of his homelands."

Most great books, she claimed, were blasphemies. To change perceptions—the distinction between greatness and mere excellence—some pieties must be destroyed. Although it was really a minor part of his book, Rushdie made the charge of blasphemy easy to support. Where Islam held sway, uncomplimentary mention of the prophet was blasphemy. The mullahs and the mullah-minded had historically mandated the obliteration of *any* contradictory or competitive image or idea in their path.

"As a great disillusioned hater, Rushdie plays in a different league from anyone in America; he's up there with Joyce and Solzhenitsyn, an educated, implacable, remorseless dissenter from deep inside the family."

Bharati Mukherjee told me she had met Rushdie in New York and had dinner with him and exchanged observations about the immigrant experience on their different sides of the Atlantic. As the carefully chaperoned daughter of a prosperous owner of an Indian pharmaceutical company, she was at school in London when she was twelve, two years younger than Rushdie when he went to Rugby School. Their backgrounds were similar in many ways. She said she considered the violent protests against *The Satanic Verses* an example of the world's different stages of development. "It's the twentieth century in the West, but in that part of the world it is the fourteenth in some ways. It makes Salman Rushdie Erasmus and turns some of the orthodox Islam interpreters into inquisitors. There's been a political manipulation of his book. It would be useful if the British political leaders were able to take a firm stand. The threats against Rushdie are very frightening."

D. J. Enright wrote in *The New York Reviews of Books* that Rushdie's book had been banned for being offensive to Muslims, "but in fact nobody in it is treated with very much respect: gods, angels, demons, prophets, they are all of them all too human, and most of the time unable to distinguish between good and evil. If they can't, how can we ordinary mortals be expected to?"

A. G. Mojtabai in *The New York Times Book Review* decided that "It is Mr. Rushdie's wide-ranging power of assimilation and imaginative boldness that makes his work so different from that of other well-known Indian novelists, such as R. K. Narayan, and the exuberance of his comic gift that distinguishes his writing from that of V. S. Naipaul."

In a long essay in *Harper's* magazine entitled "Prophet of a New Postmodernism," Mark Edmundson wrote, "The many commentators who have glibly dismissed Salman Rushdie's novel *The Satanic Verses* as a politically controversial but artistically minor production should perhaps think twice. They might remember that the world's tyrants have often been among its most astute cultural critics, revealing splendid intuition for picking out the work that's going to matter." Rushdie's novel was "a revolutionary piece of writing, disposed against provincialisms of the East and also (this is less frequently discussed) of the West." Not only was *The Satanic Verses* obsessed with metamorphosis; it was itself "an instance of the kind of creation it celebrates." It was without obvious imaginative precedents—"a harbinger of what I would like to call a new, *positive* Postmodernism."

He referred to Rushdie's rewriting of Muhammad, his "speeding up the work of secularization by vaporizing—in good, negative Postmodern fashion—the prophet's holy aura." But he stressed more the kind of *positive* transforming work of *The Satanic Verses*, which dramatized the blending of two cultures. "Rushdie is a Postmodern prophet of the confluence of cultures, and his overall hopefulness on this matter ought to be set against the kind of European xenophobia that's epitomized in the famous exclamation of Conrad's Kurtz confronted by the Congo: 'The horror!' "

One of the few thoroughly negative reviews was in *New York* magazine. Rhoda Koenig found Rushdie's blasphemy was "just a bit of philosophical naughtiness" and "the writing is so clotted, the detail so dense and pointless, and the narrative so stagnant that working your way through the novel is like trying to eat a rock-solid Arab sweet with a plastic spoon." Most of *The Satanic Verses* "with its labored jokes and whimsical rhetoric, is just a lot of confetti hitting the fan."

Mrs. Rushdie's novel, *John Dollar,* was also about to be published, so the *New York Post* reviewed her book and *The Satanic Verses* together. Husband and wife had dedicated their books to each other—*John Dollar* to "beloved" Salman. David Finkle, the *Post* reviewer, commented that what the sensitive reviewer wanted to avoid was "unfair comparison between the books." But he had to admit there was some "overlapping, if not duplication, of themes, possibly the most prominent being that of the place of aliens in society or, put another way, the place of everyone, in the last analysis, as an alien in contemporary society."

The *Post* reviewer added, "The difference between *The Satanic Verses* and *John Dollar* is that, whereas Rushdie has painstakingly constructed a complicated story out of myths, metamorphoses and metaphysical farce—never a combination to make the multitudes jump for joy on a Saturday night—Wiggins has come upon the kind of elemental narrative that seems to have been resting in the collective unconscious waiting for the right author to stumble over it."

John Dollar described how eight girls, English and Indian, were marooned on an island off the Burmese coast earlier in this century, with only a paralyzed captain, John Dollar, for company. It was like the women's side of William Golding's novel, *Lord of the Flies*, which described the plight of marooned boys and how civilization broke down among them as they struggled to survive.

Of *The Satanic Verses*, the *Post* reviewer commented, "Given that he has so much to say and much that is not as funny as he intends and/or is highfalutin at that, his reach may be thought to exceed his grasp frequently and perhaps ultimately. But it is a spectacular reach."

The reviewer concluded, "Rushdie and Wiggins have much to congratulate each other on when they lower their bedside lamps."

This was the kind of reception a publisher might pray for, but it further enraged the American Muslim fundamentalists, many of whom had received copies of the offending passages, although very few had read the book. The threats and hate mail increased at Viking-Penguin. If Rushdie came over, he was promised a hot reception. Peter Mayer, apprehensive about Rushdie's safety, took what precautions he could. Some of Rushdie's American friends advised him to cancel his trip. A great deal of concern was expressed on both sides of the Atlantic.

The whole situation was changed by events in Pakistan. A friend from Karachi phoned Rushdie in London with the grim news. Five demonstrators had been killed and dozens injured by Pakistani police in a clash over his novel in Islamabad, the

Pakistani capital. More than two thousand Muslim protesters had tried to storm the United States Information Center in the middle of the city. Screaming "Hang Salman Rushdie" and "American Dogs," the angry crowd threw stones and bricks and drove away police trying to guard the center. Windows were broken and demonstrators started some small fires in the two-story building. They pulled down the United States flag and burned it along with dummies representing Rushdie and the United States while the crowd cheered and chanted anti-Rushdie and anti-American slogans. During three hours of fierce clashes, the police drove back the demonstrators with rifles, semi-automatic weapons, and pump action shotguns.

But that wasn't the end. The following day Rushdie received more grim news. Another person had been killed and over one hundred people injured during a similar riot in Kashmir.

Ashen-faced, Rushdie was stunned. He had endured four months of death threats against himself, but these riots expressed more hatred of him personally than of the book. "Hang Salman Rushdie" had become a common cry in Pakistan and India.

"I feel completely horrified about what happened in Pakistan," Rushdie said in a voice that a reporter described as "still slightly breathless from shock." Rushdie added, "It's awful because the worst thing of all is that what they say about the book has nothing to do with what I wrote." He said that "Pakistan has been a very violent society for a long time. By Pakistani standards, this was not very violent. The thing about it that's very sad is that the fundamentalists should have some martyrs now. All I can do is go on saying that the book is being very seriously misrepresented. There is very little I can do."

What was clear from the riots in Pakistan and Kashmir was that Rushdie himself had become the target and would be in even more danger from Muslim extremists seeking revenge for the deaths in the riots. When this was confirmed by even more virulent protests to Viking-Penguin in New York, describing what would happen to Rushdie when he arrived, everyone involved in the publicity campaign worried about what to advise Rushdie.

Rushdie wanted to carry on as planned because he didn't wish to appear to be giving in to the threats. But gradually he was convinced of the danger he would be in. Some violent Muslim extremist might well try to get revenge. Reports from the mosques in crowded areas like Brooklyn showed that there was a good deal of violent talk against Rushdie. He would be very exposed in giving public readings, an easy target for any assassin.

Pete Hamill wrote in the *New York Post*, "Rushdie has been threatened with death. He must go to public events accompanied by a bodyguard. He will be in New York next week to promote the book and the publisher must be concerned about his personal safety. So should the New York Police Department. In this town, nobody can ever guarantee that some nut won't come out of the darkness."

Rushdie had been looking forward to his American tour and seeing his American friends again. London had become claustrophobic for him. A few weeks in the States would relax him. Publication there had a Hollywood kind of excitement lacking in Britain, at least when you were one of the stars. The alternative was to remain in wintry London and turn his home into even more of a fortress. He knew that both Peter Mayer and Andrew Wylie were concerned about what might happen. They didn't want him to take any foolish risks to sell a few books. Apart from his own publicity tour, there was also the question of what his wife should do about her own publicity tour for *John Dollar*. Harper and Row had cannily arranged the publication in February like *The Satanic Verses*. It had announced a big 50,000-copy first printing with a $60,000 advertising and promotion budget, anticipating good reviews and a successful response to the author on her tour.

The reception by American reviewers certainly justified the publisher's efforts. Apart from the *New York Post*, reviews didn't relate it to *The Satanic Verses*. The *New York Review of Books* described the novel as "mesmerizing and quite unlike anything else," and added, "One has to agree with the blurb that *John Dollar* is 'a literary *tour de force*.' It's too soon to say whether it's 'an unforgettable read,' but it might well turn out that way. Nightmares, possibly." *Publishers Weekly* called it a "literary milestone" and also used the word "mesmerizing." The Book-of-the-Month Club selected it as a featured alternate.

Harper had already informed media interviewers that "We are bringing Marianne Wiggins over from England, where she lives as an expatriate with her husband, novelist Salman Rushdie, for a national tour." Harper hoped that interviewers "will take advantage of Ms. Wiggins's time here." She would be in New York on February 27, Boston on March 2, Chicago on March 3, Seattle on March 6, San Francisco on March 7, and Los Angeles on March 8. Or at least that was the plan. But should she go to the United States by herself if Salman was persuaded to remain in London? Shouldn't she put her book's publicity on hold to be with him?

Once more events in the East—this time in Iran—changed the whole situation, and by greatly escalating the threat of violence, settled the immediate future of both the Rushdies.

4—AYATOLLAH KHOMEINI'S FATWA

THE MUSLIM PROTESTERS KILLED IN INDIA AND PAKISTAN WERE LAUDED AS martyrs, as Salman Rushdie predicted. They were given the kind of emotional public funerals that seemed to cry out for vengeance. The pressure on Muslim leaders for some kind of decisive action greatly increased throughout the Islamic countries where fundamentalists were in charge.

A demand for Rushdie to be judged by Ayatollah Ruhollah Musavi Khomeini, the revered Imam or Supreme Guide for much of the world's estimated one-thousand million Muslim population, was made in a petition by British Muslims sent through one of the Islamic embassies in London.

The Ayatollah was responsible for guiding Muslims on all important issues, so once he received the petition, he had to act. The old Muslim leader who at eighty-eight looked like an ancient Biblical prophet, with long grey hair and a long beard, was much hated in the West and symbolized everything that seemed baffling about the East. He was ascetic, his stern views based on the Islamic world of the seventh century, and a mystic who claimed to speak in the name of God. He had been a leader of the revolutionary opposition against the dictatorial Shah in Iran and denounced the United States as the Great Satan. He had expressed his hatred of the Great Satan many times by acts of terrorism and the imprisoning of Americans in Tehran. His plots had hurt two American presidencies, helping to defeat Jimmy Carter in his bid for re-election and involving the Reagan administration in its worst scandal. His followers even wondered if *The Satanic Verses* was part of an American plot to undermine Islam.

One of the Ayatollah's aides described to the old man what the offending passages in Rushdie's novel had contained. The Iranian literary newspaper, *Kayhan Farangi*, had already published a stinging review, in which it stated *The Satanic Verses* "contains a number of false interpretations about Islam and gives wrong portrayals of the Koran and the Prophet Muhammad. It also draws a caricature-like and distorted image of Islamic principles which lacks even the slightest artistic credentials." The Iranian reviewer referred to Rushdie's immense "artistic and moral degradation" and added the novel was full of "satanic-minded comments about Islam and our religious leaders, and this can only amount to the fact that Rushdie has fallen from the grace as a writer with a good knowledge of Islam to something like total moral degradation."

The Ayatollah seemed to welcome the simple case of a blasphemer after the complications of domestic and foreign politics. His revolutionary leadership of Iran had come under some heavy criticism. Passing a dramatic judgment against Rushdie, who was known to the whole of the Islamic world, would undoubtedly reassert his authority in the eyes of most Muslims.

It was Valentine's Day—Feburary 14, 1989—in the West when the news was announced. A "fatwa" or decree from the Ayatollah was read out on Radio Tehran just before the 2:00 P.M. news.

"In the name of God Almighty," read the announcer. "There is only one God, to whom we shall all return. I would like to inform all the intrepid Muslims in the world that the author of the book entitled *The Satanic Verses*, which has been compiled, printed and published in opposition to Islam, the Prophet and the Koran, as well as those publishers who were aware of its contents, have been sentenced to death.

"I call on all zealous Muslims to execute them quickly, wherever they find them, so that no one will dare to insult the Islamic sanctions. Whoever is killed on this path will be regarded as a martyr, God willing.

"In addition, anyone who has access to the author of the book, but does not possess the power to execute him, should refer him to the people so that he may be punished for his actions. May God's blessing be on you all. Ruhollah Musavi Khomeini."

The Ayatollah explained in a later message read on Radio Tehran that "the issue of the book, *The Satanic Verses*, is that it is a calculated move aimed at rooting out religion and religiousness, and above all, Islam and its clergy." He added that "God wanted the blasphemous book of *The Satanic Verses* to be published now, so that the world of conceit, arrogance and barbarism would bare its true face in its long-held enmity to Islam."

The Ayatollah pronounced Rushdie as *mahdur ad-damm* (he whose blood is unclean). He decided Rushdie was guilty on three charges, any one of which would carry the death penalty under Islamic law. Rushdie was found to be "an agent of corruption on earth," one who has "declared war on Allah," and a *murtad* (a born Muslim who has abandoned his faith and crossed over to the enemies of Islam).

This was not the first time the Ayatollah had called for capital punishment for an alleged enemy of Islam. His first edict of that kind was in 1947 when he sentenced an Iranian education minister to death. The minister was shot a few days later. After the 1979 revolution, his authority was used to cover the execution of political opponents and the assassination of several enemies abroad.

The day after the Ayatollah's death sentence against Rushdie, another Iranian cleric announced a reward for any avenger killing Rushdie: $2.6 million for an Iranian, $1 million for anyone else. The next day the reward was doubled.

Salman Rushdie was in his workroom at home on Valentine's Day when the phone rang. By then he must have tensed every time the phone rang. This time it was a journalist from BBC Radio. She said, "How does it feel to be sentenced to death by the Ayatollah Khomeini?" At first he couldn't grasp what she was talking about. It was the first he had heard of it.

He rushed downstairs to tell Marianne and they immediately closed the shutters and locked the front door. "We were both extremely alarmed," recalled Rushdie later. He had a longstanding agreement to be interviewed live on the CBS morning show on television that day, and they were sending a car for him. He felt he couldn't let them down. Later he would learn to be much more cautious, but "these were innocent days: I wasn't at all used to death threats at the time." So he told his wife he was going ahead with the TV interview, and when the CBS car arrived for him, he drove off. At least he missed the arrival of the world's media at his home a short time later. Over seventy television crews parked outside the house, and cameras zeroed in on the number of the house on the front door as if telling the world his address: Assassins, please note!

At the CBS studio, still very shaken, Rushdie was told consolingly by a journalist, "You don't have to worry about this. Khomeini sentences people to death every day, nothing ever happens. He sentences the presidents of America to death once a week." Rushdie told himself with relief, Oh, good, fine, it's just hot air. That feeling didn't last long.

His wife phoned the CBS studio to tell him not to come home because of the huge crowd of reporters and photographers waiting outside for him. So Rushdie decided to go to the London office of his British agent, Gillon Aitken, Andrew Wylie's partner, and meet his wife there. She could bring a few essentials in a bag. When he reached his agent's office, he found there were constant telephone calls from people looking for him. He had another public engagement that day—a memorial service for Bruce Chatwin who had recently died. A reporter who went to Rushdie's home just after he had received the news of Chatwin's death could well believe Rushdie's remark that Chatwin was "probably my closest writer friend." Rushdie seemed grief stricken and dismissed the protests over *The Satanic Verses*. "Now my friend is dead," he said, "So I don't give a damn about all this really." It was very important for him to go to the memorial service, but he had no way of knowing what he should do or shouldn't do in these new and frightening circumstances. He told a BBC reporter he took the threat "very seriously, indeed."

"The hell with it, let's go," he said and was off to the memorial service. Meanwhile Gillon Aitken was phoning New York to talk to Andrew Wylie and Peter Mayer about cancelling Rushdie's American publicity tour scheduled to begin in two days.

At the service in Bayswater at the Greek Orthodox cathedral on Moscow Road, English writer Martin Amis was sitting behind him and made what Rushdie remembered as a "supportive, very friendly remark." American writer Paul Theroux was also sitting nearby, and Rushdie recalled him "attempting black comedy," saying "I suppose we'll be here for you next week." Rushdie commented, "It wasn't the funniest joke I ever heard," but later he wrote Theroux a letter remarking, "I was glad he's a less good prophet than he is a novelist." A newspaper reporter with a tape recorder running came up to him in the cathedral and insisted on an interview. "Look," Rushdie told him, "I've come here to my friend's memorial service." The reporter—"a very upper-class English gentleman, silver haired"—replied according to Rushdie, "You don't understand, you can't talk to me like this. I'm from the *Daily Telegraph* and I've been to a public school." Rushdie said later, "That was probably the funniest thing that happened to me."

By then the media knew he was attending the service, and the army that had been outside his home was now outside the cathedral. Rushdie had no getaway car of his own available, but a friend drove up in his BBC limousine and pushed him and Marianne into the back and drove quickly away before anyone could stop them.

That was the last time Salman Rushdie was seen in public. *The Guardian* reported that his "vanishing act" began when "he emerged from a church so dark the mosaic saints scarcely glinted; winter sunshine blinded like a photo-flash; then he was limousined away into hiding."

He and Marianne actually dived for cover in the small apartment she had rented near their home to work in. Virtually no one knew about it. "So there we were, sitting in a hole, with no knowledge of what was going to happen, and actually being quite scared." The local police were already keeping watch on the building. "But that was a short-term thing. I had no sense of what the long-term strategy might have to be."

The news from abroad was worsening all the time. Muslim extremist terrorist teams reportedly had set out from Iran to get Rushdie. Even in Britain, Sayed Abdul Quddas, secretary of the Council of Mosques in militant Bradford, who had led the public book burning, was reported to have vowed to act on the Ayatollah's order. "Every good Muslim is after his life," he said. "I am a family man, but I would sacrifice mine."

In New York, a bomb threat forced the evacuation of Viking-Penguin's offices on West Twenty-third Street.

More than two thousand Iranians chanted "Death to England" and "Death to America" outside the British Embassy in Tehran.

Rushdie's friend, dramatist Harold Pinter, led a delegation of writers, literary agents, and publishers to Prime Minister Thatcher at 10 Downing Street, to denounce the threats and support Rushdie. Pinter said, "A very distinguished writer has used his imagination to write a book and has criticized the religion into which he was born and he has been sentenced to death as well as his publishers. It is an intolerable and barbaric state of affairs." Pinter said the British government "should confront Iran with the consequences of its statement and remind the Islamic community that it cannot incite people to murder."

Hanif Kureishi, a friend and script writer for the film, *My Beautiful Laundrette*, a popular comedy about Asian migrants in London, said Rushdie was "obviously very frightened. These people are completely nutters."

Viking-Penguin issued a statement that Rushdie's United States tour had been cancelled and that "no offense was intended in the creation or publication of his novel."

These events had obviously been taken as seriously by the British government as by Rushdie himself. As Rushdie reported, "There was apparently a discussion about this in goodness knows what high circles," and he was immediately offered protection by Scotland Yard's Special Branch. There was irony in his being offered protection by the Thatcher government when he had been one of Mrs. Thatcher's most persistent critics, but he was glad to accept. Although Marianne's publicity tour was all arranged, she decided to ask Harper and Row to cancel it so that she could join her husband in hiding. It must have been a hard decision to make because enthusiastic American reviews of *John Dollar* were continuing to appear and it was obviously a good time for her appearances.

She explained in a public statement, "Two writers are in hiding—one, to save his life; the other as a matter of her own free choice in an act of solidarity. Writers everywhere have been weighed and measured by an edict from Iran. We are a dangerous breed and always have been, because words outlive their authors, words can emanate from silence, words can find their way from hidden places. Only fear can stop a writer writing.

Only fear can stop a book from being sold. Fear dies with the individual—the written word, which we celebrate officially today, is one unleashed, colossal, unrepentant, joyous, passionate, expansive and courageous monster. Rejoice in it."

Before disappearing, Rushdie learned that *The Satanic Verses* was an even bigger bestseller on both sides of the Atlantic, but it was hardly any consolation for the grim future he now faced. He was close to being a millionaire, but what good was the money if he had to live an invisible life apart from other people? His big hope was that his disappearance wouldn't have to last long.

When the Special Branch detectives whisked him away, he had a writing task uncompleted—a book review of Philip Roth's autobiography, *The Facts*, for *The Observer*. In spite of the panicky rush, distracted by the thought that assassins might be arriving at any moment, he took the time to phone Blake Morrison, *The Observer*'s literary editor, to reassure him that, although the review might be a little late, it would arrive in due course. Morrison said that was typical of Rushdie's professionalism, and added, "Literary editors can be hard taskmasters, but Rushdie must have known that he had the strongest excuse in the history of literary journalism for missing his deadline." Perhaps reading Philip Roth, Morrison said, "whose fiction also once brought down the wrath of his fathers"—presumably a reference to the row over Roth's *Portnoy's Complaint*—would afford Rushdie "some kind of comfort. I hope so."

Morrison described Rushdie as "a brave man, not a quality much mentioned in the bitchy profiles of him at the time *The Satanic Verses* was published." *The Observer*'s literary editor said he hoped Salman Rushdie had a pen or typewriter in his refuge because then he knew the Philip Roth review would soon arrive. It did.

So the Rushdies disappeared into the secret network of the Special Branch and were soon being moved around in fast cars at night among the British government's "Safe Houses" usually reserved for defecting spies and the like. "And," Salman Rushdie summed up a little later, trying to give away no clues to their whereabouts, "we've been following this present structure ever since."

Most of the publicity concentrated on Rushdie's plight as a condemned man and gave little attention to the Ayatollah's condemnation of "those publishers who were aware of [*The Satanic Verses'*] contents" who were also sentenced to death. Peter Mayer was the only name generally mentioned in public as the publisher of Rushdie's novel. Whether the editors and other Viking-Penguin executives who had dealt with the book were known outside the company was extremely doubtful. Mayer, therefore, would be the target, although mail and phone threats to Viking-Penguin offices greatly increased. Mayer immediately cut down on his public appearances, and his visits to Viking-Penguin were no longer predictable according to a fixed routine, nor did he make a grand entrance through the front doors. He also beefed up the company's security staff and used bodyguards. Tracing him was made as difficult as possible. When I phoned Mayer at Viking-Penguin in New York, I was told he wasn't there, but I was given another phone number. This was at New American Library, which Viking-Penguin owns. Peter Mayer wasn't there either, but I was informed I could leave message for him because "he calls in for his messages." He hadn't disappeared as completely as the Rushdies, but he had become elusive even to business acquaintances, behaving as if he were fully aware that he was Mr. Penguin as far as many of the Muslim extremists were concerned. His financial gamble on *The Satanic Verses* had been won, but at what a price to both author and publisher?

5—TAKING SIDES

THE LONDON OBSERVER CALLED IT "ONE OF THE MOST CHILLING EPISODES to engulf the world of culture in recent times." According to the British Sunday newspaper, the Rushdie Affair "encompassed a myriad of complexities: two great religions, Islam and Christianity; secularism versus religious orthodoxy; artistic freedom versus State power; pluralism and tolerance versus doctrinal certainty." The two principal characters in the complex and tragic drama were the commanding figure of the Ayatollah, "an ageing cleric who had spearheaded a revolution," and Salman Rushdie, a Westernized Muslim-born writer, "who wrestles with some of the most profound issues of our times."

Time magazine quoted some Islamic experts as saying the situation was "the most incendiary literary fight in the fourteen centuries of Islamic history."

It was like a time bomb that had been ticking away for months and now had finally gone off with a big bang. The effects were worldwide. Almost overnight, Salman Rushdie became one of the best known people in the world, far beyond the fame of even a writer like Ernest Hemingway whose burly, bearded figure had been treated by the media as if he were a superstar. Millions in the East who never read novels knew the name Rushdie thanks to the Ayatollah's dramatic decree. Not long before the West would have paid little attention to an Indian-born writer being condemned by a leader of Islam. It would have been a one-day wonder showing once more how weird foreigners could be. But the large Muslim populations who had settled in the West made such detachment impossible now. There were constant reminders of the relevancy of what had happened from Bradford book burnings to New York bomb scares. The sentencing of migrant Rushdie was as important to the West as to the East, although their viewpoints were often opposed and baffling to each other. Much of the world was taking sides over the fate of Salman Rushdie.

Even within countries like Britain, the lines were sharply drawn. Before Rushdie disappeared, he told a reporter, "Frankly I wish I had written a more critical book. A religion that claims it is able to behave like this, religious leaders who are able to behave like this, and then say this is a religion that must be above any whisper of criticism—that doesn't add up." At the opposite extreme in Britain was Iqbal Sacranie of the Action Committee on Islamic Affairs, who said, "Death perhaps is a bit too easy for him ... his mind must be tormented for the rest of his life unless he asks for forgiveness to Almighty Allah." In the middle was Hesham El-Essawi of the Islamic Society for the Promotion of Religious Tolerance, whose opinion was more moderate: "We very much regret and denounce Khomeini's statement. Threats like this, or any violent response, is not the correct religious response. It is a very dangerous development and will give Rushdie sympathy where it is not deserved."

Amir Taheri, an Iranian journalist and author of a biography of Ayatollah Khomeini, tried to explain the Muslim side to readers of the London *Times*. Muslim intellectuals, especially "the tiny liberal and leftist wings," had been outraged by the Ayatollah's decree and by the book burnings, but he thought the majority of Muslims approved of the death sentence for the author of *The Satanic Verses*. "The mass of Muslim poor, who feel their religion and culture have been humiliated in the West for too long, are unlikely to consider the complex issues involved in this very complex case. Most of them live in conditions of misery unimaginable in the West and feel that all they have in this world is their religious faith."

To Muslims, wrote Taheri, religion was not just a part of life. It was life that was a part of religion. Muslims could not understand a concept that had no rules, no limits. "The Western belief in human rights, which seems to lack limits, is alien to Islamic traditions."

According to the Iranian journalist, Ayatollah Khomeini had been looking for an issue likely to stir the imagination of the poor and illiterate masses, among whom he recruited his most devoted "volunteers for martyrdom." Waving Rushdie's novel and sentencing him to death, the Ayatollah "hopes to tell his supporters that plots against Islam have not ceased."

The Parliamentary speaker in Iran, Ali Akbar Hashemi Rafsanjani, said that what had incited the Ayatollah was not just the book, but that it represented a "well-calculated and extensive plot against Islam."

The London *Sunday Times* suggested *The Satanic Verses* situation had become ludicrously out of proportion, but commented that it would be unthinkable for Rushdie to point that out. "It is not in his nature to say, 'Oh, come on, it's just a book.' He would perhaps have liked its literary importance to be its claim to attention; but significance of some sort it must have. He does not respond with grace even to the mildest criticism; his temper is apt to flare, his opinions are entrenched and passionate."

There may have been some sour grapes in this sniping at Rushdie at such a time because he did his book reviewing for the rival *Observer,* which said of him with more warmth and sympathy, "Rushdie has dared deliberately to provoke, not so as to make mischief or to insult, but as an artist"—to provoke the imagination as Rushdie liked to put it.

The Ayatollah had long been unpopular in the West, but his fatwa against Rushdie and Viking-Penguin came at a time when Britain and Iran were trying to establish better diplomatic relations. The British government had reopened its embassy in Tehran in the hope that more moderate leaders were coming to power in Iran and normalizing relations would be worthwhile. The day after the Ayatollah's fatwa, a mob demonstrated outside the embassy breaking some windows, but was kept at a distance by police.

The attempt to improve relations may have accounted for the cautious reserve in the British government's condemnation of the death sentence to be carried out on its turf. Sir Geoffrey Howe, the Foreign Secretary, said, "The death sentence is a matter of grave concern. It illustrates the extreme difficulty of establishing the right kind of relationship with a manifestly revolutionary regime with ideas that are very much its own."

Novelist Anthony Burgess, in the *Independent*, wrote that the Ayatollah was probably within his "self-elected rights" in calling for the assassination of Rushdie "on his own holy ground," but to order outraged sons of the prophet to kill Rushdie and the directors of Penguin Books on British soil was tantamount to a *jihad* or holy war. "It is a declaration of war on citizens of a free country and as such it is a political act. It has to be countered by an equally forthright, if less murderous, declaration of defiance."

British officials met with Iranian officials in Tehran. The *Independent* referred to the British government's "studied moderation." The British cabinet decided Britain would not go ahead with upgrading its embassy in Tehran and reappointing an ambassador, but would maintain diplomatic relations, at least for the time being. The Iranian chargé d'affaires in London was summoned to the Foreign Office to hear Britain's protest and was warned that no new applications for visas for Iranian diplomats for the Iranian embassy in London would be issued. After a cabinet meeting, the Foreign Secretary said Britain recognized that Muslims and others might have strong views about Rushdie's book, "but nobody has the right to incite people to violence on British soil or against British citizens." The Ayatollah's statement was "totally unacceptable."

The Dutch were the first European nation to treat the fatwa as an event of international diplomatic significance by cancelling their Foreign Minister's visit to Iran.

The Iranian embassy to the Vatican demanded that the Pope should join the crusade against *The Satanic Verses*. A senior Vatican official commented, "It's their problem, not ours. We have enough of our own, especially with all the books and films which cast doubts on Jesus Christ himself. We have never asked for Muslim help in curbing their sale."

The first mention that an apology from Rushdie might be acceptable came in a statement by a Pakistani foreign ministry spokesman, who told reporters that Pakistan wanted an apology from Rushdie and his publishers as well as assurances that no further similar books would be published. A Muslim wrote to the *Independent* in London that "even though these criminals against Islam are being protected by the British police, this protection can only delay the execution of the sentence. Who is destined to be the executioner, and when, is something that neither the police nor the fugitives can know." There was only one way out of this "rat-like existence" for Rushdie. "By recanting his blasphemies publicly, he can win a reprieve to make amend for the wrong he has done. God *is* oft-forgiving, most merciful."

President Ali Khameini took up the idea of an apology. He suggested that Salman Rushdie "may repent and say 'I made a blunder' and apologize to Muslims and to the Imam [Ayatollah Khomeini)]. Then it is possible that the people may pardon him." But he added, "This wretched man has no choice but to die because he has confronted himself with a billion Muslims and with the Imam." He also ordered that the British embassy in Tehran not be attacked.

Rushdie took up the suggestion of an apology, but, of course, he had no intention of groveling for forgiveness. In the latest "Safe House" where he and Marianne were hiding with Special Branch bodyguards, he wrote and re-wrote a brief statement that went as far as he was willing to go. The Special Branch made sure it reached the right hands with no risk to the Rushdies.

"As author of *The Satanic Verses*," wrote Rushdie, "I recognize that Muslims in many parts of the world are genuinely distressed by the publication of my novel. I profoundly regret the distress that publication has occasioned to the sincere followers of Islam. Living as we do in a world of many faiths, this experience has served to remind us that we must all be conscious of the sensibilities of others."

There was a confused response to Rushdie's statement in Iran. It was at first rejected as falling far short of a real apology, and then it was accepted as "generally seen as sufficient enough to warrant [Rushdie's] pardon by the masses," then it was rejected again.

The Ayatollah left no doubt as to his attitude. He said in a statement issued by the official Islamic news agency that the "imperialist mass media were falsely alleging that if the author repented, his execution order would be lifted. This is denied, one hundred percent. Even if Salman Rushdie repents and becomes the most pious man of time, it is incumbent on every Muslim to employ everything he has got, his life and his wealth, to send him to hell."

The Ayatollah appeared to slam the door on all attempts at a negotiated settlement. He called on non-Muslims as well as

Muslims to help carry out the death sentence against Rushdie. "If a non-Muslim becomes aware of his whereabouts and has the ability to execute him quicker than a Muslim, it is incumbent on Muslims to pay a reward or a fee in return for this action."

At a meeting of European nations, several were keen to protest more strongly than Britain had done. The twelve ministers issued a joint statement recalling ambassadors from Tehran and freezing all highlevel visits between their countries and Iran.

The Archbishop of Canterbury, Dr. Robert Runcie, called for strengthening the law against blasphemy in Britain to cover religions other than Christianity. He also condemned incitement to murder. Only the utterly insensitive, he said, could fail to see that *The Satanic Verses* had deeply offended Muslims throughout the world. "I understand their feelings and I firmly believe that offense to the religious beliefs of the followers of Islam or any other faith is quite as wrong as offense to the religious beliefs of Christians. But however great the grievance, I utterly condemn incitement to murder or any other violence from any source whatever."

Robert Maxwell, chairman of Maxwell Communications, wrote to *The Bookseller* in London offering $10 million "to the man or woman who will, not kill, but civilize the barbarian Ayatollah, the test of which shall be that Khomeini shall publicly recite the Ten Commandments, with special reference to the sixth ('Thou shalt not kill') and ninth ('Thou shall not bear false witness against thy neighbor')."

Joseph Brodsky, the Russian Nobel laureate now living in the United States, also mentioned turning the tables on the Ayatollah, and summed up, "On the whole this lifts the veil on Islamic fundamentalism. They execute people left and right and nobody gives a squeak."

On February 21, a week after the Ayatollah's decree, the United States, Canada, Sweden, Australia, Norway, and Brazil all supported the twelve European nations' strong statement. But it seemed only to have the effect of uniting the various divided groups in Iran. The Iranian Parliamentary speaker, who was a leading moderate, issued a statement that "the present confrontation will end once again with our victory."

In Britain, more moderate Muslim leaders, who claimed to represent the majority, opposed the Ayatollah's fatwa. The West

Yorkshire police decided they would not bring charges of incitement to murder against Muslim demonstrators in Bradford. There was insufficient direct evidence and such a prosecution wouldn't be in the public interest. Britain's chargé d'affaires in Iran returned to London, and the Iranian chargé d'affaires in London prepared to leave.

The Nigerian Nobel laureate, Wole Soyinka, condemned the threat against Rushdie as cowardly, criminal, and blasphemous.

President Mitterand in Paris told his weekly cabinet meeting that "all dogmatism which through violence undermines freedom of thought and the right to free expression is, in my view, absolute evil. The moral and spiritual progress of humanity is linked to the recoil of all fanaticism."

President Khameini on a tour of Eastern Europe said there was no difference between him and the Ayatollah over Rushdie. "The arrow has been launched towards its target," he added.

The Ayatollah said, "As long as I am alive, I will never allow liberals to come to power again, nor shall I allow any deviation from our policy of 'neither East nor West,' and I will continue cutting off the hands of all Soviet and American mercenaries."

On February 24, ten more people died and about fifty were injured during anti-Rushdie rioting, this time in his birthplace, Bombay. That would have special significance for Rushdie in his hiding place.

Practically alone in the world, Japan insisted on remaining neutral. *Publishers Weekly* commented, "Reports from Tokyo told of that country's reluctance to defend Salman Rushdie's life or his right to publish; once more, staying on good terms with trading partners got priority."

Politicians in many countries were criticized for being overcautious, but Rushdie's fellow writers were criticized, too. Norman Podhoretz, editor of the influential American journal, *Commentary*, greatly upset the literary establishments on both sides of the Atlantic by complaining that literary lions in New York and London "hesitated long and hard before emitting so much as a growl" in Rushdie's defense. Writing in a column published in the *New York Post*, Podhoretz added that "the Anglo-American literary community broke into a heavy sweat over the prospect of incurring the wrath of the Ayatollah

Khomeini." He quoted one unnamed writer as saying, "My wife said she doesn't want to see my name in the newspaper in this climate."

Lady Antonia Fraser, as president of English PEN, made an indignant statement claiming Podhoretz's criticism that the British literary establishment had been slow to support Rushdie was "totally untrue where English PEN is concerned." She listed the activities of English PEN on Rushdie's behalf and added that English PEN would like to take the opportunity to pay tribute to "the heroic determination of Salman Rushdie's publisher not to be cowed by threats and above all to the steadfastness of British booksellers, who have continued to make *The Satanic Verses* available. That is after all the whole point: freedom to publish, sell and read (or not read) within the law. It should be recorded that our firm but non-inflammatory position has received widespread Muslim support."

Although most British writers who spoke out supported Rushdie wholeheartedly, there were a few prominent exceptions. The American writer Susan Sontag told me that she thought Britain was the only Western country where there was some conflict between writers over Rushdie.

Author John Berger wrote, "I suspect that Salman Rushdie, if he is not caught in a chain of events of which he has completely lost control, might by now be ready to consider asking his world publishers to stop producing more or new editions of *The Satanic Verses*. Not because of the threat to his own life, but because of the threat to the lives of those who are innocent of either writing or reading the book. This achieved, a number of leading Islamic leaders and statesmen across the world might well be ready to condemn the practice of the Ayatollah issuing terrorist death warrants. Otherwise a unique twentieth century Holy War, with its terrifying righteousness on both sides, may be on the point of breaking out sporadically but repeatedly—in airports, shopping streets, suburbs, city centers, wherever the unprotected live." Berger described *The Satanic Verses* as "a rather arrogant fiction about playing at being God and would, in my opinion, have been forgotten in a few years, had it not provoked the present furor."

Yusuf Islam, the musician who performed as Cat Stevens before converting to Islam, said that rather than go to a demonstration to burn an effigy of Salman Rushdie, "I would have hoped that it'd be the real thing." He was taking part in a British television discussion that showed, according to *The New York Times*, "how divided British liberal intellectuals remain over the affair. British writers and publishers have signed petitions backing Mr. Rushdie's freedom to write what he wishes, but there have been no public readings of his works."

Fay Weldon said she was offended by Yusuf Islam's remarks, which incited people to violence. Dr. Kalim Siddiqui, director of the Muslim Institute in London, also took part in the discussion, saying "I wouldn't kill him, but I'm sure that there are very many people in this country prepared at the moment. If they could lay their hands on Rushdie, he would be dead."

Roald Dahl, one of Penguin's bestselling authors, who once had police protection himself after receiving death threats, called on Rushdie to withdraw *The Satanic Verses* and pulp all copies "to save lives." Dahl said, "If the lives of the author and the senior editor in New York are at stake, then it is better to give in on a moral question when you are dealing with fanatics. If I were Rushdie, then for the sake of everybody threatened, I would agree to throw the bloody thing away. It would save lives." Four years before, Dahl was given a police bodyguard after death threats from Jewish factions. He had criticized the Israeli bombing of Beirut in 1982.

Dahl also wrote about Rushdie in a letter published in the famous correspondence column of the London *Times*. "I have not yet heard any non-Muslim voices raised in criticism of the writer himself. On the contrary, he appears to be regarded as some sort of hero, certainly among his fellow writers and the Society of Authors, of which I am a member. To my mind, he is a dangerous opportunist."

Dahl added in his letter, "Clearly he has profound knowledge of the Muslim religion and its people and he must have been totally aware of the deep and violent feelings his book would stir up among devout Muslims. In other words he knew exactly what he was doing and he cannot plead otherwise."

Dahl wrote that "this kind of sensationalism does indeed get an indifferent book on to the top of the bestseller list," but he thought it was "a cheap way of doing it." It also put a severe strain on the very proper principle that the writer had an absolute right to say what he liked. "In a civilized world we all have a moral obligation to apply a modicum of censorship to our own work in order to reinforce this principle of free speech."

John le Carré, the best-selling author of *The Spy Who Came in from the Cold* and other spy novels, and a former member of Britain's intelligence service, also criticized Rushdie. In his novel, *The Little Drummer Girl*, set in the Middle East, le Carré had taken a middle-of-the-road attitude toward the controversial Israeli and Arab positions. His novel aroused no outcry from either side and was later filmed without trouble, a tribute to le Carré's diplomacy. He was reported in *The New York Times* as saying that he thought the death sentence was outrageous, but "I don't think it is given to any of us to be impertinent to great religions with impunity. I am mystified that he hasn't said: 'It's all a mess. My book is wildly misunderstood, but as long as human lives are being wasted on account of it, I propose to withdraw it.' I have to say that would be my position."

I asked Dahl and le Carré if their views had changed at all. Dahl referred me to his *Times* letter and added, "I do not wish to make any further comment." But le Carré was clearly anxious that he make his attitude perfectly clear, and he wrote me a long letter. "When the death sentence against Rushdie was first pronounced, I saluted his courage," le Carré wrote. "As time went by and I had a chance to think, I realized that I had less and less sympathy with Rushdie's position, though obviously I am appalled by the wretchedness of his existence."

Le Carré then summarized his views. He mentioned the growing argument over whether or not there should be a mass market paperback edition of *The Satanic Verses*. As such a cheap edition would sell much more widely, it was feared that Muslim extremists would respond with even more violent protests.

"Rushdie is a victim," le Carré wrote, "but in my book no hero. I am sorry for him and I respect his courage, but I don't understand him. In the first place, anybody who is familiar with Muslims, even if he has not had the advantage of Rushdie's background, knows that, even among the most relaxed, you make light of the Book at your peril. I don't think there is anything to deplore in religious fervor. American presidents profess to it almost as a ritual, we respect it in Christians and Jews. What we are speaking of in Rushdie's case is incompatible concepts of freedom. For long periods of Christian history, freedom was limited by what was sacred. That is still the case in Islam today. Therefore while I despise the self-serving antics of the Ayatollah and his mullahs, I am not surprised by them nor particularly shocked. I am also unclear about the extent to which Rushdie, perhaps inadvertently, provoked his own misfortune. His open letter to the Indian government seemed to me to be of an almost colonialist arrogance.

"Absolute free speech is not a God-given right in any country. It is curtailed by prejudice, by perceptions of morality and by perceptions of decency. Nobody has a God-given right to insult a great religion and be published with impunity.

"But all of this is academic, perhaps, beside the human mystery that Rushdie continues to present to me. How can a man whose novel, for whatever twisted reasons, has already been the cause of so much bloodshed, insist on risking more? Anybody who wanted to read this book has had ample opportunity to do so in the countries where it has been published. A great many more people who will never manage to read it have already bought it out of some sense that they are furthering a great cause. Yet we are being invited to believe that paperback publication of *Satanic Verses* is somehow more important to us than, for instance, the lives of innocent young men and women who work at the outer fringes of publishing—in the mailrooms and stockrooms of Rushdie's publishers—in bookshops and in public postal services. At this point, my judgment becomes totally subjective. I could not live with the thought that, by continuing to insist that my book be published, I would be inviting further bloodshed. And that is where Rushdie leaves me completely. Again and again, it has been within his power to save the faces of his publishers and, with dignity, withdraw his book until a calmer time has come. It seems to me that he has nothing more to prove except his own insensitivity.

"A peculiar justification used by Rushdie's most vociferous defenders is that his novel has great literary merit—some insist it is a masterpiece. I see this as a most dangerous argument, and a self-defeating one. Would the same people have leapt to the defense of a Ludlum or an Archer? Or are we to believe that those who write literature have a greater right to free speech than those who write pulp? Such elitism does not help Rushdie's cause, whatever that cause has now become."

Other British writers saw the situation quite differently.

Novelist Melvyn Bragg ignored Rushdie's critics and suggested he had created "a global community of authors." Bragg added, "It is difficult to think of any writer who has provoked such a closing of ranks. His isolation has triggered our sense of common purpose. In Britain particularly, it has encouraged and enabled writers at last to break through that barrier which forbade them to be serious in public on public matters."

Novelist Iris Murdoch said "Wars end. The night will end."

Playwright Trevor Griffiths thought "the only question left in the Rushdie Affair is how soon, and in what way, Salman will be returned to the fray." Rushdie's "important voice," raised for a decade against the deep racism of British society, was much missed. Why couldn't his life be guarded without "this total (and damaging) isolation?" There had been at least one contract out on Mrs. Thatcher for several years, but her liberty hadn't been unduly curtailed.

Novelist Martin Amis, son of novelist Kingsley Amis, commented, "Novels do not change the world, except by accident; equally, novelists are not responsible for the runaway phantasmagoria known as current affairs." He despairingly said to Rushdie that "I pity his situation, that I miss his presence and that I admire his work."

Kathy Acker, an American novelist living in Britain, said, "The fact that two friends and writers whose works I respect are forced to have their privacies interrupted violently, radically, perhaps even irredeemably, makes me both angry and frustrated." She said she was Jewish and the tradition of the Talmud was profoundly one of arriving at knowledge through argument, discussion, controversy, rather than that of acquiring knowledge through decree.

Michael Foot, a writer as well as a Labour Party leader, compared Rushdie to Montaigne, Swift, and Voltaire. "Montaigne's books were put on the Papal index; Swift was accused on the highest regal or ecclesiastical authority of defaming all religions;

many of Voltaire's volumes were actually burnt. So Salman Rushdie keeps good company. He is a great artist, even if, like Swift or Voltaire himself, he does not possess all the virtues, too. But no shield against religious intolerance off the leash can always prevail."

Sir Geoffrey Howe, the Foreign Secretary, also assumed the role of literary critic. British government officials had spoken out against the Ayatollah's death sentence, but had been curiously detached about Rushdie and his book. Speaking in a BBC interview, Sir Geoffrey described *The Satanic Verses* as offensive to Britain as well as to Islam. He said there was "a huge distance between ourselves and the book," a remark that was generally taken to be an attempt to appease Muslim outrage and the first tentative move toward a settlement with Iran. "The British government, the British people, do not have any affection for the book," he said. "The book is extremely critical, rude about us. It compares Britain with Hitler's Germany. We do not like that any more than the people of the Muslim faith like the attacks on their faith contained in the book. So we are not sponsoring the book. What we are sponsoring is the right of people to speak freely, to publish freely."

The decision to criticize the book in this way followed a cabinet meeting at which the Rushdie Affair was a leading item on the agenda. Critics of the Foreign Secretary's statement wondered whether he had been influenced by the fact that Rushdie had long been opposed to the Thatcher government.

Prime Minister Thatcher soon followed her Foreign Secretary in speaking against Rushdie's novel. "We have known in our own religion people doing things which are deeply offensive to some of us ... and we have felt it very much. And that is what has happened in Islam."

Salman Rushdie hadn't been heard from since his apology, but these remarks by Prime Minister Thatcher and Foreign Secretary Howe worried him as to whether they meant the British government was "weakening in its resolve." He broke his silence to contact by phone the Liberal and Social Democrat Party leaders to express his concern. They promised to watch the government closely and challenge any apparent weakening either towards the Muslim extremists or his protection.

Max Madden, Labour member of Parliament for Bradford (West), tabled a motion in the House of Commons urging Rushdie to instruct his publishers to stop producing more editions of the book so that the protests could end and its author could live in peace and safety.

Letters and advertisements signed by writers in support of Rushdie appeared in British newspapers. I noticed that one huge newspaper list of international names, ranging from Chinua Achebe of Nigeria to Carlos Fuentes of Mexico, included Graham Greene (who was credited to the "UK" although he had made his home in the south of France for many years). When I was a boy, Graham Greene was regarded as a blasphemer by many conservative Catholics I knew. His whiskey priest who fathered a child in his novel, *The Power and the Glory*, was considered a scandalous attack on the Catholic clergy and even the Catholic faith, and Greene's implication that the whisky priest was a saint only made it worse. French bishops twice reported on the novel to the Vatican. Ten years after the book's publication in 1940, the Cardinal Archbishop of Westminster read Graham Greene a letter from the Holy Office condemning his novel because it was "paradoxical" and "dealt with extraordinary circumstances." Greene commented in his autobiographical book, *Ways of Escape*, "The price of liberty, even within a Church, is eternal vigilance, but I wonder whether any of the totalitarian states, whether of the right or of the left, with which the Church of Rome is often compared, would have treated me as gently when I refused to revise the book on the casuistical ground that the copyright was in the hands of my publishers. There was no public condemnation, and the affair was allowed to drop into that peaceful oblivion which the Church wisely reserves for unimportant issues."

Years later, when Graham Greene met Pope Paul VI, the Pope mentioned that he had read *The Power and the Glory*. Greene told him it had been condemned by the Holy Office.

"Who condemned it?" asked Pope Paul.

"Cardinal Pissardo."

The Pope repeated the name "with a wry smile" and added, "Mr. Greene, some parts of your books are certain to offend some Catholics, but you should pay no attention to that."

I wrote to Graham Greene at his home in Antibes reminding

him of his past as an alleged blasphemer like Salman Rushdie. As Greene was eighty-five, I didn't expect him to answer or to take much interest in the Rushdie Affair. But he replied, "I have already signed several petitions against Salman Rushdie's condemnation and I feel that is all I can do."

I wondered how Graham Greene felt when a Vatican official condemned Salman Rushdie for blasphemy and spoke in what *The Tablet* called "curiously ambivalent tones of the threat to his life." The statement was in an unsigned article in the Vatican's official newspaper, *Osservatore Romano*, but as the article carried three stars, this could mark a statement by the Pope himself or at least, according to *The Tablet*, "someone of very high rank."

The Tablet said it was incredible that Pope John Paul, who had consistently spoken out in defense of human life, or anyone who shared his mind would actually endorse the savage threats to Rushdie's life. But perhaps Graham Greene wouldn't have found it incredible; at least he had been very critical of Pope John Paul. One of his criticisms would have interested Rushdie with his preoccupation with doubt. "I don't think [the Pope] has doubt," Greene told John Cornwell in an interview published in *The Tablet* and widely reprinted. "I don't think he doubts his own infallibility. He reminds me a bit of Reagan, you know. He's always on television, isn't he?"

Greene added that he had always believed that *doubt* was a more important thing for human beings than belief. "It's human to doubt. We're now entering a period where Marxism is being doubted by Marxists. I mean, he's no longer infallible, Marx. And the Pope is no longer infallible," though the present Pope was "attempting to re-establish infallibility."

Three hundred years ago Graham Greene would have been tortured on the rack and then executed as a dangerous heretic for remarks like that, not to mention much of what he has written. The same might be said of many contemporary writers in the West. Umberto Eco, the Italian professor and author of two best-selling novels, for example, would certainly have been considered a blasphemer for passages in both his novels, *The Name of the Rose* and *Foucault's Pendulum*. Asked to comment on the Rushdie Affair, Eco addressed himself directly to Salman

Rushdie: "Nobody can ignore your ordeal, for at least three reasons. First (and once again) a man is being persecuted for having written a book. Second, for the first time in the history of this century, the death penalty is extended beyond the borders of a single country, in spite of the laws of other countries. Exile, the last resort of free men, does not work any longer. Third, your potential killers are summoned through the media; ironically, any medium covering the event contributes to inform and mobilize new potential killers." Eco told Rushdie, "You deserve the full and passionate solidarity of any man of dignity, but I am afraid this is too little. This story of a man alone against worldwide intolerance, and of a book alone against the craziness of the media, can become the story of many others. The bell tolls for all of us."

Peter Preston, editor of *The Guardian*, summed up the first few weeks after Rushdie's sentence: "In the second and third and fourth weeks of the Rushdie Affair, words have replaced emotions and deeds. Salman Rushdie himself has remained out of sight, the silent victim. But there has been no silence anywhere else. Because the first articles in the press expressed outrage, the second wave has niggled away at the book and its author. A repertory company of backbench MPs has begun to wonder whether this pretentious johnny, whose book they haven't read, is worth guarding from the public purse. Hon Members with Muslim constituents have twisted and turned. Sir Geoffrey Howe has set up as a literary critic." Rushdie wasn't at the heart of this macabre affair and hadn't been since the Ayatollah spoke. Rushdie was merely now a symbol of what had to be defended and protected without question or qualification by any individual, any community and any country which purported to put freedom of speech on its list of essential human freedoms.

Condemning Rushdie's book as offensive didn't prevent Foreign Secretary Howe from being put on the death list of a pro-Iranian terrorist group known as the Guardians of the Islamic Revolution, who were ready to carry out the Ayatollah's sentence against Rushdie—if they could find him. Security was officially tightened for Sir Geoffrey Howe as well as Douglas Hurd, the Home Secretary, and other senior ministers who were also threatened. The Guardians of the Islamic Revolution had claimed a series of terrorist attacks and was suspected of having organized three London assassination operations involving Muslims.

Meanwhile, the book itself continued to be a booming bestseller, sales increasing with every well-publicized terrorist threat. Even if not all the buyers read it, *The Satanic Verses* was a prestige item for display on coffee tables. A bookshop in Somerset, far from London, wanted £200 (or roughly $320), well over ten times the original price, for a signed copy of *Grimus*. A signed *Satanic Verses* would have brought even more. According to autograph dealers, Rushdie's signature had become more valuable than any other living writer's—and most dead writers, too.

6—AMERICAN DIVISIONS

ACROSS THE ATLANTIC, THE CANCELLATION OF SALMAN RUSHDIE'S UNITED States publicity tour awakened Americans to the fact that the controversy over "That Book" wasn't just a foreign affair and so much hot air. The death sentence was real and all over a mere book. Studs Terkel, the Chicago writer and radio interviewer, said, "I was going to have Salman Rushdie on my show to talk about his book. And now he's got to hide in England 'cuz they're going to kill him. Has the world gone nuts?" The continuing bomb threats against Viking-Penguin and individual bookstores underlined the growing danger in what many had formerly dismissed as a literary storm in a tea cup.

The major American bookstore chains, including Waldenbooks, B. Dalton and Barnes & Noble, who handled at least thirty percent of book sales in the United States, dithered as the W. H. Smith chain had done in Britain, and finally decided to withdraw the book from open display shelves, claiming they wanted to ensure the safety of their employees and customers. The book was still available from the behind-the-scenes stockrooms in the stores that had some copies left. Viking-Penguin was busy reprinting to fill all the new orders.

Pete Hamill, the *New York Post* columnist, wrote that he detected a sense of shame in a Dalton store he visited in New York City, and he referred to the danger of an "intellectual Munich" if support for Rushdie wasn't made clear. At the end of the first week after the Ayatollah's sentence, Hamill summed up: "It has been a bad week for courage. Everywhere, free men have submitted to the forces of stupidity and darkness. Salman Rushdie has been abandonned to the assassins. As soon as Khomeini issued his death sentence, writers, editors, publishers and booksellers everywhere should have banded together and said to this demented old man, 'I am Rushdie.' They should have stacked the bookshop windows with copies of *The Satanic Verses*."

Instead, wrote Hamill, "in too many cases, they ran. The book was pulled from the major American chain stores. W. H. Smith's 480 stores in England hid it in the basement. France, Greece, Turkey, and West Germany announced the suspension of publication. Canada stopped new copies from crossing the border. Italy stood up, as did Holland, Finland, and Norway; they deserve praise. The rest collapsed." The reason for this submission to Khomeini was fear of the fanatics, accompanied by a lot of pussyfooting language about not intending to offend Muslims. But the issue wasn't religion; it was freedom—"and freedom must be exercized in the face of risk or it dies." Hamill ended by remarking that he couldn't believe Khomeini would prevail. "You are Rushdie. I am Rushdie. In the end, our pens will be mightier than his goddamned swords."

The White House condemned the Ayatollah's death sentence, but declined to discuss the bookstores' withdrawal of the book. "Obviously we condemn targeted terrorism," said a White House official, but refused to make any further comment. Some fans of Rushdie wondered if President Bush in not speaking out forcefully in support of Rushdie personally was influenced by Rushdie's support of the Nicaraguan leftist government and criticism of United States policy in *The Jaguar Smile*.

Members of the Authors' Guild, American PEN, and the American Booksellers' Association issued separate statements condemning the bookstore chains for withdrawing Rushdie's novel. These organizations also criticized the United States government for failing to defend Rushdie. A spokesman for the American Booksellers' Association, representing 4,500 bookstore owners, said, "The United States government has got to do something. We condemn the insidious terrorist movement to suppress the book."

Islamic demonstrators continued to protest outside the Viking-Penguin offices. Employees were described as being under a lot of stress. An executive of Knopf said, "We had threatening phone calls when we published Rushdie's earlier books, but it has been much harder on Viking. One employee was asked to vacate her building and another was requested to take her child out of school. It has scared a lot of people." Even before publication day, Viking-Penguin estimated it had received about 30,000 letters of protest and a dozen bomb threats. Photocopies of the offending passages that had circulated in mosques in Britain were still being widely distributed among American Muslims.

Cardinal O'Connor of New York denounced *The Satanic Verses* as an insult to Muslims, but at the same time he condemned death threats against Rushdie as terrorism. The Cardinal told a congregation in St. Patrick's Cathedral that it would be foolish for Catholics to read the book. He believed Catholics were "mature and intelligent enough to recognize how foolish and childish attacks against another religious faith are." Cardinal O'Connor added, "We want it clear that the Catholic Church respects the faith of Islam, respects Muslims and deeply deplores any attack, any ridiculing, anything which brings into contempt any tenets of the Muslim faith or any other faith."

The Cardinal told reporters later why he decided to speak out, the first public statement by a major American Christian leader. "I think it's imperative that the Muslims here in New York know that we share with them deep distress at the attack that's been made on their faith," said Cardinal O'Connor.

He hadn't read the book, he said, and had no intention of doing so, but he had read evaluations which said it ridiculed Islam. "A huge number of Muslims have considered it [an insult]; if they consider it so, it's not for me to say that it isn't, and therefore I just wouldn't bother reading it."

He wouldn't urge Catholics to boycott the book or call for it to be censored because "I don't deal in censorship; these are government matters." He would give Catholics the same advice about the novel as he gave about the film, *The Last Temptation of Christ*: "I would personally consider it a waste of time."

Several American Catholic writers publicly disagreed with the Cardinal and backed Rushdie wholeheartedly.

An overdue series of public meetings organized by writers' groups to support Rushdie was now held in New York, Boston, Washington, Chicago, Minneapolis, and San Francisco, at which various well-known writers—including Norman Mailer, E. L. Doctorow and Susan Sontag—made militant speeches and read from *The Satanic Verses* after police had searched the audience for weapons. There were also equally militant demonstrations organized by the National Writers' Union outside the chain bookstores that had withdrawn the book and the Iranian Mission to the United Nations. Norman Mailer said the booksellers had overreacted to the threat of violence by Muslim fundamentalists. The chances of any employee being hurt for selling *The Satanic Verses* was "more than 6,000 to one" according to Mailer.

But, like other American writers heard from in public, Mailer didn't call for a boycott of the booksellers. As the three chains controlled such a large part of the book market, often deciding which books should become bestsellers, a boycott could threaten writers' livelihood, even though most of the independent booksellers were continuing to sell the book.

The police search for weapons certainly made the writers attending the public meeting in New York City appreciate the grim reality of Rushdie's position. Some of the audience seemed to think themselves courageous just for being there. The organizers were a coalition of American PEN, the Authors' Guild, and Article 19, an international organization which fought the censorship of writers. Readings from *The Satanic Verses* were the highpoint of the meeting. At the start of the readings, most of the audience seemed to hold their breath, sitting forward tensely and looking around for Muslim opposition to Rushdie's words. But the meeting was peaceful. Norman Mailer thought the Ayatollah's sentence offered writers "an opportunity to regain our faith in the power of words and our willingness to suffer for them." Mailer added that maybe writers were even willing ultimately to die for the idea that serious literature, in a world of dwindling certainties, was the absolute they must defend. He said that if Rushdie was "ever killed for a folly, we must be killed for the same folly, and we may need be, since we will then vow to do our best to open all literary meetings with a reading of the critical pages of *The Satanic Verses*." Other speakers included Susan Sontag ("We want to show our refusal to be intimidated.") and E. L. Doctorow ("Why murder? Why not serene spiritual counselling or excommunication?")

*   *   *

Columnist Pete Hamill complained that Arab intellectuals were not speaking out in support of Rushdie and singled out Professor Edward W. Said, Rushdie's friend. "Where is Edward W. Said, who has argued so persuasively in so many books against Western stereotypes of Islam? We have seen some Muslim leaders on TV, humorless, devoid of irony, mouthing the conventional (and ferocious) pieties. But the silence of Said and other modern, secular Arabs is morally outrageous."

Hamill was doing Said an injustice. Said had already signed letters of support for Rushdie published in American newspapers and had spoken at public meetings ("We cannot accept that the democratic freedoms need to be abrogated to protect Islam"). He also wrote a long article about *The Satanic Verses* that was published in the London *Observer* and the *Washington Post*. He described Rushdie as writing "both in and for the West" and added that if he had accepted Rushdie's help as a writer in the past, "we should now be ensuring his safety and his right to say what he has to say. To dispute with him, to engage with his work does not, cannot, be the same thing either as banning it or threatening him with violence and physical punishment."

I met Professor Said in his office in the philosophy building at Columbia University in uptown Manhattan. He told me, "I spoke with Salman Rushdie on the phone recently. I admire his work a lot and I've always been very fond of him. I met him first in the early eighties in London just after *Midnight's Children*. I'd read some of his essays in *Granta*. My wife and I spent July 4 in 1987 with him and Marianne in London. He also came to New York and we had a party for him and introduced him to various writers and Indian students who wanted to meet him. He phoned me from his latest hiding place when I was in London recently. He sounded as if he was in good spirits. He was hopeful that the Iranian injunction would be lifted in time. No sign of that at present. He didn't anticipate what Khomeini did. My impression was he was expecting the novel to have an impact, but not that big. He showed it to me in manuscript. He said it would shake up the Muslims. But he never expected it to bring about a threat to his life."

Professor Said explained his own view. "I think the Rushdie Affair is much more important than many people think. It can be seen as reflecting the history of the modern relationship be-tween Islam and the West. I am one of the people who believe that *Satanic Verses* for all its irreverence and spoofing of the Islam world has been done with a certain amount of affection, not at all vituperative but done with tongue in cheek, knowingness and inwardness. It suggests he was in no way trying to get rid of the world he's lived with all his life and continues to do so. The novel is an astonishingly brilliant piece of work. It's not one of those things easily reduced to just a Western insult to Islam. But we can't speak for all Islamic reactions. We're in the middle of an extraordinarily turbulent period.

"I was in Egypt recently and after one lecture, the first ques-tion was about *The Satanic Verses*. I said exactly what I'd said in New York. The audience was full of Muslim fundamentalists. It's easy to speak out in Greenwich Village or Soho, but not before such an audience in a country where the book was banned. I didn't get any vehement or hateful responses. What I said was greeted with polite silence. I gave a rudimentary summary of the book, and people were intrigued because they had no idea of what was in the banned book. Egypt is a rich place for writers, but the ones I saw decided they were not going to say anything because they couldn't get the book. Those leaping to denounce it didn't make sense because there was no Arabic translation and not many people I met knew English. Naguib Mahfouz, Egypt's Nobel Prize laureate, had spoken in defense of it. Salman told me in our recent phone talk that Naguib Mahfouz had been friendly, but his attitude seemed to have changed." (The Egyp-tian writer had been put on the defensive by being threatened with death for supporting Rushdie. Already under attack for his own book, *the Children of Gebelawi*, published in 1958 and prosribed by religious authorities, Naguib Mahfouz said his real offense was that he had defended Rushdie against the Ayatollah. "I said at the time that [Khomeini] was acting against the laws of the world and the laws of Islam.")

Professor Said told me, "A number of people think *Satanic Verses* shows a falling off from his early work. I think it's a cut above *Shame* and as good as *Midnight's Children*. I wasn't so impressed by *Shame* which didn't seem as well thought out as the earlier book or *Satanic Verses*, which is a wonderful book and deals with the whole migration thing. He deals wonderfully with the overlap between England and India. He used to be an actor and is a great mimic, and it comes out in his writing. He's a great talker, a brilliant conversationalist. He entertains with rather fantastic monologues taking all the parts. He has an ego like us all—a powerful one like all writers—but as a man, he's rather gentle and kind."

I mentioned the common criticism that *The Satanic Verses* was difficult to read and wouldn't have become a big bestseller without the Ayatollah's death sentence.

"He's no more difficult to read than Garcia Marquez," replied Professor Said. "He's easier to read, I think, than Kundera. The only difference is that he's dealing with stuff largely unfamiliar to Western readers. A lot of what he has to say about Mahound and the story of the early years of Islam are to be found in early Islam texts, gossipy and malicious in character, most of it poking fun at divine providence. It's incredibly familiar to any Muslim. You can still buy on the streets of Rabat or Cairo scurrilous books, spoofs of Islam depending on early Islam accounts. It could be that people were over affected by the notoriety of the book. People heard of the scandal and of Khomeini's reaction and just flipped through the book quickly. They weren't familiar with Post-Modernist fiction."

Susan Sontag was also in touch with Rushdie. The message she had for him was "I hope you are getting some exercise and listening to music, dear Salman. And writing. Write another book. And another."

When I talked with her, she was concerned not only about Rushdie personally but about the effect on publishing. She told me, "Publishers are going to be much more cautious. It has renewed the power of censorship. A militant minority can have a very intimidating effect. So can fanciful lawsuits. It doesn't mean a different relationship between publishers and writers, but people with corporate responsibility will be increasingly cautious. I don't know of a book that discusses Islamic issues that has been turned down, but I heard of a film about Muslims in the United States that hasn't been shown at a film festival in California following threats. The greatest danger is self-censorship.

"There was a difference between the reaction of American and British writers. Some British writers made astonishing statements. Of course we don't have a Bradford in the United States, neither do we have blasphemy laws.

"I don't think Salman anticipated the risks he was running. No one could have. I don't think you can attribute all that has happened to the book. It's part of an angry struggle in the Muslim world. There are many communities and factions. To put it crudely, there is a struggle between fundamentalists and modernizers. The book was taken up as a rallying point and that could very well not have happened if it didn't have to do with political developments in Iran particularly and in Pakistan and India and the situation in Britain.

"I was in London recently and I read in the papers there a story about continuing agitation in Bradford that wasn't reported here. People here in the United States are unaware of such recurring agitation over there.

"Everybody here was frightened to begin with. Rightly or wrongly, they feared violence. There was an impression that Muslims everywhere—the Middle East, Iran, Pakistan—were the same thing. A Muslim cleric and his secretary were assassinated in Brussels when he said that under Muslim law, Rushdie couldn't be sentenced without first receiving a trial.

"People are likely to cave in to violence. Great fear was the initial reaction, but then nothing too awful happened. Two bookstores in Berkeley were bombed which seemed to be connected to the Rushdie Affair. People here became more courageous. It was very different in Britain. Writers like Roald Dahl and John le Carré took the position the book should be withdrawn. But in this country I didn't hear any writer say that. We seem to take the position here that people have a right to write books that offend and get them published. Of course nobody is forced to buy or read them! I think Britain was unique in having writers so divided. In no other country as far as I know did writers suggest the book should be withdrawn.

"But the situation isn't Rushdie's fault. I have a private theory that if the book hadn't had the title it did, it couldn't have been so manipulated. If it had been called, for example, *The Mountain and the Valley*, it couldn't have been so manipulated, but calling it *The Satanic Verses* was like calling it *The Devil's Book*. Millions who hadn't read it were worked up as if they were being asked 'Are you a fan of the Devil's?'

"Salman Rushdie's a very proud man. He wants to go on living as a writer. Most people don't understand what being a writer, a committed writer like he is, really means. He's also a very social man. He enjoys dinner parties and good talk. I can't see him giving up his identity and using some disguise. He's not like a spy who comes in from the cold and takes another identity. He is who he is. Everyone now knows what he looks like. That is his difficulty.

"I'm in touch with him. He's writing, but he's very unhappy. He wants to go somewhere else if only for a short time and he is going to do that, I understand.

"I had a role in mobilizing people here to become aware of the issues—that censorship can come about in other ways than through government actions. Intimidation by militant groups is a sad business, particularly sad for Salman. His life in a certain way has been ruined. I can't imagine even ten years from now that he could comfortably go to a movie or a restaurant or get on a normal plane. There may always be people who will be after him. He will have to live an ultra-secluded way of life for an indefinite period. It will be very difficult for him to move around. But I can't see him changing his appearance or taking another identity.

"Nor unfortunately can I see the Muslim leaders withdrawing the sentence. They don't have to push it, but I can't see them withdrawing it. There's nothing to gain. It would be like admitting it was wrong."

Roger W. Straus of Farrar, Straus and Giroux was also concerned about the effect on publishing standards. He told me, "What has happened is bound to have certain chilling effects. An Islamic book would probably now be read with rubber gloves. In the conglomerates, house lawyers will be much more tough. I had dinner recently with the French publisher of *The Satanic Verses* and he had a bodyguard with him. But he sold out the first week.

*　　*　　*

The New York Times Book Review published messages for Rushdie from fellow writers.

Chinua Achebe of Nigeria said, "What does one say? I think probably all I can say is: Don't despair. The world has become a very dangerous place, but it is our responsibility to keep fighting for the freedom of the human spirit. It's not just for writers that we must do this, but for everyone. If we secure this freedom, the whole world benefits."

Anita Desai of India: "Silence, exile and cunning, yes. And courage."

Nien Cheng, born in China, now living in the United States: "You must be firm and be brave, because in some ways your position is worse than being in prison. You cannot identify your enemy."

Elie Wiesel, born in Rumania, now living in the United States: "Any attack on you is directed at us all. Censorship in literature is the enemy of literature and death threats, addressed for whatever reason, if they succeed in silencing the author, would mean not only the end of literature but the end of civilization."

Nadine Gordimer of South Africa: "There is no precedent for this at all; it is the ultimate, the very last measure, of dictatorship. I can understand that some people's sensibilities might be offended by the book, and even that Muslim countries might ban it, but they cannot tell the whole world what to do. I don't know what to tell you to do. I can only assure you of my horror and my full support."

Ralph Ellison of the United States: "Keep to your convictions. Try to protect yourself. A death sentence is a rather harsh review."

Rumer Godden, born in India, living in Britain: "As someone who lived for so many years in India, I think you should have been more aware of what you were doing to offend Muslims, because they are exceedingly sensitive. Anything to do with their religion provokes a tremendous response, as it does with many committed Christians of the very orthodox type. Whatever you have done, probably you wrote it as a good story. I tremble for your safety."

Derek Walcott, born in St. Lucia, now in the United States: "The madness in *The Satanic Verses* has been misread as yours and not that of your characters. All writers are endangered if they are to be judged by the characters they create: Shakespeare would be a racist, Dante a bigot."

Robertson Davies, Canada: "To raise the future inevitably provokes the malignity of the past. We are sorry for your distress but we would not wish unsaid what you have written, for the task of all of us is to say what entrenched opinion considers unspeakable."

Octavio Paz, Mexico: "We are seeing a disappearance of the modern values that came with the Enlightenment. These people who condemn you are living before the Enlightenment. We are facing a historical contradiction in our century. I would say to you, remain firm. I defend the writer's right to be wrong."

Bharati Mukherjee, born in India, now living in the United States: "I should like you, Salman, to know that we care more about your personal safety and about the preservation of your books and your message than we do about the chain bookstore owners' angst, which unfortunately has seized the media headlines. The religious establishment seems to have proved itself to be the source either of threat or of cowardice. I hope in spite of everything your next novel will be so scaldingly blasphemous that even liberals will cringe."

Thomas Pynchon, United States: "Our thanks to you and to Marianne Wiggins for recalling those of us who write to our duty as heretics, for reminding us again that power is as much our sworn enemy as unreason, for making us all look braver, wiser, more useful than we often think we are. We pray for your continuing good health, safety and lightness of spirit."

George Konrad, Hungary: "I will be speaking in Budapest on behalf of both you and Vaclav Havel" (the dissident Czechoslovak playwright who was in jail at the time for protesting in Prague, but was later released and became President). "I believe your causes are linked. It is absolutely irrelevant what is in your novel because a novel cannot be the object of any moral or legal judgment. It is an elementary question of the freedom of writing and I believe we writers have to share the responsibility you took, and we do support the publication of your work."

And from Australia, Thomas Keneally, who remembered "the day you and Bruce Chatwin were setting off together from Adelaide to visit Alice Springs in central Australia. Now Bruce is dead and you are under a tyrant's sentence of death. All I can say is what I heard a number of authors crying in the streets of New York recently during a demonstration in favor of your right to free expression. 'I am Rushdie.' We all are." And many more.

And the book was back on the display shelves of the chain bookstores. In early March, 300,000 copies were either in print or on order for reprint. Waldenbooks declared in a full-page advertisement in *The New York Times* that "We have never taken the book off sale ... We will continue to sell the book when it comes back in stock ... We will continue to use discretion in displaying the book ... We admire the courage of our people who have gallantly performed in the face of bomb threats and unfair castigation." B. Dalton removed the book to have time to consult all its store managers and most of its employees, and more than ninety percent said Dalton should sell the book so back it went on the shelves. Was it true Stephen King, one of the chain bookstores' biggest bestsellers, phoned and threatened to pull his own books from the stores? Yes, King called, but he didn't threaten, just expressed concern.

Early in March, too, the office of the *Riverdale Press*, a New York City weekly newspaper, was fire bombed and all but destroyed after publishing an editorial entitled "The Tyrant and His Chains", defending the right to publish, to distribute and to sell *The Satanic Verses*.

Perhaps the most effective reply to the Ayatollah from American writers came from James A. Michener, who had lived in or visited extensively every Muslim nation except Saudi Arabia, from Indonesia westward to Spain, which had been Muslim for centuries. Michener called the death sentence "a fearful error and a step back to the time of the Crusades." He warned his Muslim friends that "it is absolutely unacceptable for them to inject themselves into the international writing and publishing scene with their calls for assassination and it is equally unacceptable for us to surrender to such terrorist blackmail."

Michener said he spoke only to the Muslim leadership abroad and in the United States: "Do not persist in this folly. You make yourselves look ridiculous. You damage your reputation and that of your religion. You make sensible Americans ask: 'Have these men gone mad?' Accept Rushdie's regrets. Argue against the book in your own countries. But do not try to ban it in ours."

The United States Senate unanimously passed a resolution supporting Rushdie, condemning the Ayatollah's sentence as "state-sponsored terrorism," and applauding publishers and booksellers who "have courageously printed, distributed, sold and displayed *The Satanic Verses*."

But on the Muslim side, none of this might have happened. They still flatly condemned Rushdie without allowing any arguments from Muslims who believed in non-violence. Typical was a letter addressed to Rushdie from S. Nomanul Haq, a tutor in the history of science at Harvard University, which was published in *The New York Times*. "Your response to the uproar," Rushdie was told, "has been wavering and inconsistent, and your defense has the odor of self-righteousness. You say that people who have not read your book have no right to criticize it. But do you really think that reading the book will drastically alter their opinions? Then you talk about freedom of expression. Free speech is a tricky issue and cannot be taken too literally. What do you think the response of black Americans would be if you were to mock the Rev. Dr. Martin Luther King, Jr? Or the reaction of the Jewish community if you were to eulogize Hitler? Or the anger of a pious Hindu if you were to present a graphic description of the slaughtering of a cow?" The writer concluded that he was saddened that a bounty had been placed on Rushdie's head and that a great writer like him, rather than presenting himself to the public, was in hiding. "You have elicited the rage of entire nations. This is a pity. But, Mr. Rushdie, you have cut them and they are bleeding: Do something quickly to heal the wound."

It was now over six months since *The Satanic Verses* had been first published in Britain, three months since the book first became available in American bookstores, over a month since the Ayatollah's death sentence. To Salman Rushdie in hiding, there must have seemed no end in sight.

Brad Leithauser in *The New Yorker* summed up Rushdie's situation: "What has befallen Salman Rushdie in recent months defies encapsulation. Time and again, the furor surrounding *The Satanic Verses* apparently crested, only to erupt in a more vehement, madder guise. One can usually depend on a loose network of contemporary social conditions (among them, the primacy of film over written words, the accelerated turnover of news in our media, and the general din of modern life) to dilute and diffuse any literary controversy, but things have gone otherwise with this novel." When Ayatollah Khomeini issued his sentence of execution, "a sort of infernal standoff was forged: somewhere, in hiding and under police protection, Mr. Rushdie goes on living, but those who would annihilate him remain unplaced. Meanwhile, borders of all sorts—of national sovereignty, of logic, of civilization itself—have given way. The horrors that have grown up around *The Satanic Verses* make it almost impossible to recollect the time when Rushdie's book seemed merely one controversial novel among many new novels. Yet less than four months ago (to Rushdie, it must seem like four lifetimes ago) he felt free to compose a spirited self-defense for the London *Observer* ..."

And how many lifetimes was it going to take before Rushdie could come out of hiding?

7—BREAKING THE SILENCE

AT FIRST SALMAN RUSHDIE THOUGHT IT WAS GOING TO BE ONLY A COUPLE of weeks. "How could something like this last for a long time?" The first few days in hiding were "the most off-balance I've ever felt in my life." One of his sisters received an anonymous phone call the day after it all began. A man's voice just said, "Now is your brother scared?" Rushdie commented that the answer was "Yes, he was."

It was only gradually as the weeks went by that Rushdie began to feel that the damage that had been done was so huge that it was going to take "an awful lot of undoing." One of the problems of unleashing that quantity of hatred, he said, was that it was very difficult to put it back in the box. Once crowds had been whipped up in so many countries to march down streets demanding somebody's death, it was very difficult to say, "Well, actually we were wrong, we don't really want to kill him after all."

Scotland Yard, however, never seemed to expect a quick end. The Special Branch from the beginning treated the Muslim threats even more seriously than those of Irish terrorists because the Muslims were less predictable. Two armed men were with Rushdie twenty-four hours a day and he was seldom in the same "Safe House" for more than a day or two.

He and Marianne became television addicts, spending much of their time in front of a TV set, waiting for the latest news from the outside world. After a few weeks, Rushdie told himself, "I am not going to spend the rest of my life watching people abuse me on television."

He had gone into hiding with nothing but the clothes he wore. Eventually the police arranged for Marianne Wiggins to go to

192

their narrow, terraced house in Islington for a very hurried visit with bodyguards to collect some things they both needed—a few books, typewriters and sacred objects that Salman liked to have near him when he was writing.

She turned off the gas and electricity and packed some woolen socks and wellington boots for what promised to be a long winter away from home. She also took pictures of their children and a dictionary for each of them—a Collins English dictionary for Rushdie and a Random House American dictionary for herself. They kept the two dictionaries by their bedside. It became their favorite reading. "We just read down the columns, comparing definitions," recalled Wiggins later. "Just like some couples read *Winnie the Pooh* to each other." She felt finding a twin soul for bedside reading was a good indicator of an ideal partnership. She also took an atlas—"I spent so much time just gazing at it, it brings the world alive"—and Salman's useless passport. "He'd look at all his visas in and out of India, the country he can never ever go to again. He is a completely deracinated person." She never went back to their house which remained dark and empty because their attempts to sell it didn't work out—"Local estate agents somehow fail to see the appeal of 'Salman Rushdie's house' on their books."

Among the sacred objects she took to him was the little block of Indian silver engraved with the map of unpartitioned India and Pakistan that his father's friend had given him as a baby—"my oldest possession"—and a small primitive Haitian painting, "a very simple little thing of a rural scene," given him by a friend, "which I've always kept in front of me on the desk where I write." It was less than a foot tall by eight inches wide. So he had a few of "my little totems" with him in hiding. But in the first few weeks, "when the heat of the affair was so intense," he found it impossible to do any writing except for trying to keep a journal about what was happening to him.

It was necessary, however, not to disappear completely—to become a totally invisible man as far as the public and literary circles were concerned—or he would gradually be forgotten, and perhaps in time even the government would lose interest and withdraw the Special Branch protection. To show the world he wasn't finished and to try to get back to writing, he phoned

Blake Morrison at *The Observer* in a roundabout way that satisfied the Special Branch's stringent security screen, and he told
the literary editor that he would like to continue writing book
reviews for him. The Special Branch could arrange safe methods
of delivery. He wanted to get back to the discipline of regular
writing again to show he was still functioning as a presence in
literary life and also perhaps as therapy during this incredibly
tense time.

For the first three months, until May, he did nothing more
ambitious than the journal, a few book reviews, and occasional
short poems. But in time he felt ready for something more
ambitious and began to write a long fable for children, which
had been on his mind for the last three years as something he
wanted to do next. It was a very long, very fantastic story that he
found "very pleasurable to write," perhaps because it had such
obvious connections with the *Arabian Nights* stories of his boyhood and had few reminders of the grim reality he was living
through. He had originally planned the story for his young son,
Zafar, and he used to read an early version to the boy in
serialized form at the boy's bedtime. "It was part of the deal so I
could finish *Satanic Verses*," Rushdie once said. "He asked why
all my books were for grown-ups and I didn't have an answer."
But when Rushdie was deeper into the fable, he didn't find it so
very different from writing his "grown-up" novels. "Once you set
the tone of your voice and the idea for a fable going, you don't
really have to write in any different way than you normally
would. You just tell the story, and you make it as interesting as
you can because the thing about children is, if they're bored,
they tell you. They shut the book."

Both he and his former wife, Clarissa, did their best to protect
Zafar from the media. They didn't want him to be affected by the
perilous situation, if it was possible to keep him out of it.
Rushdie's young son was rumored to have been sent away to a
boarding school, but no one was saying whether this was true or
if it was, where the school was. The Special Branch was also
arranging for the boy to see his father occasionally. Clarissa was
working for one of the oldest, most respected literary agencies
in London, A. P. Watt Ltd, but she also kept out of the news as
much as she could. A newspaper executive who sat next to her

in a London theater described her as "beautiful and distinguished, a real English lady, but with an underlying tension."

Rushdie thought his writing experience ("A novelist is very used to extended periods of time being by himself") should have prepared him for his life in hiding. "What I do most of my life is sit in a room by myself. The only difficulty is that this time I don't actually get out of it." He thought Marianne was better at coping with solitude than he was.

Seeing his friends was "incredibly difficult." It was much safer to stay in touch through phone calls from safe places arranged by the Special Branch. He had never enjoyed long phone conversations, but he had to learn how to become chatty. It was usually his only means of communication with the outside world. One of the advantages was that you could choose whom to talk to because no one could call him. People often didn't believe he was actually calling and thought it was a practical joke. There were many Rushdie jokes going around. A typical one was about passengers on a plane who suddenly learn Rushdie is one of them. Panic! Sometimes people did phone pretending to be Salman, and for that reason he often had to prove he was really himself and he found that was really difficult on the phone.

What he discovered that he missed most were the ordinary things of life that he had always taken for granted—walking in public, browsing in bookstores, going shopping or to movies. He loved movies, but he hadn't been in a cinema for several months. He loved driving fast cars of any kind, but now he had to sit in the back with the Special Branch occupying the driver's seat. When the tiny things that made up real life were no longer possible, that was the biggest deprivation.

He tried to spend the day working and then, in the evening, watched a lot of bad TV and videos. Apart from Marianne, the only company was a detective with a gun.

The biggest drama of those first few months involved his bad lower wisdom teeth. The bottom-left wisdom tooth broke shortly before he was supposed to set off on his American publicity tour. His dentist recommended waiting to take it out until after he returned from the United States. But instead of going on the tour, he had had to disappear into hiding places in and around London and visiting the dentist was regarded as too risky. The

Special Branch arranged instead for his teeth to be pulled in what Rushdie called "one of the most impressive of the many impressive things" that the detective bodyguards had done for him. The police secreted him into a hospital, reportedly in an ambulance with his face covered. He was placed under an anesthetic, which he found scary. The teeth were pulled out, he recovered from the anesthetic, and then was taken out of the hospital without his presence being generally known.

He spent some of his time alone reading *The Satanic Verses* with great care. Normally he didn't like to read his books once they were published, but he wanted to be sure he wasn't wrong about his book. "I'm happy to stand by it," he decided after almost learning the huge book by heart. This was an important decision for him. If he had felt the novel had engendered the kind of offense so many people had taken, he was to say later, he would have felt differently about everything—about what should be done in the future, about whether the present position should be maintained. Did his mind linger over the passages that seemed to predict his present position? It was true, he admitted later, that some passages had acquired a prophetic quality that alarmed even him. He was struck particularly by that passage in which Mahound said, "Your blasphemy, Salman, can't be forgiven." It was uncannily close to what had happened to him. But, he said, to write a dream based around events that took place in the seventh century of the Christian era was very different from "somehow knowing, in advance, that your dream is about to come true, that the metaphor is about to be made flesh, that the conflict your work seeks to explore is about to engulf it, and its publishers and booksellers, and you." Did he brood perhaps over another passage that involved the two main characters confronting each other and asking what was "unforgivable"? Chamcha examines his hatred for Gibreel—"Never mind about excuses ... to hell with mitigations and what-could-he-have-dones; what's beyond forgiveness is beyond. You can't judge an internal injury by the size of the hole."

What's beyond forgiveness—it wasn't a passage to brood over when he was feeling depressed. But he couldn't believe that what he had written merited the treatment it had been given. As for whether the Ayatollah's sentence would be withdrawn, he had to remain hopeful that this nightmare he was living through would end one day soon.

The latest news from Tehran was that the Ayatollah was seriously ill in the hospital, but medical bulletins were optimistic about his condition. Rushdie followed every news broadcast because his future seemed closely linked to the Ayatollah's. Death appeared to threaten both of them now.

But then events in Britain took over the headlines. A mass Muslim demonstration was held in the center of London on Saturday, May 27. Police considered the demonstration a security nightmare because of the large number of militant Muslims who wished to enter Britain to take part. Scotland Yard feared that the demonstration could provide cover for fanatics who were seeking to assassinate Salman Rushdie. Leave for thousands of police officers was cancelled, and the Special Branch guards with Rushdie were alerted.

The organizers of the demonstration, the British Muslim Action Front, who had united the many Muslim sects and communities in Britain for the first time, had distributed publicity leaflets in mosques abroad, and there had been a big foreign response. More than 10,000 Muslims from France, Germany, the Low Countries, Turkey, and the Indian subcontinent were expected—if Scotland Yard allowed them in. But like most of the estimates for the demonstration, that seemed to be a very much exaggerated total.

More than 150 coaches brought demonstrators from Bradford, Birmingham, Leicester, and other parts of Britain where altogether at least a million Muslims lived; their exact number very hard to calculate at that time of crisis. About 20,000 Muslims according to the police—and many more according to the organizers—marched from Hyde Park to the prime minister's residence at 10 Downing Street, where the leaders handed in a demand for a revision of the blasphemy laws to cover Islam. Young militant pro-Iranian demonstrators called for the execution of Rushdie and hanged an effigy of him, complete with dark suit, from a hastily erected gallows.

Fighting broke out in Parliament Square between Iranian and Iraqi groups encouraged by British racists in the watching crowds. Stones and bottles were thrown, and police in riot gear formed a circle round the violent groups. At one point in the battle, the police lost control and spectators ran for cover. Eighteen police were injured and 101 arrests were made before the fighting ended.

Another effigy of Salman Rushdie was burned and torn apart while banners with such messages as "Rushdie Burn" and "Kill the Bastard" were held aloft and crowds chanted "Rushdie die, Rushdie scum." *The Sunday Telegraph* reported that "many of the tens of thousands of demonstrators expressed violent hatred of both author and publishers." A small group of women demonstrated against Islamic fundamentalism, but needed police protection.

The London police blamed a young militant group of over four hundred who took over the front of the marching procession for most of the violence. The demonstrators blamed the police for starting it by overreacting. Among the demonstrators' influential supporters was the Labour Party member of Parliament for Leicester East, Keith Vaz, who had been running a parliamentary campaign to get the book banned. He described the demonstration as a "great celebration of freedom." The Rushdie Affair had caused a split in the Labour Party with M.P.s disagreeing over whether the book should be banned or not. But the organizers were keen to distance Action Front from the violence, stressing that it was intended to be a peaceful rally to press for the withdrawal of the book and the revision of the blasphemy laws.

The Guardian reported that "it would be wrong to think the young street fighters were anything but utterly serious about Salman Rushdie's supposed blasphemy. As the crowd heaved toward the police line at the entrance to Whitehall, one teenager explained: 'We are still here because this is jihad—you know, Holy War.' Asked why they were attacking the police, another said calmly: 'Because they are the devil dogs who protect the devil Rushdie—like the media does.' "

The organizers said the next day they "very much regretted" the violence, but they stressed it would not deter them from their campaign against the book and they didn't rule out further marches and demonstrations and even widespread strikes. A spokesman for Action Front blamed "inexperienced young police officers" for mishandling the young militants' protests and added "It was not until arrests were made that sticks and bottles began to be thrown. This was a natural reaction to seeing our colleagues dragged away." He admitted some of the demonstrators became excited and over-enthusiastic, but said some people who "didn't want us to protest against Rushdie" created trouble which led to arrests.

Scotland Yard denied the allegations against the police and blamed militant young Muslims for what happened. Sir John Stokes, a Conservative M.P., said, "The British public will not stand for this disgraceful behavior. Those who settle here must obey our laws and customs." The Bishop of Bradford, the Right Rev. Robert Williamson, was "disappointed, saddened and very disturbed" by the violence.

It was reported that *The Satanic Verses* had now sold more than 90,000 hardback copies in Britain and was second on a leading bestseller list. In the United States, more than 700,000 copies had been sold.

But these very impressive sales figures must have offered little consolation to Salman Rushdie watching the violent protests against him and his book on television, especially the sight of his effigy being hanged and torn apart. As the crowds demonstrated their hatred of him, he must have been close to despair, feeling this nightmare would never end.

But the news wasn't all bad. Among the supporters who spoke up against the demonstration was Arnold Wesker, well-known for his plays about English working-class life, who was one of the most forthright and persistent authors on Rushdie's side. As a member of the International Committee for the Defense of Salman Rushdie and his Publishers, Wesker commented: "The march ended in violence and a call for Salman Rushdie to be hanged. This is an appalling situation around which the Government is pussyfooting. Medieval bigotry is being allowed to take root."

Wesker, in a letter to *The Independent*, wrote that the International Committee supported the right of Muslims to march and freely express their views of Rushdie's book. But the Muslim community must understand that Rushdie was exercising his identical right to free expression when he wrote the book. "You cannot demand freedom of expression for one and take it away from another." The Committee called upon the Muslim community to make clear "their condemnation of the Ayatollah Khomeini's absurd and medieval fatwa demanding Rushdie's death."

Although the Committee agreed with the Muslim community that the British blasphemy law was discriminatory, Wesker wrote, it disgreed with the call for an extension of the law, which could involve a massive increase in censorship and self-censorship and thus limit the democracy which the English had evolved, argued and died for.

Wesker thought a more precise way of describing the issue at stake than "freedom of expression" was "the freedom to question one belief from the basis of another that is under threat." That was a freedom central to a democratic society. The only protection against religious and political charlatans was to keep free the right to question, debate and ridicule all belief. "The horrifying fact is that fear has already begun to eat into the soul of this society. An artist is in hiding; public personalities have to be protected; printers are refusing to print; workers in Penguin offices around the world are in fear of their lives. And this is intolerable. It is also infantile. The view that violence is a way of asserting your belief is an infantile view." Wesker added that "the Khomeini cry for the execution of Rushdie is an infantile cry." He said that his many Muslim friends were very ashamed of the furor their brethren had created. "They fear that the community is in the hands of immature minds who are using the Rushdie book as a means of gaining power over the community. I would ask the silent majority in the Muslim community to stand up and be counted among those who reject fanatical fundamentalism and to quote the words of the prophet Muhammad who said: 'The ink of the learned is holier than the blood of the martyr.'"

The arguments over the demonstration were ended by the worsening news from Tehran. The Ayatollah's doctors were no longer so optimistic. It was known that the Ayatollah, who was eighty-nine, had undergone surgery to stop intestinal bleeding on May 23. But Radio Tehran had continued to stress that he was in good condition, although no details about his operation were given. There were persistent rumors in the West that he had cancer of the stomach. The Ayatollah had been seen last in public in February on television when he met the Soviet Foreign

Minister and said he wanted closer ties with the Soviet Union to counter what he called "devilish acts of the West." In March he had ousted his heir apparent, Ayatollah Russein Ali Montazeri, who had suggested that Iran's revolution was going off course. With no designated successor, there was certain to be a power struggle between Islamic radicals who were in favor of a militant anti-Western policy and more moderate Iranian leaders who were more conciliatory to the West. The old Ayatollah's son, Hojatolislam Ahmad Khomeini, was mentioned as a leading contender for the succession.

After the Ayatollah's operation, members of the Komitch, the urban militia controlled by the Interior Ministry, suddenly took charge outside strategic public buildings, at important crossroads and on highways leading into Tehran, the capital. This was obviously to prevent any possible coup and was a sign that the old Ayatollah was dying. The stern-faced, bearded old man regained consciousness, although he couldn't speak to the relatives and top officials at his hospital bedside. He whispered prayers. The Islamic Republic News Agency quoted reports that "as the night moved closer, the Imam slid further into silence, and finally at about midnight, the long spirit of God joined celestial heaven." The Agency reported that the body of the Ayatollah, "washed and shrouded according to Islamic laws," was taken to a mortuary. It was Saturday, June 3, 1989.

The Rushdies were awakened by a guard. "Somebody started knocking on the bedroom door," recalled Marianne Wiggins. "Usually the police would let us have privacy from the bedroom door onward." But the news might change their lives. "We were jubilant," she said

Iran's clerical leaders quickly named forty-nine-year-old President Ali Khamenei as supreme leader to replace the Ayatollah. The eighty-three-member Assembly of Experts, charged by the constitution with deciding the leadership, elected him by more than two-thirds of the Assembly according to Iran's official media. However, he was judged to lack the Ayatollah's dominant religious and political authority, and he suggested himself he might only be an interim leader.

Even the West's media had huge obituaries of the man *The Guardian* called the "Mightiest of the Mullahs." *The Independent* in London summed up that the Ayatullah "was elevated to sainthood by followers and enjoyed a semi-prophet and God-like status while his detractors saw him as a blood-thirsty dictator, Lucifer and Satan incarnate." Large pictures of the familiar stern, bearded features were spread across the West's front pages.

An estimated three million mourners crowded around the burial site in a frenzy of grief during the funeral on June 6. *Time* commented that the funeral "ignited an emotional outpouring from his fanatical followers that Westerners found as bizarre, frightening—and ultimately incomprehensible—as the passions he stirred during ten turbulent years as leader of Iran. Even after his burial, Khomeini excoriated his enemies in the outside world, raging in his will against 'the atheist East' and 'the infidel West,' branding Jordan's King Hussein a 'criminal tramp,' accusing the leaders of Egypt and Morocco of 'treason,' and denouncing the United States as an 'inborn terrorist' organization." While his body lay in state inside a refrigerated glass box, the crush of mourners was so great that eight people were killed. As a helicopter brought the open wooden coffin to the cemetery, some of the mourners managed to reach the casket causing the body to fall out according to *Time*. By the end of the funeral, more than five hundred people had been hospitalized and another ten thousand treated for injuries. It was as if the Iranian people realized Khomeini had united the country, dominating the political radicals and the religious extremists, and now Iran might be in for a long, bitter struggle. Even some of the Islamic moderates opposed to the Ayatollah regretted his passing at this time.

To Salman Rushdie watching on television somewhere in London, the frenzy of grief must have been especially frightening. That was the kind of feeling he was up against. Some of Rushdie's supporters expressed cautious optimism that the new leadership might grant him a reprieve, but others thought the Ayatollah's death would have no effect because what he had said against Rushdie had become "an orthodoxy."

Marianne Wiggins said the funeral convinced them there was going to be no change. "A light at the end of the tunnel went out for us."

Hanif Kureishi, the filmmaker and friend of Rushdie's, said he didn't expect Rushdie would be able to leave his hiding places in the near future. He expected the Rushdie Affair would have long-term effects. "We are only at the first stage of a series of conflicts that have been set off between the Muslim and the secular communities in this country." The Bradford Council for Mosques issued a statement expressing sadness at the Ayatollah's death and adding "We pray that the Iranian leadership will continue to pursue and fulfill the aspirations of Imam Khomeini with undiminished zest."

It wasn't long before the new leadership in Iran confirmed the death sentence against Rushdie. While on a visit to Moscow late in June, the Speaker of the Iranian Parliament, Hojatolislam Hashemi Rafsanjani, was completely unyielding on whether the Islamic faithful should execute Rushdie at the first opportunity. "This is not the kind of prescription that can be reversed," he said of the death threat.

Nothing had changed. There was to be no reprieve for Rushdie. It was already over four months since he had gone into hiding and no end was in sight. Scotland Yard had been right. It was going to take a long time. He worried about the solitary way of life Marianne was forced to live with him. He tried to carry on with his children's fable, escaping into the world of his imagination for a time. As for Marianne Wiggins, she was beginning to feel "stunted" as a writer. "For him to be in that situation is existentially what has to do, and he will write about it wonderfully." But it wasn't a subject for her. She was beginning to miss living a full life "like crazy."

8—"THE CURRENT LEVEL"

TWO OF SALMAN RUSHDIE'S MOST FORMIDABLE WESTERN CRITICS, ONE in the United States and the other in Britain, particularly seemed to upset him—former United States President Jimmy Carter and fellow best-selling novelist John le Carré.

Jimmy Carter had surprised many of his admirers on both sides of the Atlantic by refusing to defend *The Satanic Verses*. During his one presidential term from 1977 to 1981, he had acted as a dedicated go-between in negotiations between Israel and the Arab world, and he had become friendly with President Anwar Sadat of Egypt who was later to receive a death sentence himself from his enemies and be assassinated.

Carter's Arab friendships possibly influenced his attitude in the Rushdie case, although he might have been expected to be down on Iran after the American hostage debacle which contributed to his failure to win a second presidential term and his overwhelming defeat by Ronald Reagan.

Carter said of the Rushdie Affair, "This is the kind of intercultural wound that is difficult to heal. Western leaders should make it clear that in protecting Rushdie's life and civil rights, there is no endorsement of an insult to the sacred beliefs of our Muslim friends."

Rushdie was bitterly upset by Jimmy Carter's statement, probably because Carter had been the most liberal of recent United State presidents and he had expected support from him. Even eight months later he still felt strongly enough about both Carter and le Carré to reply to them in biting terms.

It was "almost comic," he told *Newsweek*, that Jimmy Carter of all former presidents of America should say that he understood how the Iranians felt about *The Satanic Verses* "after having enjoyed as we all know such intimate and *successful* relationships with them."

But this sarcasm was very low-key compared to his reply to John le Carré. He completely rejected le Carré's argument about the threat to the bookstores and the necessity to withdraw the book. He wasn't putting the bookstores through it, that was the work of the people running the terror campaign. "It seems to me there's been fantastically disproportionate interest in what le Carré has said, because for every le Carré there's been a hundred people who think that what le Carré said was contemptible. I would hope that John le Carré's views were not tempered by the fact that I gave his last novel a bad review. I'm sure he's entirely above that." For Brutus is an honorable man—it was yet another example of Rushdie's not-so-gentle art of making enemies and showed his bitter feeling about le Carré's criticism of him.

There had been more to upset him in Britain. The House of Lords discussed the high cost of protecting him with round-the-clock Special Branch guards. Viscount Massereene-Ferrard asked Her Majesty's government: "What has been the approximate cost to date of the protection provided for Mr. Salman Rushdie by the police and how much longer they envisage this protection will be continued?"

The Earl of Arran replied for the government: "My Lords, it would not be proper for me to disclose information about police protection which would indicate its scale in a particular case. It is envisaged that Mr. Rushdie will continue to receive protection while the threat to him remains at the current level."

Viscount Massereene-Ferrard replied that he fully appreciated that it was a "delicate question." However, didn't his noble friend—the usual House of Lords' elaborate way of addressing fellow members—not agree that Mr. Rushdie, "whom I understand to be a British citizen," had, through his writings, "which in my opinion are scurrilous and blasphemous," greatly offended the Arab world and caused great offense to many devout Muslims? "Does my noble friend not also agree that presumably Mr. Rushdie has made a lot of money out of his writings and that this matter has impaired our relations, certainly in the Middle East, with the Arabs? May I also ask—"

Noble Lords: "No, no."

The Earl of Arran: "My Lords, perhaps I can take the general tenor of my noble friend's questions. I point out straight away that Mr. Rushdie's private means are totally immaterial. His life has been threatened in a way which entitles him to request protection. The police have taken the action which they consider to be appropriate in the circumstances."

Lord Mishcon: "My Lords, is there any monetary limit which a civilized state should adopt in endeavoring to protect the life of a writer, however misguided or not he may be, who is being officially and publicly threatened merely because of what he has written?"

The Earl of Arran: "My Lords, the Noble Lord, Lord Mishcon, has posed an extremely difficult question to answer. The point is that, at the end of the day, it is a matter of morals and ethics. It is an interesting question and of sufficient interest, in my humble opinion, for me to pass it on to my right honorable friend, the Home Secretary."

Baroness Strange: "My Lords, does not my noble friend the Minister agree that Mr. Rushdie has written for personal gain? Therefore, does he not further agree that it might be a kind gesture for Mr. Rushdie to contribute some cash from that gain to the long-suffering British public?"

The Earl of Arran: "My Lords, I can only say that that must be the opinion of my noble friend."

Lord Mellish: "My Lords, is it not time to put this matter in its proper perspective? If the police were not protecting Mr. Rushdie they would still be employed doing something else."

Under the House of Lords' quaint formality, there were several remarks that probably upset Rushdie. In apparently firmly defending the government's protection of him, the Earl of Arran said it would continue while the threat to him remained "at the current level." Later he said the police action was "appropriate in the circumstances." But what would the government consider a change in the "current level" and the "circumstances"? And what would happen then? At what "level" and in what "circumstances" would police protection be withdrawn? Rushdie's imagination, fed by the high degree of paranoia all prisoners suffer from, must have played with all kinds of answers. Would the time come, he must have wondered, when the government would suggest that he might like to spend some of his takings from *The Satanic Verses* on hiring a private security company and he would be on his own against the assassins? The cost to British taxpayers had been estimated at well over $1 million a year, but there was also the question of the effect on foreign policy. *Blitz* commented: "As Iranian demands for Rushdie to be handed over persist, the author's safety is obviously at the mercy of British government policy. Rushdie will be praying that Whitehall does not become too enthusiastic too soon about re-establishing diplomatic ties with Iran at his own expense." Most Britons interested in the Rushdie Affair insisted Rushdie couldn't be sacrificed in that way, but stranger decisions have been made in the shadowy world of politics when something has been judged profitable.

Would-be assassin groups had reportedly been trailed from the East across Europe and stopped before they could enter Britain. But some inevitably got through. Two floors of the Beverly Hills Hotel in the Paddington area of London were destroyed in early August when a Middle-Eastern visitor on a French passport apparently blew himself up while priming a powerful device. The Organization of the Strugglers of Islam claimed his mission was to kill Rushdie. Other groups boasted that they, too, had teams on the way with a similar mission. British extremist groups caused sporadic violence through the summer of 1989. As none of these hunters could locate Rushdie, crude arson and bombing attacks were made against several bookstores, the most serious being outside the Liberty department store in central London in September when a woman passerby was seriously injured in a bomb explosion.

Death threats were also renewed against Egypt's Nobel Prize-winning novelist, Naguib Mahfouz. As *Newsweek* reported, Islamic scholars had long ago banned his allegorical account of Muhammad, Jesus and Moses wandering through contemporary Cairo, and "now in a new age of Islamic intolerance, Mahfouz, like Salman Rushdie, has been singled out for death by fanatic preachers." But at seventy-eight, thirty years older than Rushdie, the Nobel laureate seemed unconcerned as he continued his daily routine in the same flat by the Nile he had lived in for much of his life. He didn't worry about the fundamentalists, noted *Newsweek*, and he refused to have bodyguards unlike Rushdie. "At my age, a threat of death is not really that frightening," said the old Egyptian writer. "I might receive a threat on Sunday and die on Monday of natural causes." The death threats against him received little publicity outside Egypt. Unlike Rushdie, he didn't find himself boosted into international bestsellerdom. The fact that an American edition of *Palace Walk*, the first volume of his great Cairo Trilogy, was being published was due to the interest in his writing stimulated by the Nobel Prize, not the death threats.

There was obvious envy on the part of many writers of Rushdie's worldwide fame (and notoriety) and the huge sales of *The Satanic Verses*, but none of them would have been willing to change places with him. A young Indian writer told me, "I have been horrified by the jealousy expressed by many older writers who have never had anything but a small Indian readership. Salman Rushdie made a lot of enemies among them, notably by his success but also by his criticism of what was happening in India, making no attempt to flatter or please. They often take the attitude that 'It serves him right.' Some of Rushdie's novel offends my religious feelings. I think he went too far, but since listening to the response of some Indian writers, I think we needed to be awakened to the fact there is more than one opinion in the world and everyone has a right to their own. The world needs free-thinking writers to teach us this every few years in case we forget it."

September meant it was a year since Rushdie's novel had been published in Britain. The paperback edition of a popular novel was usually published a year after the hardback, so Viking-Penguin faced a barrage of inquiries from the international media as to why no paperback edition of *The Satanic Verses* had appeared and, according to bookstores, had not yet even been announced. Elusive Peter Mayer insisted in New York that a paperback edition would be published eventually, but he couldn't say exactly when. After all, the hardcover edition was still selling briskly. Rushdie and Andrew Wylie were reportedly in touch with Mayer about it, trying to get a commitment to a definite publication date for the paperback in the very near future. There were rumors of an angry disagreement between the beleagured publisher and author in hiding, but both denied it.

The regular public readings from *The Satanic Verses* proposed by some American writers came to nothing, but comedians such as TV talk show host, Johnny Carson, felt free to make jokes about the novel with all kinds of play on the title, about Rushdie himself and his role as invisible man, and even the Ayatollah. There were very occasional Muslim outbursts in the United States, but the real action was in Britain where there were continual reports that Rushdie had been seen—in Covent Garden, in Oxford, and even in Scotland—and rumors that more terrorist groups had sneaked into Britain hunting him. During a visit to China, the Ayatollah's successor, Ayatollah Ali Khamenei, confirmed the death threat was still in force—"This is a bullet for which there is a target. It has been shot. It will one day sooner or later hit the target."

But to militant Muslims in Britain, it seemed to be a case of much "later" if ever. The more moderate Muslims were increasingly being heard from, condemning Rushdie's novel but also rejecting the death sentence. The militants needed to reassert their dominance with some kind of effective action, but further attempts to bring Rushdie to trial in London on blasphemy charges failed again. The knowledge that Rushdie was somewhere close by, perhaps in the center of London only a few miles away from the headquarters of some Muslim organizations, acted as a continual irritant for the extremists. It was like a parody of *The Scarlet Pimpernel*—They seek him here, they seek him there. Those Muslims seek him everywhere. Is he in heaven? Is he in hell? That demmed, elusive Rushdie! But the author in his latest hiding place, watching television devotedly for the latest developments, would hardly have appreciated the humor of that.

The difficulty of his situation was that he was caught in the middle of a unique event. There were no precedents to guide him as to what his fate was likely to be. "Nothing on the scale of this controversy," as he was to point out himself, "has to my knowledge ever happened in the history of literature." The next development could happen anywhere in the world where there was a Muslim community. Of course, he lived constantly with the nightmare of assassins invading his latest hiding place with no warning, but there were possible shocks for him from almost any country. He kept waiting for some positive change in Iran, but so far there was still no sign of it.

The next move came in New York where John F. Baker, the respected editor-in-chief of *Publishers Weekly*, wrote an editorial urging Viking-Penguin to give up any plans for a paperback edition. "It seems to us," Baker commented, "that, as a sober decision taken on the purely economic merits of the case—the question of freedom of expression no longer being at issue—Penguin would be well advised to consider honor satisfied at this point, and to do its best to resume a normal life: without a paperback."

A recent informal survey of American booksellers had indicated that despite their fears, they were anxious to have a paperback version to sell—as much for the principle as for the potential profit. But, wrote Baker, American booksellers had not suffered anything like British booksellers. "And it is safe to say that nobody, other than the author himself, has suffered the kind of disruptions that Penguin has during much of the past year, with its executives and personnel distracted and obsessed by the threats that continue to loom, and the burden of the enormous security costs."

Normally, a paperback version followed a successful hardcover, "but nothing about this publication is normal, and to publish a paperback of *The Satanic Verses* is an appallingly difficult decision." Certainly it maintained freedom of the press under threat, "but so does keeping the hardcover in print and available." Baker added that hopes that the threat would eventually just fade away and everything could proceed normally had been dashed by recent events in Britain—"There is no doubt that real dangers still exist." Could a major publisher like Viking-Penguin continue indefinitely to have its energies dissipated, its focus blurred, by one overriding preoccupation? And what about the moderate Muslims whose feelings had been hurt by the book but had not marched or threatened—were their patience and restraint to be rewarded by a paperback edition that would get the offending book to a much bigger audience and act as a further incitement? The issues were so controversial that members of the *Publishers Weekly* staff couldn't agree on a common position any more than London's *Bookseller* and *Publishing News* could, and it was easy to imagine similar arguments among Penguin executives.

Baker's editorial was widely discussed on both sides of the Atlantic, praised and condemned but above all argued over. The Authors' Guild in New York stated that if Viking-Penguin didn't publish a paperback, it would be "breaking faith with authors everywhere." An official of Media Coalition in New York wrote to *Publishers Weekly* that the "terrorists" threatening Rushdie would consider it a victory if Penguin didn't publish a paperback. It would only encourage more terrorism against authors, publishers and booksellers. Officials of Academy Chicago Publishers Ltd. backed Baker and wanted to know how many members of the Authors' Guild were willing to stand at the paperback racks in cities with large Muslim populations—"We're talking about literal war here, not some peaceful, if acrimonious, literary battle fought in the press." They denied Muslims would consider cancelling the paperback a victory. "The offense they feel—backed up by far too much violence already—is a strain they will wear like stigmata. It's hardly worth our helping them glorify their extremism with further trouble."

This was only the beginning. The paperback controversy erupted all over again, a welcome outlet for all the accumulating frustrations on both sides. Once more, all the arguments for and against *The Satanic Verses* were aired and brought up to date.

In Britain, Muslim leaders were soon heard from. Shabbir Akhtar, a member of the Bradford Council of Mosques and the author of a short broadside about the Rushdie Affair, *Be Careful with Muhammad!*, wrote in *The Independent* that "if Rushdie decides to cancel the paperback and engage in a dialogue with people whom he thus far contemptuously dismissed as ignorant and anti-intellectual, there is scope for reconciliation. All Muslims look forward to the end of the Liberal Inquisition. Islam is a religion of militant wrath as well as conspicuous mercy. The magnanimity which has been denied to both parties may yet seek an occasion." He added that a paperback "would fuel extremism in the Muslim camp. There may even be acts of political terrorism. It will be seen as a further provocation to Muslim sensibilities already severely bruised. There have been two dozen Muslim deaths already. After the death threat, Rushdie admittedly has no chance of resuming a normal life. But those who are dead have no chance of resuming any kind of life. It is not self-evident that an author's right to publish whatever he pleases takes priority over the right of Muslims to live with dignity as believers."

*Rushdie admittedly has no chance of resuming a normal life—*that couldn't have made encouraging reading for Rushdie, but at least the controversy was at an intellectual level, which was more promising if it could be kept there.

Hugo Young was critical in *The Guardian*. He found "the greatest free speech issue of 1989" was a "dialogue of the deaf." Author and publisher didn't pay attention to moderate Muslims who wanted it stressed that the book was fiction and not a history of Islam. The fundamentalists then continued the "non-dialogue" with their public protests, demands and threats. An author, whose work was not in print to the extent of far more than a million copies and in at least fourteen languages, could hardly be said to be "laboring under the cruel imposition of forced silence." Regarding the paperback, Young suggested it would be magnanimous for Rushdie to ask himself quite how entitled he was to insist on risking other lives than his own for the sake of a principle which in this case had long since ceased to be imperilled.

Liz Calder, Rushdie's first editor whom he dropped, was in favor of a paperback, but thought that to take some of the pressure off Penguin, it could be published, as in Germany, by a group of publishers. Playwright Arthur Miller suggested "a consortium of all the major British and American publishers." Writer Julian Barnes said if Penguin didn't publish a paperback, then the British Government, who lectured people smugly about not bowing to political intimidation, should publish it through Her Majesty's Stationery Office.

The Observer reported that a secret date for publication of a paperback edition had been agreed on, but for security reasons Penguin was not revealing when it was, though it was likely to be no later than early in 1990. Penguin quickly denied that any date had been fixed and that its plans remained the same—a paperback edition would be published when it would not endanger Penguin's staff and the bookstores.

Rushdie let it be known through literary editor Blake Morrison of *The Observer* and later *The Independent*, that he was still hopeful Penguin would publish a paperback. Allowing for some "ups and downs" and considering the "incredible pressure" of the fear campaign, "our relationship is very good." It had been suggested he should insert a prefatory note pointing out the book was a work of fiction, not a study of Islam. "I've no strong feelings about this," but it apparently seemed unnecessary to him as the book was already identified as a work of fiction on the hardcover jacket and it was impossible to read even the first page without knowing it was a novel.

Rushdie also had no strong feelings about the suggestion that a consortium should publish the paperback. If Penguin wanted that, it would be "acceptable to me." But as for the proposal that the paperback should be dropped as a peace gesture of some kind, "it's not me who is waging the war." There was also the point that as the book had been originally published in paperback in countries like France and Spain, a paperback edition already existed. But the real point was that for everyone except hardback publishers, the major publication of a book was its paperback edition. It was the only way to keep a book in print for any length of time, the only way it could receive the judgment of posterity and be studied in colleges, "and any book that's been involved in a controversy on this scale should be studied—already some Islamic scholars have defended my book and it's important that that process continues."

His main reason for wanting the paperback was to prevent his book from being banned "by the back door." If in a few years' time the paperback didn't exist, the book simply wouldn't be there for anyone who wanted to read it. "It will, in all practical terms, have been suppressed."

Rushdie was right, of course, that paperback editions already existed in some other languages. His friend, writer Tariq Ali, was also concerned at the black market price in the Muslim world that had banned the book. He pointed out that a paperback would stop the "appalling un-Islamic activity" by which a hardback edition cost $100 in Pakistan, Kuwait, and Dubai. But the irony of the often heated arguments about an English language paperback was that Penguin had already secretly printed a paperback edition as a weapon against pirate editions, according to the London *Observer*. Most of these paperbacks were eventually pulped and only a few dozen copies were inadvertently sold and became an instant collectors' item.

The Observer quoted a Penguin spokesman as stating "We wanted to have them available so that they could be sent to India if a pirate edition appeared there." This apparently was before the Indian government banned the book and Penguin executives then decided to pulp the books, but through an office error, 1,300 copies were shipped to European distributors. "We were asked to send them all back," said a Maltese distributor, but by then a few dozen copies had been sold in Malta and Switzerland.

There had also been a quality trade paperback already from the Quality Paperback Book Club, a division of the Book-of-the-Month Club in New York, but priced at $9.95, or roughly half the hardcover price, it was not a cheap mass market paperback and was available only to members.

So the paperback situation was still murky—it was still part of Viking-Penguin's future plans, but that was all Peter Mayer and his beleagured staff were admitting. "It's not a matter of *whether* we shall publish but of *when*," Mayer told his senior staff. "I'm not prepared to publish a book that will put lives at risk." Viking-Penguin's staff and their families in London, New York, and cities in several other countries had to live in a continually intimidating atmosphere. Security was heavy even by the standards of American presidents, with twenty-four-hour police surveillance, bomb curtains in their sitting rooms, and children escorted to and from school.

Peter Mayer was still the only Viking-Penguin name widely known—the only identifiable target—so when a newspaper reporter in a story named two senior members of the company who had helped to handle *The Satanic Verses* and had not been publicly identified before, there was "a terrible effect on the company," according to an insider. Protection had to be immediately extended to cover staff members who had not been guarded before. The cost for this widespread private security went up and up for Viking-Penguin and was reportedly well over $3 million a year, more than the company's profits from *The Satanic Verses*. Peter Mayer was in danger of losing his gamble on the book.

In Rushdie's more paranoid moments, he must have wondered, as he did about the British government's similarly large security expenses for him, whether Viking-Penguin would eventually decide it couldn't afford to go on like that. At the rate of over $3 million a year, how long would it take the company to go bankrupt? But there was no sign of such an attitude in Peter Mayer's occasional friendly, supportive public statements about him. An anonymously written profile of Mayer in *The Independent* suggested, for example, that Rushdie had deceived his publishers over the meaning of certain passages in his novel. The anonymous writer claimed that "Rushdie was asked twice, once before Penguin bought the book and again afterwards, what the now notorious Mahound chapter was supposed to mean. He seemed curiously reluctant to explain. 'Don't worry,' he said at one point. 'It's not terribly important to the plot'."

Rushdie wrote indignantly to *The Independent*: "I am acutely conscious of Peter Mayer's present anguish, as I'm sure he is of mine. It is therefore disheartening to find your anonymous profile writer attempting to make things worse." He'd like to think that *The Independent*'s readers found the description of his present situation ("Still in hiding and with nothing to lose") more than a little distasteful. Leaving such matters to their good judgment, he would comment only on the most blatant untruth in the piece.

After quoting the passage about his being asked about the Mahound chapter, Rushdie commented, "This passage is a lie. As Penguin editorial staff in London and New York know, I discussed the background to *The Satanic Verses* fully, answering all questions. That I failed to anticipate the distortions and falsifications to which my novel was subsequently subjected is another matter. That I might have said that some seventy-five pages of the novel (two notorious chapters, not one) were 'not terribly important to the plot' is simply risible.

"The implication that I deceived Viking-Penguin is wholly unjustified, and, in the present circumstances, injurious. Character assassination is also a sort of murder."

When this exchange was reported in *The New York Times*, Peter Mayer wrote to that paper: "It has been of concern to me that a number of people still believe that Salman Rushdie had in some sense deceived Viking-Penguin about sections of his novel that have subsequently proved contentious. None of us at Viking-Penguin believe that Salman made any attempt to mislead us. Nor do we believe he or we could have anticipated the furious and distorted response to which his novel has been subjected."

The New York Times headed the letter: "No Blame to Rushdie."

Rushdie and Mayer were not only in disagreement over the paperback, but also over the value of publicity. Mayer, according to a report by Bharati Mukherjie and her husband, Clark Blaise, in *Mother Jones*, believed that "all media attention has been harmful. It has kept the pot boiling." Rushdie himself realized that he needed "thing's said in my support." While he was under the spotlight, he would receive official protection and be as safe as possible. Without all the media attention, he would quickly be forgotten and left to his fate.

9—FIRST ANNIVERSARY

NOTHING MUCH HAD BEEN HEARD FROM MARIANNE WIGGINS WHILE SHE WAS in hiding with Rushdie. Even the predictions that the marriage would break up soon had been dropped when no evidence was available. Then suddenly in late summer, her British publisher, Secker and Warburg, released a statement from her with the news that she had been living apart from her husband for the last four weeks.

No reason for the separation was given, but the statement added, "Scotland Yard security arrangements for the protection of Mr. Rushdie have been reordered since then and Ms. Wiggins does not know where he is." That presumably was to prevent any would-be assassins from pursuing her to learn Rushdie's current address.

The statement ended: "Ms. Wiggins requests privacy. She is not prepared to discuss the matter further."

A spokesman for her publisher said, "We have no idea of her whereabouts or of her future actions. Nobody knows where she is or what she will be doing." A Scotland Yard official declined to say if separate protection was being provided for her.

The gossip columnists on both sides of the Atlantic crowed, I told you so. Some of them had reported that the marriage was in trouble even before the Rushdies went into hiding. Cindy Adams in *The New York Post* claimed that Marianne Wiggins had "returned to him" just before the Ayatollah's death sentence. "The Rushdies have split before," she remarked, "but at this moment they're stuck like Krazy Glue." Well, apparently they weren't if her publisher's statement was telling the whole truth.

There were countless analyses of the negative effects on the marriage when the couple was isolated together for so long without a settled home. There were also rather bitchy suggestions that it had been hard on Marianne Wiggins to watch Rushdie getting all the attention. Her novel, *John Dollar*, had quickly been forgotten in the fuss over *The Satanic Verses*. Few of the media reports of Rushdie's activities in hiding ever mentioned her. Presumably, when Rushdie was reported to have dined secretly with friends, she was there, too, but most reports never bothered to say so.

But on her own now, she began to assert her separate identity as a writer. She arranged with Harper and Row to bring out a collection of short stories in the United States late in 1990, entitled *Learning Urdu*. On a seven-city tour of the U.S. to promote the paperback of *John Dollar*, she said she and her husband learned what the effects of enormous isolation extended over a lengthy period of time could do to their relationship. She was now back in the world without protection. The U.S. government hadn't offered any, but then she hadn't been threatened. Her next novel was to be about Thomas Jefferson and the Bill of Rights. She didn't plan to write anything about her life in hiding. "So much of the information is classified that I don't have the freedom to do it, and also I want to have some part of my life that isn't known."

She informed interviewers that she and Rushdie had moved fifty-six times since the Ayatollah's death sentence. They had slept in more than fifty different beds in half as many weeks. MI5, the British Government's domestic counter-intelligence agency, was known to have some fine country houses, and there was speculation as to whether some of these mansions were included as the Rushdies' overnight stopping places. The cooking, like the wine, was said to be worthy of the elitist intelligence service, and the Rushdies were depicted as living like country squires against a background of infra-red cameras, fierce guard dogs, and endless armed patrols. Marianne Wiggins was not willing to discuss the security side of her experience because it might still affect Salman.

"The thing about this situation," she said, "is that one is

completely of good health and yet living the life of a paranoid schizophrenic." About the death sentence, she remarked, "We only talk about that during very intimate moments." She and her husband were keeping diaries, she said, and they stayed in touch with their families and with world events, and always had at least one armed guard with them. Their occasional dinner guests included people like Neil Kinnock, leader of the Labor Party, but these occasions had become fewer at the insistence of their guards.

She had given Salman an ornate candlestick on their first wedding anniversary, but it was difficult to give each other presents "in limbo." But when in interviews she was constantly asked about Rushdie, she sometimes responded impatiently, pointing out, "I'm here to talk about *my* book," adding that "It seems I have got to defend the fact that before all this I was already a very highly known writer in the United States where Salman was never a big seller until *Satanic Verses*."

Her separation from her husband was carefully organized. For a month she was hidden away alone while Rushdie was moved twice so the trail would go completely cold. "And then I was free." She obviously thought she had nothing to fear personally. Unguarded, she went to Amsterdam, to the Berlin Wall (she brought back a piece of it), and all over London—trips her husband yearned to take. "Rip Van Winkle's wonder at the world has nothing over mine as I move unseen and ghost-like through this city that I loved enough to leave my country for"—like Rushdie, too. She couldn't disassociate herself from the history of *The Satanic Verses* much as she wanted her own career. "But I am not tied in any way to its production. It is his book, no other mind produced that wonder." She had a delayed reaction to being free. "I would stop on the street and just have the weeps. This brilliant man is removed from society. And I could only imagine him now, just as our friends have had to."

All the media's sympathy seemed to be with Rushdie. He was truly alone at last. He was pictured staring at a TV set for hours in silence like a gloomy statue or desperately trying to make conversation with his guards. There was gossip that he had become so tense and nervously irritable as to be unbearable to live with and had finally driven her away.

But such gossip was stopped by further revelations from Marianne Wiggins, who corrected the impression that they were heading for a divorce. In an interview with the British *Mail on Sunday*, she stated that they had mutually decided that she could resume something of a public existence. "I have become his foreign correspondent sending dispatches back," she said.

She spoke emotionally of their three extraordinary years: one year living together, one year of marriage, one year in limbo. Their happiest time was when, with the synchronicity of true minds, they both finished their books in the same week: one destined to obscure the other. They went off at once to honeymoon in Mauritius. They still communicated, believing in the erotic power of correspondence.

She told *The New York Times* the marriage was "intact" and that she missed her husband "like crazy." She intended to settle in London because "my emotional center is there although I don't know where he is. "As soon—when, if, ever—as the circumstances change, we'll pick up the pieces and go forward."

As if to add to the confusion, she published a magazine article in *The Tatler* about Valentine's Day, the time for your loved one, and she wrote very obliquely and ambiguously about the Rushdie Affair. "Most people live and die alone," she wrote, "so let's be fools for love for one day of the year." Her only reference to her recent experiences was a vague, offhand "Having lived what I've lived through" and an even vaguer remark, "Talk about your fundamentalism" (perhaps joking Rushdie that he wasn't the only one to suffer from fundamentalists as her father had been one, too). She called the article "My Funny Valentine." For all it revealed to readers, she might have been communicating with Rushdie alone in some personal code of their own. She even quoted a song about someone with laughable looks that sounded like an echo of Rushdie's own jokes about his nose. *The Guardian* called it a "peculiar" Valentine to him.

Rushdie published some new writing of his own, not a Valentine but a short poem describing his state of mind. He called the seventeen lines "6 March 1989." His friend, Bill Buford, editor of the Cambridge literary magazine, *Granta*, suggested the title referred to when he wrote it. But when the poem came quite unexpectedly to *Granta* with no message from Rushdie beforehand, it was four months later.

Rushdie was friendly with Buford, and with Mario Varga Llosa, he had accompanied the *Granta* editor to his first game of soccer, which became one of his great passions. *Granta* had not only a Cambridge connection which was appealing to Rushdie, but it had become a platform for literary London's latest stars and was backed by Viking-Penguin. Rushdie had published essays in *Granta* to clear his mind while he was working on *The Satanic Verses*. In one essay entitled "Outside the Whale," Rushdie claimed "the modern world lacks not only hiding places but certainties," which later seemed yet another of his prophetic pronouncements.

His poem described his thoughts in hiding, especially about such enemies as the sixties pop singer Cat Stevens, who under his new Muslim name of Yusuf Islam supported the Ayatollah's death sentence. Rushdie called him "the Cat." The poem referred to the insulting descriptions of Rushdie, such as opportunist, self-aggrandizer and Satan, and to the hanging of his effigy. If "the Cat" got his tongue, Muftis, politicos, his "own people" and hacks would rejoice. But he had no intention of being silenced in that way. He declared:

"... here's my choice:
not to shut up. To sing on, in spite of attacks."

The London *Daily Mail* headlined its account of the poem's publication: *Rushdie the Poet Defies Muslim Fanatics*. But, although the poem's conclusion was upbeat, Rushdie's general tone was rather melancholy, obsessed in its concentration on his enemies' attempt to destroy his good name and end his life. That was surely understandable, but suggested he was beginning to feel the great strain he had been under all these months.

Rushdie also still wrote occasional book reviews that inevitably reflected the life he was living. He paid tribute in one review to his friend, the late Raymond Carver, the American short story writer and poet, who had survived alcoholism only to be felled by lung cancer after years of heavy smoking. In reviewing Carver's posthumous poetry collection, *A New Path to the Waterfall*, Rushdie recalled a memorial meeting after Carver's death held in "some suitably 'high tacky' club" in London a couple of months before he went into hiding. "A bunch of us" read out pieces for and by Carver, and at one moment Rushdie remembered looking along his row "and the truth is we were all blubbering, or close to it, except for Ray's widow, the poet Tess Gallagher, who reminded me of my grandmother refusing tears after my grandfather died."

Rushdie drew attention to a poem of Carver's entitled "My Wife" in which a wife had left him, and "We find the idea of having to 'account for' one's life." Was that what had occupied Rushdie's thoughts over the last year? "Many of Carver's poems seem to use narration as a process of arriving at a profit-and-loss understanding of life, complete with bottom line." Another poem described a doctor's death sentence ("He said it doesn't look good") that perhaps reminded Rushdie of the Ayatollah's fatwa. Rushdie summed up that Carver's death was "hard to accept, but at least he had lived." Throughout his review, there was an eerie sense of Rushdie hearing echoes of his own situation, a reflection of his obsessed state of mind.

A review of Thomas Pynchon's *Vineland*, the American writer's first novel for seventeen years, which Rushdie wrote for *The New York Times Book Review*, pointed out the resemblance to his own life much more directly. Pynchon had influenced Rushdie's writing and had written in his support after the Ayatollah's death sentence. But the two writers had never met. Pynchon lived a secret life, turning down any kind of publicity, refusing to be photographed and not even letting people know where he lived. He was often compared to J. D. Salinger, who had retired to New England to live a completely private life as far as the media would let him. The main difference was that Pynchon continued to publish books whereas Salinger didn't, though he was apparently still writing.

Rushdie called Pynchon the "old Invisible Man," a nickname they shared. "One thing that has not changed about Mr. P. is his love of mystification," wrote Rushdie. "The secrecy surrounding the publication of this book—his first novel since *Gravity's Rainbow* in 1973—has been, let's face it, ridiculous. I mean, *rilly*. So he wants a private life and no photographs and nobody to know his home address. I can dig it, I can relate to that (but, like, he should try it when it's compulsory instead of a free-choice option)."

He should try it when it's compulsory—once more Rushdie referred to his own situation. He also found rampant paranoia in Pynchon's writing—"The shadowy invisible forces, the true Master of the Universe" were behind everything—but there was something new to report about Pynchon, some faint possibility of redemption, some fleeting hints of happiness and grace. Pynchon "like Paul Simon's girl in New York City, who called herself the Human Trampoline"—this was Rushdie showing off his hipness in hiding—was bouncing into Graceland. Was Rushdie, a changed man perhaps, too, also bouncing there? He summed up *Vineland* the way many people summed up *The Satanic Verses*: "It either grabs you or it doesn't, I guess. It grabbed me. I laughed, many times, out loud." Like Raymond Carver, Pynchon to him was "one of American's great writers."

As he was writing for American readers, he couldn't resist poking fun at some old targets. It was interesting, he wrote, to have in *Vineland* at the end of the "Greed Decade" that rarest of birds: a major political novel about what America had been doing to itself, to its children, all these many years. And most interesting of all was that hint of redemption suggesting that community, individuality and family might be counterweights to power. "These are values the Nixon-Reagan era stole from the sixties and warped, aiming them back at America as weapons of control."

It was such biting remarks against conservative targets that made *The Guardian* comment that Rushdie's political commitment on the Left was intact and active. But many Rushdie readers were far more inclined to think of his personal predicament than his political stance. Typical was *The New Yorker*'s view of the Rushdie Affair in terms of "our interconnectedness." When we imagined Rushdie writing *The Satanic Verses*, "we visualize a normal-scale human being, part of a society of equals in which he is participating by sharing his thoughts and feelings—the very stuff of interconnectedness. But with this explosion of murderous intolerance he has had to disappear, and in his disappearance he seems tiny, silenced, and, above all, isolated. That isolation by terror from the rest of humanity is in itself a kind of death sentence."

*   *   *

There was a new round of rumors that Rushdie had been seen in London, the Scottish Highlands, and even Bradford, where no assassin would think of looking for him among the militant Muslims. He was compared to the Loch Ness monster, which was forever being seen if only in people's imaginations, but was never found.

When Gabriel Garcia Marquez wrote a too-realistic portrait of Simon Bolivar, the Great Liberator of Latin America's struggle for independence, the bitter attacks were compared to the Rushdie Affair. *The New York Times* reported that "Thus far, however, the controversy has fallen short of the heights of passion reached in the Islamic world following the publication of Salman Rushdie's *Satanic Verses*. No one has yet threatened Mr. Garcia Marquez's life, but he recalled the Rushdie case in replying to those who have accused him of blasphemy or unpatriotic conduct." Defending his novel, *The General in the Labyrinth*, Garcia Marquez said, "The real crime against the nation, against its health and destiny, is to satanize a book and condemn its author. That is what other ayatollahs are doing to instigate regional rivalries and border discord in a country that so urgently needs peace and calming reflection." Following Rushdie's example, he spent several weeks at a hideout in Cuba, out of reach of his angry critics and the media. Asked for an interview, he told a reporter cautiously, "Maybe next year." There was also another resemblance to the Rushdie Affair. The curse words that his Simon Bolivar used and that had so offended purists came from three years of preliminary research into thousands of letters and historical accounts—which recalled Rushdie's defense of his portrayal of Mahound in *The Satanic Verses* that he said was based on extensive research during his Cambridge days.

Two books about aspects of the Rushdie Affair ran into trouble with publishers, recalling the predictions of its "chilling effect" on anything to do with Islam. Collins in London signed a contract for a book entitled *The Rushdie Dossier*, a collection of media reports edited by Rushdie's friend, Lisa Appignanesi, and Sara Maitland. Hilary Rubinstein, the agent involved, claimed Collins had already accepted the typescript enthusiastically "and then got cold feet." He added, "First we were told that the book might exacerbate problems for Penguin, but when Penguin's managing director, Trevor Glover, phoned Collins to say that he could have no objection to the book's publication, they shifted their ground and said that they had taken soundings from leading booksellers and wholesalers and were convinced that the bookshops wouldn't back the work. Their grounds for abandoning the book were, we were told, purely commercial. Now they say it was insufficiently objective, though that is the first time such a charge has been made." Collins insisted their decision was based solely on commercial considerations. The Fourth Estate eventually published the book in Britain as *The Rushdie File*. In the United States when commercial publishers turned it down, Syracuse University published it. It was a book of record rather than a contributor to what *The Listener* in London called the "battle still vociferously joined."

Another book contract concerning Rushdie was also cancelled, this time in the United States. Basic Books, a subsidiary of Harper and Row, part of the News Corporation owned by Australian billionaire Rupert Murdoch (who also owned Collins), signed scholar Daniel Pipes, director of the Foreign Policy Research Institute in Philadelphia, to write a book exploring why *The Satanic Verses* had prompted such intense reactions. Pipes, the author of three books on the Middle East, submitted a manuscript entitled *The Ayatollah, The Novelist and the West*, and was informed that it was rejected. A spokesman for Harper and Row said the contract had been cancelled because the marketing department concluded the book would not be profitable. He denied that Harper and Row had any prohibition against books about Islam or the Rushdie Affair. Birch Lane Press, a new publishing company, then accepted the book, which was given a new title of *The Rushdie Affair—the Ayatollah, the Novelist and the West*. Defending his book in a newspaper article, Daniel Pipes argued that "Not only do Salman Rushdie's life and career remain upended," but free speech remained imperilled in "a host of ways, large and small, in distant places and at home." His many examples ranged over much of the world from Austrian students who were refused permission to read from *The Satanic Verses* on university grounds to a Pakistani woman television rock singer who was harassed by Muslim fundamentalists and commented, "Everything in Pakistan, even the way you sing a song, is highly politicized now."

When the young Japanese British novelist, Kazuo Ishiguro, won the twenty-first Booker Prize for his short novel, *The Remains of the Day*, about an old English butler, he thanked his agent, Deborah Rogers, once Rushdie's agent, and his editor at Fabers, Robert McCrum, and paid tribute to Rushdie. "It would be improper for us not to remember him this evening, and think about the alarming significance of the plight he is in." In the advertisements for *The Remains of the Day*, praise from Rushdie was quoted: "A brilliant subversion of the fictional modes from which it at first seems to descend ... A story both beautiful and cruel." At least Rushdie and John le Carré could agree over this novel because there was also a plug from le Carré: "A diamond of a book, perfectly cut, with splendid and uncountable facets, deceptively modest." There were suggestions, however, that the Booker shortlist had exemplified a "middlebrow conspiracy" against innovation, intelligence and imagination, and that it stressed the adventurousness of a novel like *The Satanic Verses.*

As the first anniversary of Rushdie's disappearance approached, the media prepared to commemorate it and try to show whether Rushdie had been changed by his experiences.

When Dostoevski escaped the firing squad, he was profoundly affected for the rest of his life by this near encounter with death. He wrote in *Crime and Punishment* that someone condemned to death thinks "If he had to remain standing on a few square inches of space for a thousand years or all eternity, it would be better to live than to die. Only to live, to live, to live, no matter how." After coming out of prison in Siberia, Dostoevski was a changed man, becoming an outspoken conservative, a staunch supporter of the Czarist regime, and the Russian Orthodox Church, and suffering from epilepsy.

Had Salman Rushdie been affected as deeply?

Although the anniversary was not until the middle of February, *The Guardian* began early by interviewing his friends in January. John Cunningham wrote that "even his friends, consoled by his strength and integrity, say his success contained self-souring elements. Hanif Kureishi says 'He's been like a brother to me. At the same time he's tough and prickly. He seems to know about everything: he's read everything.' "

Cunningham discovered that a friend of Rushdie's left messages for him with a telephone answering service. The friend refused to give the answering service's number, but agreed to leave a message asking Rushdie to phone *The Guardian*. A few days later Cunningham's phone rang. It was Rushdie, and "for the first time since he went into hiding, Rushdie allowed the contents of a conversation to be reported."

Rushdie made it clear he wouldn't say anything about whether the Special Branch considered his situation any less dangerous beyond commenting: "You shouldn't assume that I have very much freedom at all."

As for the effect of the last year, Rushdie said, "It would be impossible not to be affected by this degree of hostility, which is totally misplaced. I am not the enemy of my own people. I do not feel like the enemy of my people." He added, "I don't think one is as self-sufficient as all that. I'm very grateful for all the support I've received. It's nice to know that there is something other than anger aimed at one. I do get a great many letters of support, including some from Muslims who've read the book."

He saw no end to his plight as he neared the first anniversary. "One would wish a thing to come to an end. But I'm not the maker of the problem. I think if some of the people who protested about the book took the trouble to read it, they would see that it is not unsympathetic to them. The main characters are British Muslims and they are not treated unsympathetically." There was no question of backing down or withdrawing the book or going to another country where he would be no more safe from the Islamic threats. "One of the things this has shown is that the world is very small."

The Guardian asked Dr. James Thompson, senior lecturer in psychology at London University, about the possible effects on Rushdie. Anyone faced with a death threat, said Dr. Thompson, would be fearful and anxious, in a heightened state of vigilance, with all that putting a strain on relationships. "My feeling, without knowing Mr. Rushdie at all, is that someone in his position would be showing anxiety responses which I would see more strongly in cases of post-traumatic stress disorder."

The Observer also consulted a psychologist—Dr. John Potter, who advised business corporations on kidnap victims. Dr. Potter said, "He is likely to be affected by paranoia, becoming worried by shadows and noises. His wife's decision to leave him must have created unbearable stresses. No doubt he communicates by telephone with his friends, but he has lost a great deal by seldom being able to talk to them face-to-face. Body language is very important." Dr. Potter added that Rushdie was "a strong character who will find it very difficult to make any concessions. In a life-threatening situation, he will see these as a sign of weakness, especially with few people around him to bounce ideas off."

But Viking-Penguin sources quoted by *The Observer* suggested Rushdie was showing the effects of his grim experience in their dealings with him. "Our relations with Salman are strained," said one Penguin source. "It's impossible to have a normal conversation with him. He's become totally obsessed with the need to go ahead and publish the paperback now. He can talk about no other topic."

Friends also told *The Guardian* they noticed a change in him, that although he *sounded* like the Salman of old—"pugnacious, amusing, completely unbowed"—events had marked him "and he doesn't talk of anything else." In discussing the paperback, Rushdie told a friend he felt that he was facing "a Conradian moment"—like the tragic hero of *Lord Jim* perhaps who had to prove his courage even if it meant losing his life. But wasn't this rather a high-flown comparison providing critics of Rushdie's ego with more ammunition?

Rushdie's friend and fellow writer, Tariq Ali, said that he had met Rushdie for "a very nice meal together far, far away from London." He refused to be more specific about the whereabouts of the meeting and the security arrangements, but he added, "I think he is in a relaxed mood." Rushdie had phoned him many times since he went into hiding and "clearly doesn't like being so private and all that gets on his nerves. But in general he is in good spirits and laughing and joking and discussing everything going on in the world, as well as his own situation." He was also very excited about the children's book he was working on.

As for future prospects, Ali said, "The problem is not just the Iranian state. The problem is in Britain itself, where you have a group of fanatics who could inspire someone to do a dirty deed. I think he knows he will always have to live very carefully."

Literary editor Blake Morrison, who was regularly in touch with Rushdie about book reviews, said that although Rushdie was coping extremely well in the circumstances and showed "extraordinary resilience," his moods "fluctuate according to the situation, whether it be a new death threat or the latest position on whether the paperback edition will be published, which has been putting him under strain for weeks or months."

I phoned Andrew Wylie in New York to ask him if any decision had been reached about the paperback.

"I'm not discussing anything to do with Salman Rushdie," he said.

Not even to check facts?

"No."

According to *Blitz* magazine, Wylie had upped the advances for future Rushdie books reportedly in case Rushdie eventually had to fund his own security. Rushdie's French publisher was said to have rejected a request for an advance of over $1 million, "prompting what one observer described as a 'tantrum' on the part of Rushdie's agent." *Mother Jones* reported that Wylie wanted a $14 million advance, presumably for world English language rights, for three books—the children's fable, a new novel, and a nonfiction account of the year in hiding—but so far there had been no takers.

Perhaps the brief *Guardian* interview had shown Rushdie that he wanted to express his thoughts at greater length, to mark the first anniversary with a full defense of himself and his book. He put aside the children's story temporarily and wrote a long essay that he called *In Good Faith: Reflections on a Year of Controversy*. It was altogether seven thousand words long or about twenty pages of the average book. It was published in the *Independent on Sunday* in Britain on February 4, 1990—well before the anniversary—and on the other side of the Atlantic in the issue of *Newsweek* dated February 12.

Blake Morrison, now literary editor of the *Independent on Sunday*, had a meeting with Rushdie at a pre-arranged place arranged with Special Branch approval. They talked over cups of tea in a room with curtained windows. Rushdie looked healthy and relaxed and felt writing the long essay had lifted a burden from his shoulders. It had been the "hardest piece of writing I've ever done," he told Morrison. Rushdie said he had written the essay now because he hoped the time had come "when people would be ready to listen again." He expressed indignation that people who called publicly for his murder, even on television, were not being prosecuted. "As the object of the attack I find it upsetting," he said.

Morrison commented that Rushdie was "a far more engaging companion than newspaper profiles suggest." He seemed to have shown remarkable resilience in the face of intense psychological pressure, "but no one should doubt that he has suffered appallingly: he was always gregarious and the denial of ordinary human pleasures has been hard."

His friends agreed that the ordeal had changed him, Morrison added, and perhaps even improved him—had there at least been "the consolation of learning about himself?"

Rushdie told him: "You make the best of the situation but it doesn't mean it's a positive experience. If you'd told me in advance this and this and this is going to happen over the next year I'd not have been very confident of my ability to cope with it. You don't find out until you're in the situation whether you can stand up to it. Fortunately so far I have. But I don't recommend it. As a way of learning about yourself, there must be better ones."

Writing helped him to cope. The children's book was nearly finished, he was putting together a collection of essays, and he had the synopsis for a new novel, "one without any magic noses or cloven hooves"—the end of magic realism for him—and not likely to be politically controversial. "But then I thought *The Satanic Verses* was a personal and inward novel, not a political one—obviously that's not how it turned out. Some mistake, surely."

He had re-read *Moby Dick, Ulysses,* and *Tristram Shandy*, and a lot of poetry, including American poetry, and writers of the eighteenth-century Enlightenment such as Rousseau, Diderot, and Voltaire, "the bedrock of European free speech," who were banned, persecuted, reviled, and accused of blasphemy, too. He also continued to watch a lot of "junk television" and became "hooked" on a series called *Capital City* about yuppie bankers, which was available when "my other fixes" like *Dallas* and *Dynasty* were off the air. "Having had a lot of late nights by myself, I've also become an addict of American football."

Referring to putdowns of Rushdie as obsessive and egomaniacal, Morrison wrote that "With me, he seemed rather keen to talk about things other than his work, not least the way the world he has been removed from has changed over the past year." Especially in Eastern Europe.

Rushdie told him: "In normal circumstances, I'd have been on the first plane to Berlin and dancing on the Wall." He felt he had missed "one of the great moments of our time." He remembered when he was young in 1968, he and his friends used to talk as if some great shift in power towards the people had taken place, but actually nothing really happened. "This time it actually did happen." What was optimistic about it was that those in power seemed intelligent and restrained. It was rather heartening to find that when the people took over, they were far more reasonable than politicians. To have a serious writer like Vaclav Havel running a country like Czechoslovakia was a sign that perhaps the world was a less hopeless place than he had thought it was. I wonder if he had the same reaction to the big changes in Nicaragua and the defeat in a free election of Ortega's government that had won his support when he visited Nicaragua and wrote *The Jaguar Smile*. Of Britain, he said "It would be nice if it happened here."

Morrison asked him if his attitude toward Mrs. Thatcher ("Mrs. Torture") had changed. Yes, at a personal level his feelings toward the British government had changed, helped by the fact that the Labor Party he had supported all his life had been "vocal in the attack on me," though there had been supporters like Michael Foot. "I think better of the Tories for this trivial reason: they saved my life."

As for the future? "I have to be optimistic about that because what's the alternative: to be pessimistic, and that's not much fun. When things seem appropriate, they will happen."

Morrison summed up: "He is a very strong, some have said arrogant person, and that conviction of his own worth has helped him to get through this experience."

But had there been moments of doubt? "Every day, more than once—of course," Rushdie replied. But he had re-read *The Sa-*

tanic Verses, and he honestly believed there wasn't a sentence he couldn't justify. "I can defend my novel's shape, the images it uses, the language it develops. That's comparatively easy. What's hard is to have to defend my life."

Newsweek also published an interview with him—the first since he disappeared, Rushdie was quoted as saying, though that wasn't correct if the exchanges with *The Guardian* and Blake Morrison were counted.

The *Newsweek* interview was conducted on the phone for ninety minutes. The reporters described him as sounding "relaxed and reflective, discussing his predicament with British understatement." Asked about his wife, Rushdie said, "It's always easier when there's somebody else there. I don't really want to say a lot about Marianne, but I do think that I would like to say that of all the people who have offered me support and strength this year, nobody has offered me more than her." She had naturally "taken more of the weight of this than any other human being, and in many ways still is. So it's easier in a way being with somebody else, but you do what you have to do."

Referring to the paperback, Rushdie said there had been a lot of very malicious rumor-mongering about Penguin and him. He felt Penguin should have published the paperback a year after the hardback and they decided not to. "The fact that we have these disagreements doesn't mean that we don't like each other. I still have faith in them as my publisher." He believed that "If we do not complete the cycle of publication, we will in some sense have been defeated by the campaign against the book. I see this as an innocent book, wrongly accused and much persecuted."

Rushdie ridiculed suggestions that he might change his appearance and identity. "It would mean that I would have to cease to be a writer. I would have to cease to be everything that I am. No, that's no life. This is more of a life than that. I simply will not accept that this is going to be the rest of my life—I have to remain an optimist in the sense of believing that solutions are possible. But one of the things that this shows is that there is such a thing as being too famous."

In the seven-thousand-word *In Good Faith*, Rushdie invited "ordinary, decent, fair-minded Muslims" to reconsider his novel in a calm, reasonable atmosphere. Describing himself as "secular, pluralist, eclectic," he denied the charge of blasphemy yet again, regretted the harm done to race relations over the past year, and hoped that "the way forward might be found through mutual recognition of mutual pain."

Rushdie wrote that those who opposed the novel most vociferously thought that intermingling with a different culture would inevitably weaken and ruin their own. "I am of the opposite opinion. *The Satanic Verses* celebrates hybridity, impurity, intermingling, the transformation that comes of new and unexpected combinations of human beings, cultures, ideas, politics, movies, songs. It rejoices in mongrelisation and fears the absolutism of the Pure." Like many millions of people, "I am a bastard child of history. Perhaps we all are, black and brown and white, leaking into one another, as a character of mine once said, *like flavors when you cook.*"

Rushdie added, "What is freedom of expression? Without the freedom to challenge, even satirize all orthodoxes, including religious orthodoxes, it ceases to exist. *The Satanic Verses* is, in part, a secular man's reckoning with the religious spirit." He had said it before, but the continuing outcry showed that many people hadn't been listening.

The two books that were "most influential" on the novel's shape didn't include the Koran, wrote Rushdie. They were William Blake's "The Marriage of Heaven and Hell," a classic meditation on Good and Evil, and Mikhail Bulgakov's *The Master and the Margarita*, the great Russian comic novel in which the Devil descends on Moscow. Bulgakov was "persecuted by Soviet totalitarianism. It is extraordinary to find my novel's life echoing that of one of its greatest models."

"I am not a Muslim," Rushdie added, stressing a point he had made many times before, and therefore he didn't accept the charge of blasphemy because, as a character in *The Satanic Verses* said, "Where there is no belief, there is no blasphemy." He didn't accept the charge of apostasy because he had never as an adult affirmed any belief.

He had expected that "the use of fiction was a way of creating the sort of distance from actuality that I felt would prevent offense from being taken. I was wrong."

Would he have written differently if he had known what would happen? "Truthfully, I don't know. Would I change any of the text now? I would not. It's too late."

He paid tribute to publishing people and booksellers and to his Special Branch bodyguards—"my protectors who have done such a magnificent job and who have become my friends."

The one real gain for him in this bad time "has been the discovery of being cared for by so many people. The only antidote to hatred is love."

He felt as if he had been plunged like Alice into the world beyond the looking glass, where nonsense was the only available sense. "And I wonder if I'll ever be able to climb back through the mirror."

He added, "Please understand, however: I make no complaint. I am a writer. I do not accept my condition; I will strive to change it; but I inhabit it. I am trying to learn from it.

"Our lives teach us who we are."

That was the end of his essay—of his speech for the defense.

There was nothing to do then but wait for the Muslim reaction.

10—TO SING ON

IF SALMAN RUSHDIE EXPECTED HIS LONG ELOQUENT DEFENSE TO HAVE THE effect he wanted—to persuade his enemies to bury the hatchet and begin a reasonable exchange—he was destined to be disappointed. There was, of course, little in his essay that he had not said before he went into hiding, but he was hoping the past year had made everyone more receptive and willing to understand why he had written *The Satanic Verses*. But the general Muslim reaction was reminiscent of Sydney Smith's old joke about two women who were shouting at each other across the street from their front doorsteps. "Those two women will never agree," remarked Sydney Smith, "because they're arguing from different premises." So it still was with Salman Rushdie and his Muslim critics.

Newsweek's readers were typical, being split between those who saw hope for Rushdie—"If the Berlin Wall can crumble," wrote one woman, "then there is hope for all impossible situations" —and those who thought Rushdie lived in "a hell of his own construction." Even an editorial in the friendly *Independent on Sunday*, headed "A Time for Reason," was not too encouraging, suggesting that Rushdie's effort might not be enough. "If he could find some way, in addition to the writing of this essay, of making a conciliatory gesture towards the Muslim community, it would not compromise either the freedom to publish or his role as an artist."

Tariq Modood, a Fellow in politics at University College, Swansea, described the reasons for the mixed Muslim reception. He wrote in the *Independent* that the tone of Rushdie's essay was "unreservedly to be welcomed. It is a tone which is absent from *The Satanic Verses*, absent from Mr Rushdie's dismissal of Muslim petitions and incompatible with the demand to bring out the paperback." But that incompatibility would "nullify the good that Mr. Rushdie seeks to do with the essay."

Several Muslim leaders in Britain said Rushdie's public defense would only inflame Muslim anger. Liaqat Hussain, the general secretary of the Bradford Council of Mosques, accused Rushdie of being "arrogant and ignorant" over his book and called on him to come out of hiding and defend *The Satanic Verses* in person "even if that means losing his life." Sayed Abdul Quddus, president of the Al Mujahid movement for the protection of Islam, said, "Only if the book is banned and the British government extends the blasphemy laws will there be a way of getting this problem solved. Rushdie should be tried in this country or taken to a Muslim country and tried according to Islamic law."

In Iran, Ayatollah Ali Khamenei declared that the death sentence remained in force "and must be carried out." Later the Speaker of Iran's Parliament, Mehdi Karrubi, said, "However much Salman Rushdie may be kept under guard, eventually a Muslim will carry out the edict."

A statement supporting Rushdie was signed by over one hundred well-known writers and distributed by the International Committee for the Defense of Salman Rushdie and His Publishers.

Some moderate Muslims argued that a religious decree was not valid if its pronouncer was dead and the accused had not had a trial. Much of British Muslims' efforts now concentrated on trying to change the blasphemy laws so Rushdie could be brought to trial in Britain. Although the Muslims had been turned down at all levels over this, they persisted. In arguing that the blasphemy laws were unfair in covering only Christianity, the Muslims were fond of referring to the 1977 private prosecution for blasphemous libel successfully brought by Mary Whitehouse against the editor and publisher of *Gay News*, which had published a poem about a Roman centurion's homosexual love for Christ at the crucifixion. The Muslims wanted to bring the same kind of legal action against *The Satanic Verses*. Dr. Syed Pasha, general secretary of the Union of Muslim Organisations, said, "Ideally, we would like to see Salman Rushdie tried in a Muslim country.

However, the British Government can do a service by changing the laws of blasphemy so they cover all religions. If they do so within six months, it could be in time to ensure that Rushdie goes before a British court. If this happens, it could solve the problem."

The British Muslim Action Front challenged in the High Court in London the refusal of the chief Bow Street magistrate, Sir David Hopkin, to issue summonses for "blasphemous and seditious libel under common law" against Rushdie. Rushdie's lawyer argued that trying Rushdie for blasphemy would merely result in his acquittal, but it would not satisfy the people "orchestrating these demonstrations." Would it satisfy the Government of Iran? "It is idle to expect that a trial would do anything more than exacerbate the problems that arose when this book was made a scapegoat by people with their own political purposes and axes to grind." Only Parliament could extend the blasphemy laws to cover all religions, and it could lead to a "quagmire" in which all kinds of groups would claim protection. The Action Front's representative said that Britain was a signatory to the European Convention on Human Rights, which guaranteed freedom of religion to all citizens in equal terms. When three senior judges rejected the Muslims' case ruling that blasphemy covered only the Christian religion, the next move was to be an appeal to the House of Lords and if refused, an approach to the European Court of Human Rights.

The annual meeting of the Authors' Guild in New York called on Penguin to publish the paperback "to support author Salman Rushdie, authors everywhere and the principle of freedom of expression."

Rushdie himself was heard from again. He was invited to give the Herbert Read annual memorial lecture, named for the British historian and critic, at the Institute of Contemporary Arts in London. Several journalists suggested he should deliver the lecture himself, arguing that his life couldn't be in any more danger than Mrs. Thatcher's and she appeared in public, an idea that had been voiced before to try to tempt him out of hiding. Rushdie said the same idea had crossed his mind, "and if it were up to me I'd be there. But there are people I have to talk to about this, and it's their judgment that I can't be." He could assure everyone that there is "no one more anxious to resume my life than me. If I'm not doing so, there's a reason." But he was obviously becoming more impatient and restless.

His friend, dramatist Harold Pinter, acted as his stand-in and read his lecture, "Is Nothing Sacred?," for him. There was tight security at the crowded hall. Pinter, solemn-faced in a dark suit, explained that Rushdie had considered showing up, but reconsidered on the advice of British government detectives. "It is an agony and frustration not to be able to re-enter my old life, not even for such a moment," Rushdie told the large audience via Pinter.

The lecture made only glancing references to *The Satanic Verses* and the death threats, but Rushdie advocated the freedom of the novelist to explore what others held as sacred truths. Religion, he said, "seeks to privilege one language above all others, one set of values above all others, one text above all others."

As Harold Pinter read Rushdie's precise but passionate words with the author faraway watching the event on television, the whole conflict seemed to be summed up in that strange, foolish situation. The audience applauded, but whom were they applauding—Pinter for a nice reading? The absent Rushdie? It was like a cinema audience that applauds the screen at the end of a movie. A gesture only.

Rushdie must have had the feeling by then that he had labored over his seven-thousand-word essay and his long lecture in vain. An eerie status quo had been established. Day after day he continued to sit in front of a TV set watching *Dynasty* or *Dallas* or another of his favorites, trying to distract himself while he waited. One day perhaps, if he had to wait long enough, he might switch on to watch a mini-series about himself. Who would play Salman Rushdie or, as a former actor, would he play himself, his first public appearance in over a year before an audience of millions? But perhaps TV producers would wait for a happy ending. In that case, they might have to wait a long time by all the present signs.

If the Rushdie Affair had been a mini-series, no doubt a satisfactory climax would have been reached already, a clear dramatic ending solving the situation in a striking memorable way, with Rushdie still alive and the Muslims pacified. But it was more like life to create a dramatic situation and then to let it linger on until it finally petered out through sheer exhaustion or boredom.

In a mini-series Rushdie would no doubt have been more heroic, more immediately sympathetic, more modest and more a middle-of-the-road conservative, a personality millions could easily identify with.

The real Rushdie, as seen through hostile conservative eyes, was depicted in the London *Sunday Times* by Julie Burchill. She identified him as one of the devotees of "radical chic" who had been too busy bleating self-importantly to take note of the real world. "The darlings of the international left" in Nicaragua had been voted out of power leaving their supporters, including Salman Rushdie, with few causes to cling to.

Burchill made the point that unlike writers in Eastern Europe, no modern British writers had ever known the meaning of terror "until Salman Rushdie, that is—who then ran helter-skelter into the arms of his 'Mrs. Torture' and her 'secret police,' accepting all the machinations and subterfuge that her 'police state' could offer in his protection. Mr. Rushdie's current dependence on the trustworthiness and dedication of the police force is a piece of irony so beautiful (and such a cause for national pride and laughter) that it should hang in the Tate."

She claimed that Rushdie had found the "police state" he used to condemn was "a life-support machine," and she argued that his references to "Mrs. Torture" had been an offense against language because if Mrs. Thatcher was a torturer, what did you call a leader like Pinochet in Chile? "When it comes to shameless mutilation of language and the twisting of the truth, Rushdie is up there with the big league—Ceausescu, Kissinger and Khomeini."

She also revived the old charges against Rushdie. "Don't tell me that Rushdie and Fay Weldon dumped the publishers who had nursed and nourished them, when offered serious money by big conglomerates, in the name of art. I don't blame them. I never met a massive advance I didn't like, either."

She even had a go at Rushdie's stand-in, Harold Pinter, and

his wife, Lady Antonia Fraser, for announcing their departure from their political June 20 Group—"that very epicenter of dissident Britain"—due to the "burden of work" (which roughly translated, she said, as "our brilliant careers").

Salman Rushdie was made to seem like one of those characters in the *Arabian Nights*, who were mountains of pride and had to be humbled by circumstances. Some people who claimed to be his friends even saw him that way. But if the Little Prince hadn't grown up into the Man of Destiny, it is unlikely that he could have survived for so long without a complete breakdown. His pride and colossal belief in himself kept him going. He re-read *The Satanic Verses,* approved of everything he had written, and that was all that mattered. Such an attitude doesn't win popularity polls, but it is often what enables someone to stand alone against the crowd. Although *The Satanic Verses* is still a controversial book among literary critics as well as Muslim fundamentalists, Rushdie seems to be in the company of those artists who shake up the society they live in, usually for its own good, helping people to shed blinkers and false values. Writers like D. H. Lawrence and Henry Miller are obvious examples in this century. They challenged the System and the Establishment as much by their personal behavior as by their writings. Much as some of their excesses may be condemned, there is no doubt such artists open our eyes wider to the possibilities of life.

Is Salman Rushdie that kind of artist, forcing us, Christians as well as Muslims, Westerners as well as Easterners, to face the meaning of some of our most dearly held beliefs and codes of behavior and the price of co-existence in a world increasingly a racial melting pot and a Tower of Babel?

If the answer is yes, then much must be forgiven Rushdie even by those who claim he has "blasphemed" unless they want to be condemned themselves by posterity. And Rushdie must do some forgiving, too, which obviously isn't easy for him.

Meanwhile

"... here's my choice

not to shut up. To sing on, in spite of attacks."

EPILOGUE:
PREDICTION FULFILLED

THE QUEST FOR THE MEANING OF THE RUSHDIE AFFAIR ENDS AS IT BEGAN—with Salman Rushdie still playing the Invisible Man. Lost in a rhetoric of threats and defenses, the significance of what has happened since September 1988 has become increasingly elusive, all viewpoints dependent on the character of the people involved. The evidence of witnesses varies radically whether they are rooted in Western or Eastern cultures, whether they belong to extremist or moderate groups, to conservative or liberal factions. Naturally the extremists in the East make themselves heard far louder than the moderates, and in the West the opinion makers are largely those accepted by the media as celebrated or fashionable spokesmen. It is impossible to learn what the majority of Muslims or Westerners think about the Rushdie Affair or even if it means anything to most of them. Just a few people in Islam and the West speak for all and they are not enough.

As a Westerner born of a Catholic mother and an agnostic father, I began this inquiry feeling that there should be limits to what is said about people's most dearly held religious faith. This attitude was backed up by a longstanding interest in India beginning with a boyhood correspondence with Mahatma Gandhi and much experience of the prejudice against India and Islam in the West.

But after following Salman Rushdie's development over forty-two years, from Bombay to somewhere now in England, I find my own attitude has changed, and I am convinced that no limits are possible because who is going to set them without in some way restricting freedom of expression. And when restrictions are accepted, there is no end to them.

241

I also have learned that capital punishment is not effective. I knew the last hangman in Britain and have covered executions in the United States. Official, legal murder is still murder and ultimately encourages human violence. No doubt that influenced my reaction to Ayatollah Khomeini's death sentence. Also, from my reading of the Koran, I conclude the violent side of Islam does not truly represent the faith of which Muhammad was the Prophet.

I mention this personal background merely to be fair to readers at the end of my quest, but after many years as a reporter, I am satisfied I have not taken sides in covering the events of the Rushdie Affair.

It is surely no coincidence that Salman Rushdie and *The Satanic Verses* have turned out to be the test case that E. M. Forster predicted. Such a confrontation on a world stage was only possible with a writer of Rushdie's aggressive public character, his Muslim background, and his great belief in his own role. But how is it all going to end? It seems now that some face saving will have to be contrived for both sides unless the world is to live indefinitely with this reminder of its deep divisions and uncertain future. Possible scenarios that have been suggested include: giving up the paperback in return for the end of the death sentence; a blasphemy trial in London; facial surgery and a new identity in a part of the world with no Muslims. None seem very likely at this stage.

Has the test case been a success then?

Islam and the West have certainly been forced to look at each other more closely.

Lance Morrow in *Time* argued recently that those who actually read *The Satanic Verses* "may have absorbed Rushdie's brilliant perception of what the planet has become: old cultures in sudden high velocity crisscross, a bewilderment of ethnic explosion and implosion simultaneously."

Columnist Pete Hamill wrote in *The New York Post* that "the conflict between capitalism and communism is ebbing, but religious fundamentalism is on the rise everywhere."

That seemed particularly true in the Soviet Union, the center of communism for so long, where ethnic and Muslim conflicts have shaken up the makeup of that vast country.

When settling in a Western country, Muslim immigrants seem to hold on to their traditions even more strongly than most immigrants. A recent controversy in France was a good example. Muslim women demonstrated in Paris to demand Muslim girls be allowed to wear their traditional veil called the hijab, a scarf that covers the hair, ears and neck, in French schools. Muslim, Jewish, and Christian religious leaders said they saw little harm in the wearing of the hijab, but school and union leaders came down on the side of keeping all signs of religion out of the schools, saying a secular system was one of the pillars of French democracy. Shades of Salman Rushdie!

What was missing in the Rushdie Affair was any real lead from religious leaders between the two sides. Christian and Jewish leaders, for example, have tended to condemn the death sentence while rejecting Rushdie's book. It would have helped if they had tried to persuade the Muslims that, like Christians and Jews, they will have to tolerate critics, unbelievers, heretics, satirists and even outright blasphemers without recourse to primitive violence if they are to co-exist successfully in today's global village.

I go back to my conversation with E. M. Forster to try to get some perspective on what appears up close to be merely an unending state of drift with both sides in a stalemate. Forster didn't think of the test case as a great big solution that would settle everything. He saw it as something that would make the world more *aware* of the situation that threatened it. That is the true meaning of the Rushdie Affair. It has made us more aware of the danger we face in being so divided at the end of the twentieth century. It is the best—and worse—kind of culture shock.

SELECTED BIBLIOGRAPHY

Books by Salman Rushdie:
Grimus, novel, Overlook Press 1979
Midnight's Children, novel, Knopf 1981
Shame, novel, Knopf 1983
The Jaguar Smile, non-fiction, Viking-Penguin 1987
The Satanic Verses, novel, Viking-Penguin 1989

Books about Rushdie:
The Rushdie File, edited by Lisa Appignanesi and Sara Maitland,
Syracuse University 1990
The Rushdie Affair: The Ayatollah, The Novelist and the West
by Daniel Pipes, Birch Lane Press 1990

General Reading:
As Salman Rushdie has been a great reader since boyhood like
many writers, the books which have influenced his own writing
would make a library and include most of the principal Indian,
British and American classics. But the following should be on an
essential short-list: *The Koran, The Bible, Thousand and One
Nights* (Arabian Nights), *Anthology of Indian Literature* edited by
John Alphonso-Karkala, Laurence Sterne's *Tristram Shandy*, Nikolai
Gogol's *Dead Souls*, Charles Dickens' *Bleak House*, Herman Melville's
Moby Dick, E.M. Forster's *A Passage to India*, James Joyce's *Ulysses,*
Günter Grass's he Tin Drum, Vladimir Nabokov's *Lolita*, Thomas
Pynchon's *Gravity's Rainbow*, Gabriel Garcia Marquez's *One
Hundred Years of Solitude*, and anthologies of Indian, British and
American poetry. Several other ancient and modern classics, which
influenced *The Satanic Verses*, are mentioned in the narrative.

ACKNOWLEDGMENTS AND SOURCES

I have tried to give my main sources in the narrative because that seems easier for general readers. The most important informants have been people in India, the United States and Britain, most of whom, as I mentioned in my author's note at the beginning of the book, do not unfortunately wish to be named. All writers like to credit their sources, but the Rushdie Affair is unique in my experience for the atmosphere of fear it has created.

I would like to thank particularly Liz Calder, Salman Rushdie's first editor, and his former U.S. and British agents, Elaine Markson and Deborah Rogers, for being willing to answer my questions and not requesting anonymity.

I regret that Rushdie's present agent, Andrew Wylie, refused to answer any questions concerning Rushdie, even to check facts, or to respond to the criticisms of him in the publishing industry.

I am very grateful to Professor Edward Said for talking about his friendship with Rushdie and the significance of the Rushdie Affair.

Susan Sontag was very helpful in a long interview as was Roger W. Straus, president of Farrar, Straus and Giroux.

I am grateful, too, for talks over the years with Peter Mayer and for the help of his Viking-Penguin assistants.

Other American publishers of Rushdie—Knopf, Avon and Overlook Press—were also very helpful.

Sonny Mehta of Knopf provided some valuable background knowledge, and I am grateful to answers to my questions from Graham Greene, John le Carré, Roald Dahl, John F. Baker, Fay

Godwin, W. L. Webb, John Cunningham, Richard Gott, Robert Silverstein and Ram V. Singh.

I remember, too, with gratitude some very helpful long lunch-time discussions with my editor, Kent Carroll, at Carroll and Graf, and some shrewd early reactions from Herman Graf at the same company. Thanks, too, to James Mason there for helping to recover the time lost when I was ill by speedily getting the book into production.

Salman Rushdie talked in much the same way about his life and work to many reporters and acquaintances. He was very consistent in this way over the years. Remarks he made to me at a short meeting in New York I have read in more or less the same form in newspaper and magazine interviews. I have used my own notes whenever possible. I also like to quote an author's books in conveying his/her viewpoint, but I have restricted my direct quotations from Rushdie's works to what is generally considered fair usage because this is copyrighted material.

Although Bill Buford, editor of *Granta*, refused to let news-papers quote any of the brief Rushdie poem describing his thoughts in hiding when it was published in *Granta* in late 1989, he gave me permission to quote two lines summing up Rushdie's state of mind that were impossible to paraphrase adequately.

For such a public drama as the Rushdie Affair, the world's media have been useful in following what has happened over the last fifteen years since Rushdie published his first book. I am especially grateful to British, American and Indian newspapers and magazines and have mentioned some of them in the narrative. But I would like to draw attention particularly to the regular coverage and special articles in the following: *The Guardian, The Independent, The Observer, The* (London) *Sunday Times, The International Herald Tribune, The Daily Mail, The Daily Tele-graph,* The *Times, The New York Times* (including its Sunday Book Review and Magazine), *The Washington Post, The Los Angeles Times, Time, Newsweek, The New York Review of Books,* and *The New Yorker.*

All these sources were helpful in making the bricks with which I built my portrayal of Salman Rushdie and my account of the Rushdie Affair. If a source is not named, it means the information came from my own reportage or from an individual who didn't wish to be named, and I thank all these anonymous helpers, most of whom were delightfully free of prejudice even though the subject stirred their deepest emotions.

INDEX

A

Academy Chicago Publishers, 211
Achebe, Chinua, 174, 187
Acker, Kathy, 172
Adkins, Dr., 25
Advertising industry, and Rushdie, 32–33
After the Last Sky (Said), 58
Ahmad, Faiyazuddin, 129
Aitken, Gillon, 113, 156
Akhtar, Shabbir, 211–12
al-Tabari, 26
Albee, Edward, *Zoo Story*, 28
Aldiss, Brian, 37, 46–47
Ali, Tariq, 213–14, 228–29
American Booksellers' Association, 178
Amis, Kingsley, 37, 128
Amis, Martin, 156, 172
Appignanesi, Lisa, 224
Arabian Nights, 11–12, 35, 40, 43, 50, 194, 240
The Arabian Nights, 97, 99
Arran, Earl of, 205–06
Article 19, anti-censorship group, 181
Asari, Zamir, 128
Attenborough, Richard, *Gandhi*, 82
Australia, Rushdie in, 81–82
Authors' Guild, 178, 181, 211, 237

B

Babe (Wiggins), 85
Badawi, Dr. Zaki, 130
Baker, John F., 210
Bakewell, Joan, 46
Bandung File, 142
Barness, Julian, 212
Basu, Shrabani, 127
BBC debate, Rushdie-Essawy, 137–38
The Beginning of Spring (Fitzgerald), 136
Bellow, Saul, 53
Berger, John, 168
Beverly Hills Hotel in London, bombing of, 207
Bloomsbury, 113–14
Bombay, Rushdie boyhood in, 9–15
Bonadio, Candida, 110
The Book of the Fir (Rushdie), 33
Book-of-the-Month Club, 214
Booker Prize for Fiction, 45–46, 65–69, 135–37, 226
Booth, James, 25
Bradbury, Malcolm, 46, 64
Rates of Exchange, 66
Bragg, Melvin, 172
Brick Lane, 139–40
British government, and Ayatollah death sentence, 164
and Rushdie protection, 205–06

251

British Muslim Action Front,
    197–99, 237
Brixton riots, 59
Brodsky, Joseph, 166
Buford, Bill, 111, 220–21
Burchill, Julie, 239–330
Burgess, Anthony, 45, 163–64
Bush, George, 178

C

Calder, Liz, 35–38, 42, 47, 63–64,
    68, 74, 115–16, 212
    and Bloomsbury company,
        108–09, 113–14
Cambridge,
    Rushdie at, 20–28
Campden Hill Mob, 83
Carey, Peter,
    Oscar and Lucinda, 136–37
Carson, Johnny, 209
Carter, Angela, 65, 125
Carter, Jimmy, 204–05
Carver, Raymond,
    A New Path to the Waterfall,
        221–22
    "My Wife", 222
Charter 76, 94
Chatwin, Bruce, 81, 188–89
    memorial service for, 156–57
    Utz, 136
Cheng, Nien, 187
The Children of Gebelawi
    (Mahfouz), 183
Clarke, Arthur C., 37
Coetzee, J. M.,
    Life and Times of Michael K,
        66–67
Collins,
    The Rushdie File, 224–25
The Comfort of Strangers
    (McEwan), 45
Conrad, Joseph,
    The Nigger of the Narcissus,
        14
Crime and Punishment
    (Dostoevski), 226
Cunningham, John, 226–27

D

Dahl, Roald, 169–70, 185
Darkness (Mukherjee), 146
Davidson, Robyn, 82
Davies, Robertson, 188
Desai, Anita, 187
Dhondy, Farrukh, 57–58
Doctorow, E. L., 181
Dostoevski, Fyodor,
    Crime and Punishment, 226

E

Eco, Umberto, 175–76
    Foucault's Pendulum, 175
    The Name of the Rose, 175
Edmundson, Mark, 148
Ellison, Ralph, 187
The Enigma of Arrival (Naipaul),
    55, 57
Enright, D. J., 147
Essaway, Hesham, El, 129, 137–38,
    162

F

The Facts (Roth), 159
Faiz, Ahmed Faiz, 11
Falklands War, 52–53
Faqir, Fadia, 139, 141–42
Fatwa. See Khomeini, Ayatollah
    Ruhollah Musavi
Faulks, Sebastian, 136
Finkle, David, 148–49
Fitzgerald, Penelope,
    The Beginning of Spring, 136
Flying to Nowhere (Fuller), 66
Foot, Michael, 135–36, 172–73,
    231
Footlights Club,
    at Cambridge, 23–24
Forster, E. M., 27, 33, 244–45
Foucault's Pendulum (Eco), 175
Frazer, Lady Antonia, 83, 168,
    239–330
French, Phillip, 136
Fuentes, Carlos, 174

Fuller, John,
    Flying to Nowhere, 66

G

Gallagher, Tess, 140–41
Gandhi (Attenborough), 82
Gandhi, Indira, 40, 47, 560–51
Gandhi, Rajiv, 76, 127–29
Garcia Marquez, Gabriel, 11
    The General in the Labyrinth,
        224
The General in the Labyrinth
    (Garcia Marquez), 224
Glover, Trevor, 225
Godden Rumer, 187
The Godfather (Puzo), 110
Godwin, Fay, 91
Golding, William, 45
Good Behavior (Keane), 45
Gordimer, Nadine, 54, 132–33, 187
Gottlieb, Robert, 44
Granta, 221
Grass, Gunter, 11, 53–54
Greene, Graham, 33, 174–75
    The Power and the Glory, 174
    Ways of Escape, 174
Greer, Germaine, 23
Griffiths, Trevor, 172
Grimus (Rushdie), 35–38, 119
The Guardian, 52, 54, 117,
    125, 131–32, 139, 141, 143,
    157, 176, 198, 212
    death threat anniversary arti-
        cle, 226–29

H

Hamill, Pete, 151, 178–79, 182, 244
Haq, S. Nomanul, 190
Hare, David, 23
Hattersley, Roy, 82
Havel, Vaclav, 188
Herr, Michael, 140
Herself in Love (Wiggins), 85, 113
Hopkin, David, 237
A House for Mr Biswas (Naipaul),
    56

Howe, Sir Geoffrey, 163, 173, 176
Hughes, Thomas,
    Tom Brown's Schooldays, 16–18
Hurd, Douglas, 176
Hussain, Liaqat, 236

I

The Illusionist (Mason), 66
*In Good Faith: Reflection on a
    Year of Controversy* (Rushdie),
        229–30, 232–34
The Independent, 215
India,
    independence from Britain, 10
    Muslim-Hindu conflict, 77
    partition of Pakistan and, 10
    and Rushdie, 76–79, 92–93
    and *The Satanic Verses*, 127–33
International Committee for the
    Defense of Salman Rushdie
    and his Publishers, 199–200,
        236
"Is Nothing Sacred?" (Rushdie),
        238
Ishiguro, Kazuo,
    The Remains of the Day, 226
Islam,
    Rushdie view of, 93–96
Islam, Yussuf, 135, 168–69, 221

J

*The Jaguar Smile—A Nicaraguan
    Journey* (Rushdie), 74–75
Jain, Madhu, 127
James, Clive, 23–25
    My Week Was in June, 22
Janklow, Morton, 110
Japan,
    response to Rushdie death
        threat, 167
John Dollar (Wiggins), 86–87, 113,
    134, 148–49, 151–52, 218
John Paul, 175
Jonathan Livingstone Seagull,
    121
June 20 Group, 240

K

Karrubi, Medhi, 236
Kashmir,
    demonstrations against *The
        Satanic Verses*, 150
Keane, Molly,
    Good Behavior, 45–46
Keneally, Thomas, 188–89
Khamenei, Ali, 165, 167, 201, 209,
    236
Khan, Sherafsal, 138
Khomeini, Ayatollah Ruhollah
        Musavi, 153, 162–63
    death of, 200–201
    funeral of, 202–03
    international reponse to, 164–67
    Rushdie death sentence pro-
        nouncement, 154–55
    and Rushdie statement, 165–67
    Rushdie death sentence pro-
        nouncement, 154–55
    and Rushdie statement, 165–67
    and *Shame* (Rushdie), 63
Khomeini, Hojatolislam Ahmad,
    201
Kilmartin, Terrence, 66
King, Stephen, 189
Kings College. See Cambridge
Kipling, Rudyard, 33
Knopf, 178–79
Koenig, Rhoda, 148
Konrad, George, 188
Krantz, Judith,
    Princess Daisy, 110
Kureishi, Hanif, 158, 202–03,
    226–27

L

Labour Party,
    and Rushdie, 82, 198
Lady Chatterley's Lover (Law-
    rence), 128
The Last Temptation of Christ,
    130, 139
Lawrence, D. H.,
    Lady Chatterley's Lover, 128

le Carré, John, 170, 185, 205,
    226
"Learning Udru" (Wiggins), 218
Lee, Hermione, 46
Leithauser, Brad, 190–91
Lessing, Doris,
    The Sirian Experiments, 45–46
Liberty department store,
    bombing of, 207
Life and Times of Michael K
    (Coetzee), 66–67
The Little Drummer Boy (le
    Carré), 170
Lodge, David,
    Nice Work, 136
Loitering With Intent (Spark), 45
London, Rushdie move to, 29–34
The Lost Father (Warner), 136
Luard, Clarissa. See Rushdie,
    Clarissa Luard

M

McCrum, Robert, 226
McEwan, Ian,
    The Comfort of Strangers,
        45–46
Madame Rama (Rushdie), 38, 100
Madden, Max, 174
Magic realism,
    and Rushdie, 99–100
Mahfouz, Naguib, 207–08
    The Children of Gebelawi, 183
Mahoud,
    character in *The Satanic Verses*,
        95–96
Mailer, Norman, 53–54, 181
Maitland, Sara, 224
Markson, Elaine, 44, 53, 65, 74, 81,
        86, 114–15
Marzorati, Gerald, 139–41
Mason, Anita,
    The Illusionist, 66
Massereene-Ferrard, Viscount,
    205
Maxwell, Robert, 166
May Week Was in June (James),
    22

Mayer, Peter, 118–22, 144, 149, 151, 160, 208, 214–16
Mayhew, Sir Patrick, 130
Media Coalition, 211
Mehta, Sony, 74, 118–19
Mellish, Lord, 206
Meredith, Scott, 110
Michener, James, 189–90
The Middleman and Other Stories (Mukherjee), 146
Midnight's Children (Rushdie), 10, 14, 16, 29, 96, 119–20
  and India, 78–79
  and Indian reaction, 50–52
  writing of, 41–48
Migration,
  theme of in Rushdie's work, 102
Miller, Arthur, 54, 212
Mishcon, Lord, 206
Mitford, Jessica, 73–74
Mitterrand, François, 167
Modood, Tariq, 235–36
Mojtabai, A. G., 147
Montazeri, Ayatollah Russein Ali, 201
Morrison, blake, 136, 159, 194, 213, 229–30
Morrow, Lance, 244
Muhammad,
  Midnight's Children portrayal of, 96
  Satanic Verses portrayal of, 95–96
Muhammad—Messenger of God (film), 130
Muhammad ibn Abdallah,
  Rushdie study of, 26
Mukherjee, Bharati, 30, 146–47, 188
  Darkness, 146
  The Middleman and Other Stories, 146
Murdoch, Iris, 172
Murdoch, Rupert, 225
muslim tradition,
  and Rushdie background, 13, 27–29

Muslim-Hindu conflict,
  in India, 77
Muslims,
  American, 149
  British, 211–12
  burning of *The Satanic Verses*, 131–33
  in Iran, 157–58
  May 27th London demonstration, 197–99
  and Modernism, 141–42
  reactions to *In Good Faith* essay, 235–36
  reactions to *The Satanic Verses* in Britain, 125–44
  Rushdie supporters among, 139
  in Western countries, 245
My Beautiful Laundrette (film), 158
"My Wife" (Carver), 222

N

Naipaul, V.S.,
  The Enigma of Arrival, 55, 57
  A House for Mr. Biswas, 56
  and Rushdie, 55–58
The Name of the Rose (Eco), 175
Narayan, R. K., 33
National Writers' Union, 181
A New Path to the Waterfall (Carver), 221–22
Newsweek,
  interview with Rushdie, 232–34
Nicaragua,
  and Rushdie, 70–75
Nice Work (Lodge), 136
The Nigger of the Narcissus (Conrad), 14

O

The Observer, 159, 194, 214, 228
O'Conner, Cardinal, 180
Organization of the Strugglers of Islam, 207

Ortega, Daniel, 72
Oscar and Lucinda (Carey), 136–37
"Outside the Whale" (Rushdie), 221

P

Pakistan, 10
demonstrations against *The Satanic Verses*, 149–50
and Rushdie, 61
and Rushdie death threat, 164–65
Rushdie family in, 20–21, 27–28
Pan Books. See Picador
Pasha, Dr. Syed, 129–30, 236–37
Paz, Octavio, 188
PEN,
in America, 178, 181
in Britain, 168
Penguin. See Viking-Penguin
Picador, 74, 120
Pinter, Harold, 83, 128, 158, 238–330
Pipes, Daniel,
The Rushdie Affair—the Ayatollah, the Novelist and the West, 225–26
Podhoretz, Norman, 167–68
Porter, Peter, 65–66
Potter, Dr. John, 228
The Power and the Glory (Greene), 174
Preston, Peter, 176
Princess Daisy (Krantz), 110
Pritchett, V. S., 42–43
Prix du Meilleur Livre Etranger, 69
Purves, Libby, 66
Puzo, Mario,
The Godfather, 110
Pynchon, Thomas, 188
Vineland, 222–23

Q

Quddas, Sayed Abdul, 157, 236

R

Rafsanjani, Ali Akbar Hashemi, 163
Rajsanjani, Hojatolislam Hashemi, 203
Rates of Exchange (Bradbury), 66
Reagan, Ronald, 70
Religion,
Rushdie view of, 29–30
The Remains of the Day (Ishiguro), 226
Rhine Journey (Schlee), 45
Riverdale Press,
fire bombing of, 189
Rogers, Deborah, 63, 113–16, 226
Rosenthal, Tom, 67
Roth, Philip, 111
The Facts, 159
Rubinstein, Hilary, 224
Rugby School, 15–19
Runcie, Dr. Robert, 166
The Rushdie Affair—the Ayatollah, the Novelist and the West (Pipes), 225–26
Rushdie, Anis Ahmed, 10, 59
Rushdie, Clarissa Luard, 31–32, 49, 67–68, 194
divorce from Rushdie, 80–81
The Rushdie File (Collins), 224–25
Rushdie Negin Butt, 10
Rushdie, Salman,
"6 March 1989", 220–21
American reactions to death threat, 178–91
and *Arabian Nights*, 11–12
at Cambridge, 20–28
The Book of the Fir, 33
book reviews while in hiding, 220–23
and Booker Prize for Fiction, 45–46, 65–69
boyhood in Bombay, 91–15
Jimmy Carter and, 204–05
and Clarissa Luard, 31–32, 80–81